HIKING THE EAST COAST TRAIL
Guidebook

T5-COB-327

Petty Harbour/Maddox Cove to Bay Bulls

By Peter Gard

book #2

PUBLISHED BY THE EAST COAST TRAIL ASSOCIATION

Copyright 2005
The East Coast Trail Association

All rights reserved. No part of this publication may be reproduced in any form or by any means without the prior written permission of the publisher, except in the case of a reviewer, who may quote brief passages in a review.

The East Coast Trail Association gratefully acknowledges the support of Human Resources Development Canada, the Atlantic Canada Opportunity Agency, and the Government of Newfoundland and Labrador.

Series Editor
Peter Gard
Associate Editor
Libby Creelman
Research/Writing
Libby Creelman
Peter Gard
Laura Kerr
Patrick Ryan
Additional Research
Clare Armstrong
Robin Chidley
Nathalie Djan-Chékar
Suzanne Dooley
Steve Emberley
Sherry Glynn
Tony Horwood
Doug Keough
Janet Kingsley
Kristina Mansson
Lisa Moore
Michelle Murphy

Laura Noel
Barry Norris
Darren Power
Christine Vickers
Jim Walsh
Susan Williams
Editorial Support
Marnie Parsons
Artistic Direction
Vessela Brakalova
Veselina Tomova
Design & Layout
vis-à-vis graphics inc.
Cartography
Steve Fagan
Dean O'Reilly
Cartographic Support
Cormorant, Ltd.
Jacques Whitford Environment, Ltd.
Printing
Transcontinental

ECTA Map & Guidebook Committee
Mark Graesser
Ed Hayden
Roberta Hicks
Elizabeth Ohle
Maggy Piranian
Marilyn Porter
Darlene Scott
Alan Stein
Roger White
Wanda Cuff Young
Funding Committee
Tim Crosbie
Keith Healey
Randy Murphy
Wayne Spracklin
Doug Youden
Cover Photograph
Hearts Point Ridge from Miner Point, Peter Gard
Author Photograph
Julia Schwarz

National Library of Canada Cataloguing in Publication Data

Hiking the East Coast Trail
Guidebook and Maps
Book 2: Petty Harbour-Maddox Cove to Bay Bulls

Contents: Bk. 2. Petty Harbour-Maddox Cove to Bay Bulls

ISBN 0-9689509-0-6

1. East Coast Trail (Nfld.)-Guidebooks. 2.Hiking-Newfoundland-Avalon Peninsula-Guidebooks. I. Gard, Peter, 1949- II. East Coast Trail Association

GV199.44.C22N48 2001   917.1804'4   C2001-902449-5

Copies of this guide can be obtained from the East Coast Trail Association, P. O. Box 8034, St. John's, Newfoundland A1B 3M7, (709) 738-4453.
www.eastcoasttrail.com

TABLE OF CONTENTS

Exploring Petty Harbour-Maddox Cove	2
Motion Path	59
Spout Path	115
Exploring Bay Bulls	171
Acknowledgments	209
Illustration Credits	210

There are walks on which we tread in the footsteps of others, walks on which we strike out entirely for ourselves.

Thomas A. Clark, IN PRAISE OF WALKING

"After traversing... moorland, we came suddenly on the verge of its seaward slope; and there in a narrow ravine between dark precipices lay the cluster of white houses called Petty Harbour. The houses surround a small creek, which receives a howling torrent that hurries over the rocks of a desolate valley just behind, and they seem so secluded and shut out from the world, and the people too seemed so well off and contented, that I was much interested with the place altogether. There was a small inn also, where I got very decent quarters."

—Joseph Beete Jukes, EXCURSIONS IN AND ABOUT NEWFOUNDLAND, 1842

The Petty Harbour Road

A cycle of the circling hills,
A shadowy bit of lake,
A clump of spruces here and there,
An opening in the brake;
A trill from some melodious throat
Not very far away—
A winding road, a pleasant cot
And haunts, where children play.

—Ellen Carberry, NEWFOUNDLAND QUARTERLY, 1903

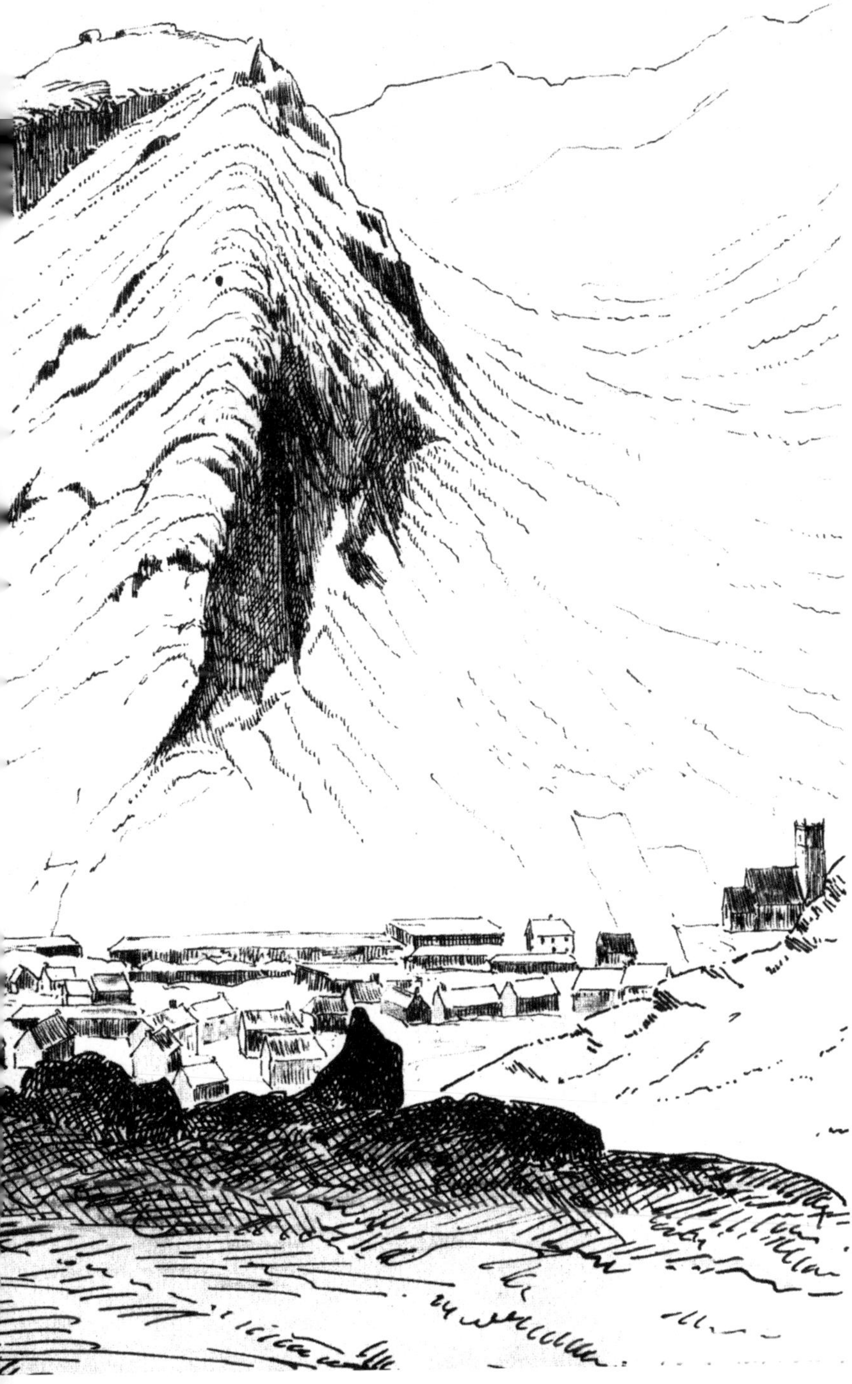

Exploring Petty Harbour Maddox Cove...

Maddox Cove

> **PLANTERS**
>
> ***Planters*** were independent contractors who came out on fishing ships and over-wintered, often for several years. Some brought families and attempted to settle permanently. War, weather and the up-and-down nature of the fishery, however, constantly disrupted the settlement process. Planters recruited workers, known as ***servants***, from the men who arrived on the ships each spring. Servants generally contracted to work for two to three years, but returned home each fall once the fishing season was over.

The name "Maddox Cove" is most likely a shortened form of "Maddick's Cove." A Petty Harbour planter named Maddick likely maintained a room in the cove, possibly John Maddick of Petty Harbour, whose name appears in a 1713 ledger kept by the Boston merchant Thomas Ruck. Another possible candidate is Thomas Maddock who, in 1771, married Ann Martin, a Petty Harbour widow. The couple still resided in Petty Harbour in 1803.

Maddox Cove was a difficult spot to fish from, but had other advantages, chiefly its access to woodland and farmland. The cove developed in the 19th century from a summer fishing station into a place where people from Petty Harbour grew vegetables and pastured livestock. The cove is first listed as a separate settlement in the census of 1857. Would-be

Petty Harbour, c. 1890

cultivators in the 1860s received both free land and subsidies for clearing land, and these agriculture-friendly policies likely spurred growth in the cove. By 1871, the community had a population of 90 and three families listed farming as their primary occupation. Late 19th-century photographs show a string of hayfields along the southwestern exposure of McGraths Hill. A track good enough for driving cattle linked Maddox Cove and St. John's, and fields were cleared along this road as well. The subdivision that has spread through the cove since the 1970s has claimed most of this land.

The cove is exposed to southeasterly storms, which are particularly common in the late summer and fall. It is said that "The Independence Hurricane" of 1775 (also known as the "Great Newfoundland and St. Pierre-Miquelon Hurricane") did so much damage in the cove that all subsequent development took place well back from the shoreline. Only in the last decade has this practice changed. Photographs dating to the 1940s show significantly more cobble and pebble on the shore and in nearby gulches; not enough material has survived recent storms to cover the rock outcrops and steeper-sloped areas. Sometime after 1900, a supply wharf was built out into the cove. Until the 1950s, local fishermen used the wharf to tie up, or haul out boats. By 1966, the wharf's planking was gone. Six incongruous concrete piers

A 19th-century room

Old Maddox Cove and Pancake Rock

ROOMS

A *room* (also called a *plantation* or *station*) was a quasi-permanent fishing property consisting of one or more *stages* for the landing, washing and salting of fish, a *dwelling house* for the planter or ship merchant, storehouses, a *cookhouse* where servants bunked down and were fed, and *flakes*, i.e., platforms made of boughs on which fish were dried. The most desirable rooms were close to fishing grounds. Year-round shelter was of little importance to the seasonal ship fishery, for rooms were claimed on a "first-come, first-served" basis, and structures destroyed over the winter were rebuilt by crews in the spring. A *planter's room* was occupied year round, but it, too, was generally of rough-and-ready construction, and in need of seasonal repair.

still marched out to sea in the 1970s, but heavy seas are unrelenting in their work and, by 2003, only one pier and a few pieces of bent iron remained.

Pancake Cove, at the westward end of Maddox Cove Beach, is most likely named for the pancake-flat rock on its shore, though some claim the whole shore is "as flat as a pancake." A cart track called Pancake Road climbs the hill above the cove and, reaching the Ridge, meets up with Old Petty Harbour Road at a level spot, also called "the Pancake." Maddox Cove and Petty Harbour were initially connected by this hill route; the road along the shore is more recent. Past Pancake Cove, Old Womans Gulch cuts close to the shore road, just before the Point. It is said that a man was driving his crippled mother home to Maddox Cove when his cart hit a bump and the unfortunate woman was thrown over the cliff.

Ruined supply wharf, 1974

The Point

A narrow chasm called Big Gulch splits the Point. Frost fracturing and waves are rapidly removing layers of shale from the gulch and the sign warning "Dangerous Gulch" should be heeded; in 2003, the post supporting the sign actually slipped through the thin layer of sod bridging the chasm. The lobster pound at the Point, owned by Bidgood's, was one of the first in the province when it opened in 1967. Mad Rock, below the Point, is used by Petty Harbour fishermen to judge if the sea is suitable for small boats; if foaming waves are breaking over the rock, the weather is too rough to go out.

The hill above the Point, sometimes called Cannon Hill, is the likely site of a battery constructed in 1778-79 by members of the Royal Newfoundland Volunteers, under the command of Captain (later Major) Robert Pringle. The battery was short-lived, for the five soldiers stationed there appear only once on the rolls. Scratched onto one of the guns were the words, "Ram me well, and point me fair and I'll drive a ball from here to Cape Spear." The inscription may have been ironic, for no gunner was assigned to the detachment.

The battery was one of many built in Newfoundland in 1778 to defend larger settlements from "Yankee privateers." However, by 1779, so many privateers had been captured that Captain Pringle's tactics changed: an American or French invasion was judged to be a more pressing threat. Most likely, Petty Harbour's five soldiers were re-deployed to Bay Bulls or Torbay, communities which had seen previous landings; or were used to guard access roads to St. John's. In 1781, Petty Harbour saw action—for the last time in its history—when a Royal Navy sloop,

Two girls in pinafores rounding the Point

RARE BIRDS (2000)

One morning, William Hurt (*The Accidental Tourist, Children of a Lesser God*) was seen directing traffic on Maddox Cove Road. He was in the cove—in the house at the bottom of Motion Head Road—filming interior shots for *Rare Birds*. Petty Harbour-Maddox Cove is featured in the movie mostly from the rear window of "Phonse" Murphy's decrepit car, as it careens from one mad caper to the next. Hurt plays Dave Purcell, a cocaine-loving four-star chef whose hare-brained dream of a gourmet restaurant on an isolated Newfoundland cliff is floundering. Phonse (Andy Jones) saves Dave's hide by convincing him to telephone an open line show with a rare bird sighting. Dave's restaurant, The Auk, fills with cold and hungry birdwatchers on the lookout for Tasker's sulphureous duck (*Aythya flagitius*). Phonse's sister-in-law Alice (Molly Parker) waits tables and steals Dave's heart. Ed Riche adapted his novel and Sturla Gunnarsson (*Such a Long Journey*) directed. Critics reserved their strongest praise for the coastal scenery, drawn, in many scenes, from the East Coast Trail.

LORD JOHN

A curious story is told of an early John Angel, that he was the son of a pirate. His father and older brother are said to have retired to England after a profitable career pirating off the coast of Spain. John found the roving life difficult, so he built a house in Petty Harbour and married. John inherited the family's English estate, but for a long time this was unknown, for the man charged with executing the will—a certain Parnell—hid the document in the back of a grandfather clock. A well-meaning St. John's merchant financed John Angel's trip back to England to claim his inheritance. The estate in question was on the Salisbury Downs, and the competing claimant, the British army, used the land for gunnery practice.

Settling the will proved difficult. On the eve of the court hearing, the lawyer pursuing the case was poisoned, and John returned to Newfoundland a broken man. Thereafter, as a sign of respect, the people of Petty Harbour called him "Lord John."

One of the stranger twists to this story is that, in 1818, one John Parnell, a widower, did indeed marry the widow Elizabeth (*née* Angel) Chafe (1765-1835). Perhaps the story came down through one of Elizabeth's six children by her first husband, Henry Chafe (1757-1814).

The Point

stationed "at the ready" in St. John's, chased two privateers into the harbour, where they were promptly captured.

In the 1790s, the colony's commanding engineer, Captain (later Colonel) Thomas Skinner, facing yet another French invasion threat, chose a strategy similar to Pringle's. He had guardhouses built, and guards stationed, at alarm points around St. John's, including, in 1793, Hayes Farm on Old Petty Harbour Road. The farm was likely close to where Old Petty Harbour Road meets Pancake Road. During the Second World War, a small American detachment kept watch from the Pancake, the flat prominence near the junction.

The Point was originally called North Point. The planter Samuel Angell was active at North Point from about 1705 to 1725. In 1734, Angell willed his plantation, as well as the small hill behind the point, then called the Mount, to his daughter Mary Watts and son John. The Mount is now called Watch Hill, "Watts" having become "Watch." The terms of the will allowed Mary to build storehouses and otherwise improve the property, without interference or claim from her brother. A third child, Ann, was left an income of £5 per annum from a plantation "formerly occupied by William Bount."

In 1794, 60 years after she inherited the plantation, Mary Watts was still living at North Point with a daughter, a female servant and five men hired to make fish. She leased out three additional rooms on the north side. Her brother John had died, but two of his sons, Edward and John, and one of his grandsons, Stephen, also occupied rooms. The family name of Angell, also spelt Angel, died out in Petty Harbour about a century ago, but there is still an Angel Gulch, immediately west of the Point, where Mary Watts' room was located.

Introducing customers to live lobster, Bidgood's, c. 1967

The Public Beach

Petty Harbour was a prime spot for catching fish, but was poorly configured for ships. To quote a 1693 description, it is "a small cove, where the ships are fastened head and stern, and have about as much water as they will draw." The narrowness of the harbour amplified sea swells, as did the shallow, rocky bottom. As there was no deep basin to anchor in, ships had to be secured to shore or to each other, increasing the likelihood of damage during storms. This state of affairs persisted until 2004, when extensive dredging conducted under the Petty Harbour Model Fishing Village project deepened the harbour sufficiently to permit keeled vessels.

A number of small ships—optimistic sources say four—could anchor in the lee of the Point. This short stretch of shore has gone through many changes. Now generally referred to as the Public Beach, it was likely formerly Admirals Beach, i.e., the room claimed by the first ship in the harbour each spring. A photograph

THE SHIP FISHERY

Early in the 17th century, as many as 5,000 fishermen crammed into some 250 vessels of 40- to 100-ton capacity and migrated annually from the West Country of England to the shoals and shores of the Avalon Peninsula. The rule of thumb was one passenger per ton capacity; the more men carried, the more fish caught. Ships were packed with workers and provisions to the point that men often slept on the main deck or, if the ship were larger, half the crew bunked down while the other half kept busy topside.

A skilled captain braved storms and sea ice to arrive in March or April, in order to claim a prime site, preferably one he had worked from before. Late arrivals had to settle for inconvenient and/or less productive sites. Before fishing began, servants cut and hauled wood, constructed flakes, stages, wash-cages, storehouses and cook-houses, and fashioned oars, boats and barrels. **Shallops** (fishing boats), too, were often constructed on site. Shallops typically had a crew of three. Two shore workers headed, gutted and split the fish as they were landed and were in charge of the **cure** (salting, washing and drying the fish) on shore.

Walking to Petty Harbour in 1670

"Having now more leisure than last year, and better stockt with books, as also our men generally healthful, I applied myself to study. There was one great impediment, which was in being compelled to go often to Petty Harbour, which is nine miles off, a very ill way, up hill and down hill, through marshes, over rocks, an in many places without paths. I once lost myse[lf] in the wood, and wandered to a beaver house. To this Petty Harbour I went nine times this summer, often by land and sometimes returned the same day. I had no other business but to look after our men on the hills between the two harbours. I could see over St. Johns, to Bellile and the Bay of Conception (called 'Consumption' by the people) to Haver de Grace."

—THE JOURNAL OF JAMES YONGE, 1670

Fishing boats, 1909

from the 1920s shows a bunkhouse above the beach. As late as the First World War, the beach still accommodated a seasonal flow of men and boats. During the construction of the breakwater in 1967 much of the old anchorage was filled in. From 1967 to the mid-1980s, Newfoundland Quick-Freeze operated a feeder plant (later, a processing plant) from the concrete wharf west of the breakwater. The plant was demolished in 1995. The wharf now serves as an informal skate park, boat storage and parking area, and is slated to become a "living museum" devoted to boat building.

The first ship's captain to arrive became *fishing admiral* for the season, and his word was law in the harbour. William Squarey ruled over Petty Harbour as a *vice-admiral* in the summer of 1731. Vice-admirals generally claimed the second best spot in a harbour. Possibly Petty Harbour only warranted a vice-admiral, for, in the days of the fishing admirals, it is likely most ships' captains preferred to anchor in St. John's, where a lively social life was guaranteed. Their fishing crews would disperse in coves along the shore as far as Petty Harbour.

In the summer of 1670, James Yonge (1646-1721), a ship's surgeon from Plymouth, repeatedly walked from St. John's to Petty Harbour to tend to the medical needs of crews scattered along the shore. In addition to caring for his own ship's crew of 50 to 100 men, a ship's surgeon anticipated—and profited from—the demand for his services from vessels without a surgeon. Yonge was paid one full share by the ship's master and received a half-crown from each crewman's share. In addition, ship owners paid Yonge 100 *poor jack* (dried fish) and contributed to his medical chest. Though largely self-taught, and engaged in a profession more tolerated than admired, Yonge rose to become first surgeon of the Naval

BY-BOAT KEEPERS

Sir David Kirke (1597?-1654), the newly created governor of the Colony of Avalon, transported a contingent of ***by-boat keepers*** to Petty Harbour as early as 1637. By-boat keepers, like planters, were independent operators who, at their own expense, acquired tackle, provisions and shallops from a ship merchant, hired servants, and sold their catch, sometimes back to the merchant, sometimes to a ***sack ship*** (trading vessel). The practice originated in South Devon and flourished in all the small harbours north of Ferryland.

It was up to the by-boat keeper to choose a location and make it profitable. If the catches were poor, the ship merchant had first claim on the by-boat keeper's fish, leaving it to the by-boat keeper to sort out how to settle matters with his servants. Petty Harbour was ideally configured for by-boat enterprise, and between 1640 and 1790 by-boat keepers caught between half and two thirds of the fish taken in Motion Bay.

A WHALE FOR THE KILLING (1980)

Shot in Petty Harbour and Quidi Vidi in the summer of 1980, *A Whale for the Killing* was at the time the most expensive television movie made by the ABC Network. Farley Mowat's lurid account of the death of a trapped whale in Burgeo inspired both the title and screenplay. New England architect Charles Landon (Peter Strauss), his long-suffering wife (Dee Wallace) and two sons are stranded by a storm in the quaint but impoverished fishing village of "Barrisway." They pitch in to help a sympathetic doctor (Kathryn Walker) and a crusty fisherman (Richard Widmark) save a trapped humpback. Barrisway's rough-cut villagers (Bruce McGill plays their leader) scheme to sell the whale to a Russian ship for $30,000, in order to buy medical equipment for Walker's clinic.

The production was plagued with problems. The whale sank, the cinematographer had a heart attack and there was a strike in the fourth week of the shoot. Rain and bone-chilling temperatures put everyone in a bad mood, particularly the 250 extras fed on cold plates; only actors with speaking parts were served hot meals. Playboy Productions and Beowulf Inc. co-produced the $4 to $5 million "telefeature" with ABC, and Richard T. Heffron (*Futureworld*, *True Grit*) directed. The film briefly hijacked three hours of prime time, and was in equal measure ridiculed and loathed.

Hospital at Plymouth, Devon, as well as a fellow of the Royal College of Physicians and Mayor of Plymouth. He is credited with the invention of the flap technique in limb amputation, life-saving advances in the treatment of skull fractures and the first reported use of vacuum extraction in obstetrics.

Great Big Seas

The seventh deadliest North Atlantic storm on record, the "Independence Hurricane" of September 12, 1775, is the first recorded "big sea" to wash into Petty Harbour. According to some estimates, the hurricane drowned as many as 3,000 Newfoundland fishermen, and the six- to ten-metre-high surge accompanying the storm caused widespread destruction. The "Great Gale of 1846," which struck on September 19, was less deadly, but caused similar damage. In Petty Harbour, a cooper named Patrick Kelly was crushed by a falling stage. In the 20th century, "great big seas" washed into Petty Harbour in 1927, 1935, 1955 and 1966. Some fishermen, like Bill Stack, rebuilt their stages three times during this period.

The storm of January 28, 1966—the same wild sea that washed out La Manche Village—destroyed 90 per cent of Petty Harbour's fish landing facilities. A roof, torn off the government wharf at the Beaches, rammed into one

Storm damage, 1966

Storm damage, 1966

structure after another, knocking them over like dominoes. Thirty-six stages were lost, including all of Island Rooms, a dense cluster of stages and flakes occupying the centre of the harbour basin. The government compensated fishermen for 60 per cent of the damage to structures and boats, but nothing was received for lost fish. Mayor Cyril Whitten's newly formed town council lobbied the federal government for a breakwater, constructed in 1967, which has yet to be tested by a storm of equal magnitude. In 1976, during the filming of *Orca—Killer Whale*, 50 extras were hired to show up for a mob scene on the breakwater. They turned up in their Sunday best and were promptly told to go home and dress like fishermen.

50 Years Ago . . .

In 1966, there were 169 resident fishermen in Petty Harbour. There were no fish plants and only limited public landing facilities. Most crews still maintained their own rooms, consisting of a boardwalk leading to a *stage head* (the part of the stage over the water,

Breakwater, 1974

Petty Harbour Flakes, June 24, 1859

"The fishing flakes completely floor the river, and ascend in terraces for a short distance up the sides of the vale. Beneath these wide, evergreen floors, upon which was fish in all states, fresh from the knife, and dry enough for packing, ran the river, a brawling stream at low tide, and deeper, silent water when the tide was in. We could look up the dark stream and see it dancing in the mountain sunshine, and down through the dim forest of slender props, and catch glances of the glittering sea. Boats were gliding up out of the daylight into the half-darkness, slowly sculled by brown fishermen, and freighted with the browner cod, laced occasionally with a salmon. In this wide and noiseless shade, these cool, Lethean realms, sitting upon some well-washed boulder, one might easily forget the heat and uproar of all cities, and become absorbed in the contemplation of merely present and momentary things."

—Louis Legrand Noble, AFTER ICEBERGS WITH A PAINTER, 1862

Tying up at a stagehead, 1974

where fish are landed), and a fish flake close by. Cod taken by hand-lining—the most important fishing method used—was turned into light dry salted fish, which was sold to St. John's merchants, or their local agents. The season began in mid-May and lasted until mid-November. Men fished one or two per boat, on the submarine shallows and ledges off North Head and Motion Head. Lines were baited with caplin until early August, after which herring, squid and mackerel were purchased from the bait depot.

Cod trap crews consisted of a crew captain, usually the boat owner, and two or three sharemen, who each received a fifth share of the catch. Twenty-three trap crews set an average of 50 traps along 21 km of shoreline, from North Head to Long Point. Trap berths were allotted by an annual draw, held in mid-June, lasted until mid-August. Traps of 110-155 metres circumference were set in 18-27 metres of water, about 90 metres from shore. Cod from traps was mostly sold fresh, and trucked into St. John's.

Michael Hearn mends a net, 1974

Beaches stagehead, c. 1909

North Side Beaches

The Newmans of Dartmouth, Devon, were 16th-century wine merchants who, in 1601, expanded their business to include the making and trading of Newfoundland saltfish. The company traded its stock of fish for wine and salt from Portugal and Spain. The company's Newfoundland operations were initially located in or near St. John's and Conception Bay. The company's Petty Harbour plantation was situated at the Beaches, a low shore immediately west of the Public Beach. In 1783, Robert Newman (1735-1803) convinced his brothers to shift the business to the Burin Peninsula and the South Coast, shores that were sufficiently remote to permit a Devon-based company to compete with Newfoundland-based suppliers. The collapse of the migratory fishery in the 1790s resulted in the withdrawal from Newfoundland of most of the old Devon-based ship merchants, but not the farsighted Newmans, who closed their last Newfoundland operation in 1907, after a record 306 years.

Many of the servants and by-boat keepers from South Devon who shipped out with the Newmans, and who worked from the Newman premises on the Beaches, or from *fishermen's rooms* (small rooms) nearby, eventually settled as planters on Petty Harbour's north and south sides. Following the departure of the Newmans, the Hearns and other Irish-born planters and by-boat keepers leased rooms at the Beaches from the company. They continued to pay ground rent to the Newmans

The Beaches, 1974

until the 1940s. The St. John's-based supplier Bulley & Job set up a premises on the harbour's south side, likely around the time of the Newman pullout.

In 1912, several descendants of Samuel Churchill, brother of the first Duke of Marlborough, filed suit stating that *their* family, not the Newmans, had once been the owners of two rooms—Calvers Room and Flag Staff Room—in Petty Harbour. According to the suit, at an unspecified date, Samuel Churchill designated the Newmans as *agents* to manage the Churchill properties. Two of Samuel Churchill's daughters eventually inherited the estate: Elizabeth, who married Richard Halfyard of Ochre Pit Cove; and Clarimond, who ran off with a young Irish servant of her father named Bolan. Descendants of the two daughters disposed of their interest in the Petty Harbour rooms in the 1820s, but failed to reach an agreement with the Newman family over the *so-called* Newman Premises on Water Street in St. John's, presently a Provincial Historic Site. The Halfyard / Bolan claim on this property remains active but unresolved.

The Big Rock

North side fishermen gathered to catch up on news by the Big Rock, below St. Joseph's Church, under the shelter of the Beaches flakes. Or they dropped into "Keiley's," the cooperage at the Beaches, run first by John Anthony Keiley (1854-1923), and then by his son "Cooper Jack" (1901-79). The cooperage made

Carpenter's plane

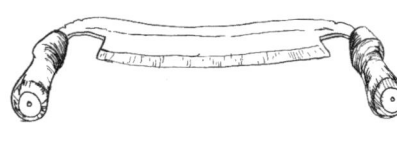

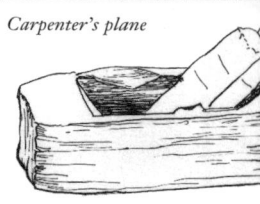

Rind stripper

standard-sized barrels holding a *quintal* (50.8 kilos) of salt fish, as well as *fish barrels* (half-barrels used to salt fish, fish heads, etc.) and *float kegs* (small barrels used as cod trap floats). The Keileys also bought used pork barrels that they resold in St. John's. John Anthony's brother, Peter Joseph Kieley (1860-1951), leased his property at the Beaches to the firm of Bowring Brothers Ltd., which erected a cod liver oil factory on the land. Later, the factory was taken over by Walter S. Munroe and his son Arthur H. Munroe.

Bidgood's

In the 1920s, John and Maggie (*née* Hannaford) Bidgood ran a small shop across from the Big Rock, where the War Memorial stands today. For 33 years, Maggie also operated a post office next to the rock. In 1948, their son Roger (1923-2004) began wholesaling groceries "up the shore," accepting produce in exchange, which he sold wholesale in St. John's. In the early 1950s, Roger and his wife Jennie relocated the family shop to a larger site next to the post office (the building housed a hair salon in 2004) and turned John Bidgood's cow barn behind the shop into a saltfish plant. The wholesale operation was moved to the Goulds. By 1957, the Bidgoods had 19 trucks on the road. Following the opening of a road system across the Island in the 1960s, the Bidgoods took a truck across the Strait of Belle Isle each year to buy Labrador bakeapples for preserves.

In 1963, the Bidgoods opened the family's best-known operation, Bidgood's Supermarket in the Goulds. For 40 years, the supermarket has sold every imaginable Newfoundland and Labrador specialty, from flipper pie, cod tongues and cod sounds, to squashberries, bakeapple jam and turnip greens. Foodstuffs purchased from local farmers, hunters and fishers are sold fresh, frozen, baked, boiled and

BIDGOOD'S WHOLESALE

"I picked a fine day [in 1948] and loaded the truck with 60 boxes of different kinds of Browning Harvey biscuits and headed up the shore. I went as far as Ferryland before I sold one box to Tommy Grant at the Southern Shore Trading Company. At that time all the shops on the shore were dealing with the St. John's merchants and money was scarce. A couple of weeks later, I loaded a truck with groceries at Barrett's Wholesale, and biscuits from Browning Harvey and went as far as St. Shotts. I traded quite a lot of groceries for eggs, etc., which I sold to Jack Ryan on Holdsworth Street. That was the start of Bidgood's Wholesale."

—Roger Bidgood, 1994

Dog delivering cookies

Roger Bidgood with fish

DEAR MRS. BIDGOOD...

"I am a native daughter of Newfoundland and I can truthfully say that I haven't had a decent meal, but a few times, since I came to live on the main in 1947. When my father was living, he used to send me saltfish and other much-longed-for goodies from home. Since his passing, I've just longed continually for some of that Newfoundland fare ... I reside in the East Kootenays of British Columbia and our city here has not got stores that carry anything like it. We've gotten so we just lunch. Nothing seems to have any taste for us. Our mouths are still watering since reading your article."

—Mrs. William Allen, *Letter to the Star Weekly*, 1971

bottled. The store's popular bakery department began when Roger Bidgood supplied the store's first baker, Mercedes Putt, with a stove just like the one she had at home. Mrs. Putt, a widow with 19 children to support, made a sign of the cross over each loaf so it would rise. For some, selling rabbits to Bidgood's provided a major source of winter income. The fish plant in Petty Harbour closed with the Groundfish Moratorium of 1992. In 1999, the Bidgoods donated the plant to the town of Petty Harbour-Maddox Cove as the future site for a fisheries museum. The deteriorating plant was pulled down in 2002 and by 2004 only a small section of the foundation remained. In 1998, a volunteer committee built a war memorial where the Bidgood home once stood.

Bidgood's plant, Petty Harbour

Dog delivering bread

Petty Harbour Dogs

Hayfields and a barn are essential to the keeping of a horse. In Petty Harbour, land of any sort was in short supply and the community was famous for using dogs rather than horses for hauling and transport. A 1910 census counted 38 ponies and horses in Petty Harbour and Maddox Cove; the dog count was 282. In the summer, dogs were turned loose to forage on caplin and fish offal, and roamed as far south as Bay Bulls, half-starved and half-wild. No one could keep sheep in Petty Harbour or Maddox Cove, for the roaming dogs would kill them. In winter, dogs were penned in cribs or under houses and fed seal meat and salt herring. All through the winter, three- and four-dog teams pulled *dog-cats* (dog-slides or catamarans) loaded with *sticks* (wood) from as far away as Bay Bulls Big Pond and Heavy Tree Road.

Petty Harbour

JOHN AND THE MISSUS (1987)

In *John and the Missus*, feisty John Nunn battles to save the mining town of "Cup Cove" from resettlement. At home, John spars with the "Missus." Petty Harbour is not a mining town but, nonetheless, its cliffs, houses and interiors are featured throughout the film. The house posing as the Nunn residence is in the Cribbies; its unusual façade echoes that of an elaborate **palace** (priest's house) that once stood to its north. Gordon Pinsent (*The Forest Rangers, Quentin Dergens MP, A Gift to Last*) wrote the novel, adapted, directed and starred in the movie, and later toured a stage production of the story. The film won Pinsent his second Genie for best actor (he won his first in 1971, for *The Rowdyman*, his first Newfoundland feature).

Pinsent employed Petty Harbour people as extras and cast professional actors from St. John's in minor speaking parts. Jackie Burroughs (*Anne of Green Gables*) played the Missus, and Jessica Steen, a promising Canadian ingenue, played Faith, the Nunns' prospective daughter-in-law. *John and the Missus* was a critical success, but did not lead to projects of similar magnitude, and Pinsent returned to television (*Red Green, Due South*), dramatic writing and sporadic supporting roles in Hollywood films (*The Shipping News*).

Eric Chafe on his "truckley," c. 1941

The main slide path followed the string of frozen ponds above the community, rounded John Pynns Hill and descended Long Run to the harbour.

Dogs also hauled goods and supplies to and from St. John's, mostly along Old Petty Harbour Road. A Petty Harbour fisherman walking to St. John's in the summer might bring along a couple of dogs hitched to a small cart, for one never knew what of value might be encountered along the way. Men from the harbour were called "Petty Harbour dogs" by the people of St. John's, an allusion to both their mode of transport and scrappy behaviour.

Smallpox Politics

The years 1832 to 1836 were a period of unparalleled turmoil and transition for Newfoundland. In 1832, the party of reform, led by William Carson and Patrick Morris, failed to gain electoral control of New-

Customer served by Maggie Bidgood, "John and the Missus"

foundland's first House of Assembly, a pioneering institution of self government that both men had been instrumental in creating. The reformers' most effective ally was Newfoundland's fourth Roman Catholic bishop, Michael Anthony Fleming (1792-1850), a wily and energetic Irish-born prelate schooled in the liberation politics of the Irish nationalist, Daniel O'Connell (1775-1847).

Bishop Michael Anthony Fleming

Bishop Fleming visited Petty Harbour three times in the year immediately before the election of 1836, a watershed event that brought the reform party to power. On July 17, 1835, the bishop arrived on the dioceses' newly christened schooner, the *Madonna*, and stayed three days with Laurence Kiley Jr. (1781?-1850). The *Madonna* carried 6-8,000 board feet of lumber destined for the community's first Roman Catholic church. A second lengthy coastal stop made that summer was at Ferryland, like Petty Harbour a denominationally mixed community, where the bishop again staged an elaborate display of ministry. Bishop Fleming received an annual grant of £75 from the governor, compared to £2,170 received by Anglican clergy, an injustice that the bishop's summer-long display of missionary zeal was designed, in part, to underscore.

Laurence Kiley Jr.

In September of 1835 the bishop returned to St. John's to a raging smallpox epidemic. He remained in town long enough to fulminate against the colony's elite, who, he claimed, aided the sick only after the epidemic had spread to their class. He also preached against Chief Justice Henry Boulton's new quarantine regulations, which prevented relatives from begging door-to-door for coffin money for the deceased. From a medical point of view, the custom was unfortunate, for smallpox spreads chiefly through close facial contact with an infected person. In November, he moved to Petty Harbour with a medicine chest and

Governor Henry Prescott

Dr. Edward Kielly

The Mass House, c. 1900

"I betook myself to that place, and as I did not wish to expose the family with whom I usually lodged to the danger of infection through me, I took possession of an abandoned cabin and having some knowledge and skill in medicine I set up my medicine chest there as the village dispensary, and I remained four months in this abandoned shed without a servant except for someone who prepared my food. And in my visits to the sick I made no difference between Protestant and Catholic in the free distribution of medicines and of the means of nutrition. When the disease finally abated, it was through the mercy of God that only two deaths occurred out of 400 cases of severe sickness."

—Bishop Michael Anthony Fleming, *Relazione*, 1837

soup tureen for a four-month stay. The bishop is remembered in the community for scorching his fine waistcoat against the stove while making soup, and for bringing nourishment to the sick and dying of both creeds, an act of kindness that inspired many conversions.

The bishop left two accounts of his stay. In one, he spent the winter in a washhouse; in the other, he inhabited an abandoned cabin so he would not infect the Kileys. Family tradition has the bishop residing in the family home, where he built an altar, said Mass and performed funerals, marriages and christenings. As the "Mass House" was then long and narrow, with attached outbuildings, all three accounts are possible. In addition to tending the sick and overseeing the building of St. Joseph's, Bishop Fleming moved the Catholic cemetery from where the War Memorial sits today, to a spot on Old Petty Harbour Road, a kilometre outside the community. He used his own funds to purchase land in front of St. Joseph's and blasted out a level area, possibly for a school or gathering place.

Bishop Fleming's sojourn in Petty Harbour was as strategic as it was humanitarian, for Governor Henry Prescott (1783-1874) had procured a letter of censure from the bishop's superiors, expressly forbidding political engagement. From his humble washhouse in Petty Harbour, the bishop could neither effectively be served the letter, nor be blamed for the outrages his subalterns, chiefly Father Edward Troy (1797-1872), committed in his absence. The bishop's smallpox ministry had a third advantage in that it embarrassed the medical establishment, particularly Dr. Edward Kielly (1790-1855) who, the previous year, had accepted the position of chief medical officer, putting the bishop's close political ally, Dr. William Carson, out of the job. Dr. Kielly was a "Mad Dog," or "Orange

The Mass House today

THE MASS HOUSE

In the 40 years before a church was built in Petty Harbour (*c.* 1795-1835) visiting Roman Catholic clergy lodged with Laurence Kailey (1745?-1821), a devout, Gaelic-speaking fisherman from County Waterford, Ireland. So many services were held in the Kailey home that it became known as the "Mass House." The easternmost half of the house survives as an oddly proportioned, large-windowed salt box across from St. Joseph's Church. Laurence Kailey's Gaelic family name, *Cadhla*, was anglicized by succeeding generations as Kiley, Keily, Kielly, Keiley and Kieley.

Mass House altar

Old St. Joseph's, 1955

1845 chalice, Petty Harbour

Catholic," terms of reproach hung on any Catholic who married into, socialized with or otherwise co-operated with the Protestant establishment. The bishop's refusal to stay—or admit that he stayed—with the Kileys of Petty Harbour may be pure coincidence, but it is more likely he was making a point. It was the case too that, by having a servant prepare his meals, the bishop was not forced to eat food prepared by Laurence Kiley Jr.'s Protestant-born wife Maria, the daughter of William Chafe and Mary Angel.

The bishop returned to Petty Harbour in May of 1836 to celebrate Mass and confirm 413 out of a congregation of 700. The bishop had reason to celebrate. As a peace offering, Governor Prescott had agreed to support the bishop's petition for a prominent cathedral site next to Fort William in St. John's. Bishop Fleming left for England and Rome forthwith, both to secure his cathedral and to refute the governor's charge of undue political meddling. The bishop left behind Father Troy as Vicar General. Troy both refused the Sacraments (including last rites), and incited voters to violent action against "Mad Dog" candidates and their supporters. In the election of 1837 (called when the election of 1836 was annulled

St. Joseph's altar, 1955

by Chief Justice Boulton on a technicality) only two of the members returned to the House of Assembly were not of the reform party. In 1837, Governor Prescott struck another truce. Justice Boulton, who had repeatedly used his office to oppose reform, would be asked to leave Newfoundland if the bishop's Vicar General was removed from the Island as well. Bishop Fleming agreed to the letter of the terms and removed Father Troy to the island of Merasheen, Placentia Bay.

St. Joseph's Church

Bishop Fleming's flurry of activity in Petty Harbour resulted in a church but no resident parish priest. In 1866, three Sisters of Mercy took up residence in quarters behind the church, though they left in 1870, as there was no priest or daily service, and sometimes no Sunday service at all. Petty Harbour's first resident priest was Father John Walsh, who performed his first baptisms and marriages in the community in 1873. In June of 1884 Dean Roger Tierney (1855-1930) succeeded Father Walsh and served the parish for 46 years. Dean Tierney was born in Drom Cashel, County Tipperary, of a poor family; it is said four of his brothers laboured as farm workers to support his

Old Petty Harbour Road, 1839

"For the first three or four miles there was a good road, but we then turned off by a narrow path over the ridge of the South Side Hill. The summit of this is a broad bare moorland, consisting partly of morass or small skirts of wood, partly of naked sheets of level rock or of round hummocks and knobs, and small abrupt ridges of rock rising up here and there along 'the strike' of the beds. There are several ponds or small lakes scattered about it: one or two of these are connected by narrow passages, and form most picturesque sheets of water; and when the eye stretches across them over the well-defined boundary of the hill just beyond, and sees far away in the distance the blue horizon of the sea, few scenes that I have beheld are more wild and striking."

—Joseph Beete Jukes, Excursions in and about Newfoundland, 1842

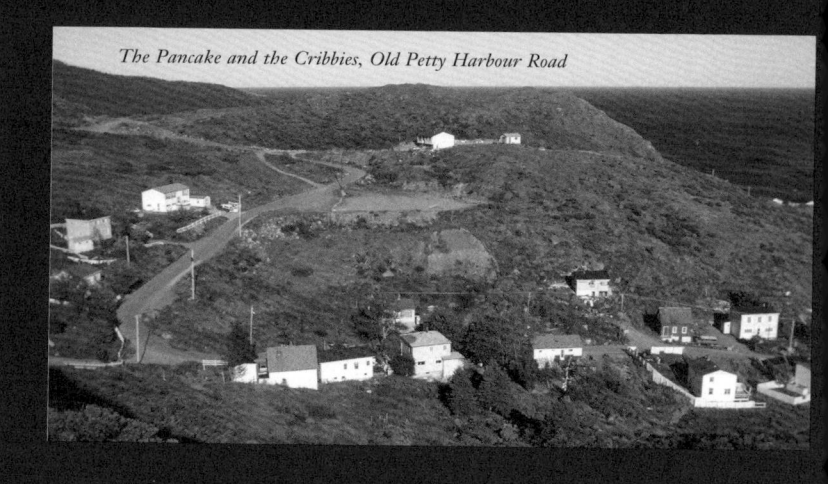

The Pancake and the Cribbies, Old Petty Harbour Road

Dean Roger Tierney

education into the priesthood. The dean made one trip back to Ireland. His parishioners celebrated his return by donning harness and pulling the dean from St. John's to Petty Harbour by sleigh.

In 1962, during the ministry of Father James L. O'Dwyer (1917-86), the old church was torn down and, for two years, Father O'Dwyer celebrated Mass in St. Edward's Roman Catholic School next door. The new church was consecrated on March 15, 1964. Its most attractive feature is the interior, where 12 laminated-wood arches, finished in natural stain, mimic a ship's hull. St. Edward's School was closed in the early 1980s and has since housed government offices, the town hall, a community centre and a volunteer-run museum.

Old Petty Harbour Road

For three centuries, Old Petty Harbour Road was the quickest route from Petty Harbour to St. John's. The path crosses the exposed highland plateau north of the harbour and comes out at Kilbride. Around 1860, the footpath was upgraded to accommodate wagons and carts. The road served for years as a favourite excursion for hikers, hunters and, above all, trouters, for there are 10 ponds along the route. Before it was dammed to supply water to St. John's, the largest, Petty Harbour Long Pond, was said to resemble the Lakes of Killarney in County Kerry.

At its Petty Harbour end, the road switchbacks through the Cribbies, a neighbourhood tucked into a steep valley. The Cribbies is too far from shore to be of value to the fish trade, so it became a convenient place to house animals and Irish servants. "Cribbies" captures in a word how the poor once lived: in "cribs," i.e., shelter resembling that provided for animals, and often shared with animals; on "crib," i.e.,

Petty Harbour Hospitality, June 24, 1859

"We descended in a zigzag way into the deep gorge, one of these cuts through the shore mountains from inland regions to the sea, which occasionally became fiords or narrow bays ... At the bottom is the little village of Petty Harbour, where the river, a roaring torrent, meets the salt tide. We alighted at a cottage, Swiss-like among the rocks, before we were quite down, and were pleased to hear Mr. [Ambrose] Shea, whose guests we were, making arrangements with a nice-looking woman for an abundant supper, or our return. Mr. S., in company with several persons who now joined us from St. John's, then proceeded to show us the lions of the place, or lion rather, for everything and everybody are run up into, and knit into one body, the fishery ...

Upon our return to the cottage on the hill-side, where we at first alighted, we sat down, with sharp appetite, to a supper of fried capelin and cods' tongues, garnished with cups of excellent tea. We ate and drank with the relish of travellers, and talked of the continent from Greenland to Cape Horn. After supper, we climbed out of the valley, in advance of the wagons and our company, to an eminence from which [Frederick William] Church sketched the surrounding scenery, more for the sake of comparison with some of his Andean pencillings than for any thing really new. He remarked that the wild and rocky prospect bore a strong resemblance to the high regions of the Cordilleras. While he was engaged with the pencil, I scrambled to a high place, and looked at the Atlantic, touched with long shafts of the light and shade of sunset."

—Louis Legrand Noble, AFTER ICEBERGS WITH A PAINTER, 1862

Visitors seated by Indian Rock

shared grub; and among people who "cribbed,' i.e., scrounged what they could. In Newfoundland, in matters Irish, feelings of pride have long replaced the pejorative, and the neighbourhood's colourful history has been whitewashed. "Cribbies" is now thought to refer to the "Caribee," i.e., the Caribbean Islands, or to the neighbourhood custom of hosting the Christmas crèche.

Irish Youngsters, Dieters and Masterless Men

During the 1700s, Newfoundland-bound fishing vessels that stopped at Wexford and Waterford, Ireland, to pick up provisions, loaded *Irish youngsters* as well as salt meat and butter. Boys and men willing to indenture to a planter for two summers were packed below decks in pitiable conditions and hired to a master upon arrival. Single women booked passage too. Most youngsters shipped home for the winter, but increasing numbers sought to stay in Newfoundland by becoming *dieters*, i.e., servants who received winter bed and board in exchange for woodcutting, field-clearing, the repair of fishing rooms and other off-season tasks. It was the custom to refuse wages and return passage to youngsters who missed five days work without leave during their contract,

CRIB LODGINGS, 1820

The pioneer Methodist missionary William Wilson (1799-1869) had first hand experience of crib lodging in Petty Harbour. Wilson joined John Pickavant (1792-1848) in St. John's in 1820. Until their mission was reduced to one man in 1821, the two young preachers made regular visits to the coves and outports surrounding St. John's. They were received hospitably everywhere except Petty Harbour. In his memoirs, written 40 years later, Wilson so vividly remembers those thankless Sabbath slogs to the community that the reader can imagine the route taken: the path over the South Side Hills in the summer; in winter, the "easier" route over what is now Old Petty Harbour Road.

"Petty Harbour is nine miles south from St. John's. For three fourths of the way, the path was over a series of high hills, many of them having an inclination of more than 45°, with large rocks and caverns almost every step; so that locomotion was necessarily very slow, and the labour very great to the wearied pedestrian. The winter path was not so exhausting, as it lay mostly over roads and level marshes. This was truly mission ground, where we both had to toil and suffer. Newfoundland is justly proverbial for its

Interior of a fisherman's cabin

whatever the reason—sickness, drunkenness, pregnancy, a dispute. The practice created a troublesome population of *masterless men*, i.e., "dieters" who over-wintered under whatever roof they could find, and under whatever terms.

Chronic winter idleness, drinking and grumbling occasionally turned to violence. In 1708, with four boats and 29 servants, Thomas Ford was Petty Harbour's most substantial planter. Ford was also the unofficial "winter governor" of the settlement. During the winter of 1720, Ford died of stab wounds inflicted by an enraged Irish servant. Awakened to the consequences of the lawless confusion that prevailed over the winter, Petty Harbour's surviving planters petitioned for a local, merchant-run winter court able officially to sentence miscreants. The Boston-born

A London press gang at work

Petty Harbour "cribs," 1886

merchant William Keen (1680?-1754) acquired Ford's plantation. Keen, who rose to become the colony's chief civilian magistrate, was murdered by a nine-member Irish gang in St. John's in 1754.

The Napoleonic Wars (1793-1815) drove the price of fish to new heights, increasing the demand for workers. English servants, however, were in short supply, for press gangs combed the countryside, netting every fisherman they could find for the Royal Navy. Newfoundland's West Country ship merchants addressed the growing labour crisis by stopping in at Irish ports. Dispossessed and desperate Irish workers were particularly numerous following the failure of Theobald Wolfe Tone's United Irishmen Rebellion of 1796-98. Wily masters engaged the most vulnerable of these political refugees as "dieters," knowing full well such men would have good reason not to request return passage.

Neither winter work nor lodging was in fact provided. At season's end, abandoned Irish servants, in alarming numbers, were left to fend for themselves. Beginning in 1799, a succession of governors instituted measures designed to rid the colony of its swelling Irish underclass. They decreed that all dieters be deported and, to discourage over-wintering, forbade the

hospitality; and, in the out-harbours, every house is, or may be, the stranger's home.

Petty Harbour was an exception. The people would come to hear us preach, but none would invite us to their table. We were accustomed to walk this terrible path on Sabbath morning early, preach twice, and teach a small Sabbath school, remain without dinner, unless we took it with us, and return the same nine miles in the evening. Often has the writer been compelled to satisfy the craving of hunger with a few berries plucked by the wayside. One Sabbath, Brother Pickavant walked this laborious eighteen miles, preached twice, and, having taken no food since the morning, he fainted as soon as he entered the Mission House. How merciful was the Redeemer, when he justified his disciples, who, being "a hungered" on the Sabbath day, began to pluck the ears of corn to eat. When the winter came on, it was not possible to return on Sabbath evening: we therefore went on Saturday, and remained generally until Tuesday morning. The writer had to sleep two, and sometimes three, nights every fortnight, during the severe winter of 1820-1821, in an open loft, on a bed of shavings, with two horse-rugs for his covering."

—William Wilson, *Newfoundland and Its Missionaries*, 1866

Skinners Hill and bridge, c. 1890

building of chimneys and hearths in any house within 600 feet (183 metres) of shore.

In 1794, Petty Harbour sheltered 32 male and 23 female dieters scattered among 53 households. Though dieters were a short-lived phenomenon, their misery left an enduring shadow. Dieters were often employed piling rock, and so-called *dieter* or *diter walls* still mark many property lines. On May 1, Newfoundlanders welcome spring by exclaiming, "Out dogs, and in dieters!" Dogs hauled wood during the winter and so were well fed and housed. At the beginning of May, however, the dogs were chased out of their cribs to forage for themselves, and dieters were *put in collar* (engaged) to prepare the cribs for the spring shipment of fishery workers, of the two-legged kind. It was widely believed that the men were not as well cared for as the dogs.

Skinners Lane

Most likely, the name Skinners Lane derives from Skinners Hill, the steepest, most exposed part of the lane. Workers called "skinners" made the best pay of anyone in the sealing industry, for they could remove blubber from a heavy seal pelt in two or three strokes of a long knife, leaving no valuable fat on the pelt. Understandably, it tempted such men to work Sundays, on which day the godless might be seen scurrying up the hill on their way to the skinning lofts of Southside, St. John's. At the top of the hill, a rough shortcut called the Protestant Path branched north. Sunday workers (if not Protestant, then soon to be so) took this route to avoid the pelting they would receive if they passed the church-abiding folk of the Cribbies.

The narrow lane with its neat houses and gardens retains the flavour of old-time Petty Harbour. The concrete foundation of Holy Name Hall is still visible on the south side of the lane, near the top of the hill. The hall, opened in 1921, was a

Seal skinner

Roman Catholic establishment that held events the whole community attended: political meetings, movies and concerts put on by the students of St. Edward's or St. Joseph's (the one-room school in Maddox Cove). Dances, numerous during the winter, were usually held in aid of the church. In the 1930s and early 1940s, Josie Everard played all-night, non-stop accordion. From the war into the 1950s, Harold LaFosse's Orchestra, or a four-man band led by Micky Michael, generally supplied the music. Hall dances drew audiences from Bay Bulls, Kilbride and the Goulds.

Immediately back of the hall is a broad rock knob called Mount Pleasant, or Break Heart Hill. Some say the name commemorates the pleasure of hauling fish up and down from its flakes. Others claim the knob was named for the beauty of the view. There are certainly fine views from the outcrop. At night the mount is dark and secluded and, being directly back of Holy Name Hall, no doubt broke hearts and provided pleasure to many.

Picnicking on Mount Pleasure

Great Big Sea

Edward Doyle moved to Petty Harbour in the 1850s, and was one of two community merchants in 1871. At that time, the name was a rare one in the community. By 1904, there were six Doyle households and today

The song "Picking Berries," popularized by the band *Great Big Sea*, goes back four generations in the Doyle family. It likely began as a spoof of, or tribute to, "Out to Old Aunt Mary's," a poem written in the 1880s by the "Hoosier Poet" James Whitcomb Riley (1849-1916). In Riley's version, two elderly brothers recall innocent boyhood visits to the Indiana home of a beloved jam-making aunt. Riley's sentimental original was widely anthologized in school readers.

Picking Berries

Well I spied a berry bush, as I was strolling home one day,
And somehow it brought back the bygone days;
Of when you and I were berrypicking many years ago,
In a little county not so far away.
How well I do remember the day when we first met,
It leaves a picture in my mind I never can forget

We were picking berries at old Aunt Mary's
When I picked a blushing bride,
As we strolled home together, I just wondered whether
I could win you forever if I tried.
Then at love's suggestion, I popped the question
And asked you to be mine.
By your kisses I knew, you'd picked me and I'd picked you
At berrypicking time.

Well, how sweet you were, that day, in your simple gingham gown,
To me you were as lovely as a queen;
When from underneath your bonnet popped a pair of golden curls
And the bluest eyes that I have ever seen.
Your lips were red as cherries, the taste was twice as sweet
It only took one kiss to make my happiness complete.

Boys from Petty Harbour with John White

there are about a dozen. So many Doyles live on Skinners Hill that Skinners Lane is often called "Doyles Lane." Four generations of Doyles have sung and played at "whatever went on"—St. Patrick's Day concerts, Christmas gatherings, rock-and-roll dances, church picnics, church services and community days. In the Doyle family, "if you laid down your guitar someone else wouldn't be long picking it up." (Tom Doyle, *ECTA Interview*, 1999)

Between 1964 and 1969, brothers Tom, Ron, Leonard and Jimmy Doyle appeared regularly on the CBC television variety show *All Around the Circle* in the group *Boys From Petty Harbour*. Also, in the 1960s, brothers Leonard, Brian, Dennis and Paul Doyle formed the *Sandells*, a rock-and-roll band that re-formed 20 years later as the *New Sandells*, when the brothers were joined by Alan Doyle, Tom's 15-year-old son. Alan Doyle sang and played his way through high school (in *First Attempt*) and university (in *Staggering Home*). In 1991, he joined three members of *Rankin Street*, Séan McCann, Bob Hallett and Darrell Power, to form *Great Big Sea*, a high-energy rock band widely celebrated for its Newfoundland roots, fast pace and party-loving fans. Over the next decade, *GBS* toured extensively through North America and Europe, averaging more than 100 concerts a year. In 2000, the band

Ellen Doyle Howlett, 1898

> Then D'Iberville pushed boldly on,
> Through woods and over rough terrain,
> And Petty Harbour next did yield,
> With thirty-six defenders slain.
>
> With six score men, all fighting fit,
> Like demons from the gates of hell
> Let loose to wreak their savage will,
> Upon St. John's the Frenchmen fell.
>
> —George Hoskins, *The Ballad of D'Iberville's Raid*, 1960

Quebec soldier

headlined the province's Millennium celebration and, in 2001, *Sea of No Cares*, the band's sixth release, débuted at the top of the Canadian charts.

French Attacks

During the French and Indian attacks on English settlements in the 1680s, the French *habitant* (settler) community in Quebec developed *petit guerre* (guerrilla) units, modelled on First Nation raiding parties. The units, composed of Indian warriors and French settlers, travelled light, living off the country or off plundered food and ammunition. Raids took place in winter to take advantage of snow cover and frozen ground. Raiders who attacked without hesitation returned with the richest booty, for they had first pick of the spoils. Following a raid, anything that could not be carried away was destroyed, and prisoners were crammed into captured vessels and deported.

In November of 1696 the Quebec-born general Pierre Le Moyne d'Iberville (1661-1706) led an attack on St. John's that was a model *petit guerre* campaign. On November 24, while his main force was pillaging Bay Bulls, Le Moyne d'Iberville sent his most trusted lieutenant, Jacques Testard de Montigny (1663-1737), ahead with 20 scouts to flush out any English lying in wait along the route to the north. De Montigny's men ran into a party of 30 English and pursued them to the outskirts of Petty Harbour. Early on November 26, Le Moyne d'Iberville's main force, carrying mortars, powder and provisions, quick-marched to Petty Harbour, following the route secured by de Montigny. The English, misled by the encounter of the previous day into thinking the raiding party was small, set up a defense position on the north side of Petty Harbour River, most likely on Mount Pleasure, which directly abutted the river in Le Moyne d'Iberville's day. The

Mount Pleasure, c. 1880

Pierre Le Moyne d'Iberville

French raiders crossed the waist-high river, outflanked and slew 36 defenders, and took prisoner many of the rest.

On November 27, heavy snow fell, temporarily preventing troop movement. De Montigny went into the woods to stretch his legs and returned with three semi-frozen prisoners. On November 28, Le Moyne d'Iberville repeated his manoeuvre. De Montigny's advance party encountered 88 defenders in a field of large boulders, 3 km outside St. John's, possibly near Blood Hill and Deadmans Pond. De Montigny held the English under fire until the main force arrived. If the Abbé Jean Baudoin is to be believed, the English lost 55 men and the French just one—their trumpeter.

The Power House

Having rejected Quidi Vidi and the Southside Hills, the Reid Newfoundland Co. picked Petty Harbour River in 1899 as the most promising site for a power station supplying electricity to St. John's. Throughout the summer of 1899, Petty Harbour echoed to dynamite blasts, issuing from the 107-metre-long tunnel being driven through Gull Hill, and a clamorous steam derrick excavated a 150-metre-long tailrace to

MONSIEUR DE MONTIGNY

"In order to face any eventuality, the dauntless officer [de Montigny], after distributing several days rations to his men, commanded them to march in battle formation. The precaution was not needless. They had only gone several leagues when they found themselves faced with a sizable English detachment entrenched behind the brush and hidden in the woods. It was necessary to pass through this corps, or perish. Communicating his drive and fervour to his little troop, Monsieur de Montigny swooped down on the enemy, sword in hand. Realizing that he did not have enough men to dislodge them, he prolonged the attack, and by the wisdom of his skillful manoeuvres, gave Monsieur Le Moyne d'Iberville time to arrive."

—Abbé François Daniel, *D'Iberville ou le Jean-Bart du Canada*, 1868

ELECTRIFYING NEWFOUNDLAND

"Gas engines will become a thing of the past in all probability. Great is the power of capital directed by science. Who could have imagined that this little stream at Petty Harbour would be made to drive the flying cars along our streets, and do all the heavy work for our machinery. Possibly it may yet be used to light our rooms, cook our food and warm our dwellings. Aladdin's wonder working lamp will be left in the shade."

–*The Evening Herald*, August 12, 1899

Drive out to see the 'Power House.'
Drive out to see the change!
The river's bed is drained and dry
Its waters elsewhere range!

–Ellen Carberry, *Newfoundland Quarterly*, 1903

Power house site, c. 1886

the harbour. About 200 men worked on the project, one of whom, Edward Thomas Lee, was killed when a rock-filled boom broke during excavation of the tailrace. On May 1, 1900, the first St. John's streetcar powered by the Petty Harbour Hydroelectric Station commenced its run. Until the construction of the Perrys Brook Power Station in Witless Bay in 1931, Petty Harbour supplied electricity for all of the Avalon Peninsula's domestic, civic and industrial needs.

To supply water to the plant, four ponds above the settlement were fitted with locks and sluices, a dam was constructed at First Pond, and a 1,006-metre-long wooden flume was dug into the slope of the Gorge. Having passed through ponds, flume and tunnel,

Completed power house and bridge, c. 1900

Reid Newfoundland Co. ad promoting electricity

water plummeted down a steel penstock into a gable-roofed power station. Inside, a 1,868-hp Victor turbine, two Westinghouse 500-volt revolving armature generators and three transformers generated a 15,000-volt electrical current that was carried by two 700-pole transmission lines—the second a backup—to a sub-station in St. John's.

In April of 1901 an ice storm downed both transmission lines, and the station's electrical engineer Frank Wing was electrocuted while attempting to control the resulting fire. A more challenging problem was the unanticipated demand for electricity. The more the turbines turned, the more summer pond levels dropped, threatening to cut off water to the flume and station. Following a citywide power failure in the summer of 1908, a more water-efficient 2,100-hp Voight turbine, manufactured in Hildesheim, Germany replaced the Victor. In 1911, Middle Pond's water level was raised by five metres, and in 1912, a second Voight and a more powerful Westinghouse generator were added to the plant. The two Voight turbines and the Westinghouse generator are still in use.

"His Excellency Sir Henry McCallum accompanied by Lady and Miss McCallum, Mrs. Hewlett, Messrs. W. D. Reid and E. P. Morris, visited Petty Harbour yesterday afternoon. Tho the visit was an informal one, to observe the progress made in the work of preparing the street railway power house, His Excellency availed of the occasion to go about among the fishermen and discuss their main industry. He visited the fishing rooms, examined the fish on the flakes, and made a tour of the pretty little village, expressing himself well pleased with evidence of prosperity around . . . The Governor's inspection of the Reid works was also satisfactory. The wooden flume is advancing towards completion, the excavating of the tunnel is making good progress, the boulders from the river are being removed and the site of the power house is being levelled . . . Refreshments were partaken of at Mrs. Jacob Chafe's and in the meantime the villagers gathered with their guns, flags were run up on all the houses, and as the Gubernatorial party left for home volleys of musketry and hearty cheers testified to His Excellency that the people of Petty Harbour were no whit behind the other sections of the Island in their welcome to him."

The Evening Herald,
September 6, 1899

Stave flume under construction, 1926-27

In 1924, a Montreal consortium, christened Newfoundland Light and Power (NLP), bought Reid Newfoundland's power plant and streetcar system. The consortium acquired a leaky flume and dam, an insufficient water supply, an antiquated transmission line and an undersized powerhouse. Only the turbines passed muster. A major overhaul was undertaken in 1925-26. The storage dam at Bay Bulls Big Pond was upgraded, the wooden dam above the plant was replaced by a higher dam built of concrete, and the near-level flume along the Gorge slope was replaced by a 975-metre-long wooden stave pipeline that descended directly through the valley. A surge tank (still existing) was erected on top of the original

Power house, 1974

steel penstock. NLP removed the power station's gable roof and extended the building to accommodate an additional 2750-hp Armstrong Whitworth turbine. The Westinghouse generators were upgraded to 2,300 volts and the transmission line was rebuilt to carry 33,000 volts. Between 1930 and 1935, NLP erected a wall of rock on the slope of Gull Hill to protect the plant and penstock from slope failure and avalanches, such as the one that destroyed 25 metres of flume and cut off power to St. John's for five days in 1921.

The station is one of the oldest active power plants in North America. It springs to life each afternoon, contributing a welcome extra boost of electricity to the evening power grid. The route of the 1899 flume and tunnel can still be traced along Gull Hill's north-facing slope. The 1926 additions to the station's walls are also visible, for they are made of concrete, whereas the 1899 walls are of local stone. In 2002, a steel penstock replaced all but the upper portion of the leaking 1926 stave structure.

THE BRIDGE

Petty Harbour had a population of 133 Anglicans and 122 Roman Catholics in 1794; however, most property was in Protestant hands and only four Catholic families owned land. The Chafes, all Anglican, occupied Big Hill, but otherwise the two faiths lived intermingled and mixed marriages were common. There were only 17 Newfoundland-born heads of household; 36 households were headed by someone English- or Irish-born.

Petty Harbour changed considerably over the next decades. Prominent Anglican families on the north side, such as the Angells, Hayes and Bidgoods, died out, moved or converted. By 1884, the south side Anglican population had doubled, to 251, but the north side Catholic population had more than quadrupled, to 556. The river now divided two communities. Petty Harbour's social life was organized around competing north and south side churches, schools, garden parties and sports teams. "We had our scuffles," as one resident put it.

In 1948, the community split over Confederation, the Anglicans on the south side voting for, and the Catholics on the north side voting against, union with Canada. During the campaign, the bridge witnessed much "yelling and dancing" as the pro-Confederates under Joey Smallwood and anti-Confederates under Peter Cashin held competing rallies. In recent years, cooperation has been

View of north side from bridge

The Chafe House

Petty Harbour photographs show gable-roofed houses to be the 19th-century norm. Flatter roofed dwellings came in with roof felting in the 1890s. Few people pass Hugh Chafe's white- and red-trimmed gable-roofed house without remarking on the beauty of its form and setting. The house was built by Edward Chafe (1859-1929) in 1878, and has changed little since then. All told, Edward Chafe built four houses. For years, his wife Harriet (1861-1934) was the town midwife. It is a Newfoundland tradition for the youngest son to look after his parents, and eventually inherit their house; in this manner the house passed, first to Edgar (1898-1985), then to Edgar's youngest son Hugh.

Chafe House, 1978

View of south side from bridge

The house's moment of glory came on September 23, 1977, when Edgar and Fanny Chafe served a cup of tea to King Baudouin (1934-93) and Queen Fabiola (1928-) of Belgium. The King and Queen were concluding a week's tour of Canada with an eight-hour stop over in Newfoundland. Boats crowded the harbour and the whole community turned out. Children from St. Edward's Elementary School and Goulds Elementary School gathered at the north end of the bridge to sing Newfoundland folk songs and a Belgian song, *The Rumbling Pot*, in Flemish. The royal couple toured a fish plant and received numerous bouquets of flowers. "It's not often you get to shake hands with a king," remarked Mike Hearn, "he's the first one ever came to Petty Harbour." (*Evening Telegram*, 1977)

Herbie's Old Shoppe

From the late 1880s to his death in 1957, John Pynn operated a sawmill below John Pynns Hill. Pynn initially ran his mill from a waterwheel in the river. He bought logs from local fishermen and supplied milled

more common than rivalry. Beneath the surface, some say, Petty Harbour was never fiercely denominational. "People had to live together and work together and get along together, the best they could, and that's just how it was." (Luke Bidgood, *ECTA Interview*, 1999)

"Babe" Chafe transporting tea in her buggy

HARBOUR SHOPS

For years, Henry J. Bishop owned a general dealership near the bottom of the Long Run. Bishop, in addition to operating the store, was at various times the community's postmaster, Justice of the Peace and undertaker. Arthur H. Munroe owned a general dealership near the bridge, and a succession of enterprising women such as Georgina "Babe" Chafe, Maggie Bidgood and Irene Cove ran small shops on the north side.

Weir's Store, 1979

lumber to the Petty Harbour area. He was also a bridge and house contractor and built boats and churches, including St. Kevin's in the Goulds. After the river was diverted to the power plant in 1899, Pynn ran his mill using a stationary engine powered by electricity from the plant. (Stationary engines were bolted in place and ran saws or other devices off a belt or clutch.)

In 1933, Pynn built his son Augustus ("Gus") an elaborate general store a few doors down from Bishops. In the 1940s, Gus opened an ice cream parlour and soda fountain in a back room of the shop that became a popular teen hang-out. Herbert

Family of Augustus and Mary Chafe, 1910

and Marguerite Weir bought Gus Pynn's store in 1955. Weir's General Store was known informally as "Herbie's." In addition to running the store, the Weirs trucked saltfish, cod tongues and cod liver oil to St. John's, and returned with coal, salt, food and household items for the community. Before telephones became common, shopping lists were handed to children who ran down to the store. Orders received on Friday night, or Saturday morning, were packed for home delivery on Saturday afternoon. In 2001, the Weir children converted the store into a craft shop. Inside, the store has changed little. In addition to crafts, it contains displays and mementos from the store's earlier days.

The Stand

In the old days, every community had one or more gathering places where men met, chatted and enjoyed a smoke or chew. North side fishermen gathered under the flakes below St. Joseph's Church. Southside fishermen gathered at the Stand in front of St. George's Anglican Church. The Stand was originally a community well and gathering spot for women; it is not known when the changeover to male chat took place. It has been said of the Stand that, "If there's not someone there, something is wrong."

THE CHAFES OF PETTY HARBOUR

"Chaffes," "Chaffeys" and "Chafees" are found everywhere in the world, but if you meet a "Chafe," the chances are they or their ancestors came from Petty Harbour. John Chafe (1686-1759) of Ipplepen, Devon, was one of a half-score West Country by-boat keepers who, by 1708, had moved into rooms in Petty Harbour emptied by three French attacks. John was of a sensible, religious disposition and, in 1729, became Petty Harbour's first constable. His descendants still possess his silver teapot and oak desk. The family Bible dates from 1749.

Three of John's four sons prospered and had large families, as did, in turn, 11 of their sons. John's oldest, Samuel (1721?-1800) had no children but his second son Henry George (1723-1801) became one of the most prosperous planters in Petty Harbour. Sons William (1725?-1812) and Edward (1727?-1824) married John Angell's two oldest daughters, Mary and Ann, and both couples had large families. It is Edward's great-grandson Jacob Chafe (1798-1878) who is the hero of the ballad, "Petty Harbour Bait Skiff." By 1894, 47 of the 96 families in Petty Harbour were Chafes.

Jacob Chafe's commemorative watch

The Stand, June 24, 1859

"The catch, as the fisher terms the number of fish taken, was small that day, and we encountered, here and there, knots of idle men, smoking, chewing, whittling and talking. For the most part, they were a russet, tangle-haired and shaggy-bearded set, shy and grum [glum] at first, but presently talkative enough, and intelligent upon all matters in their own little world. Fish were so glutted with capelin that they would not bite well. The seines did better. Among the dwellings that we passed or entered, was one of a young English woman, of such exceeding neatness, that the painter could not forget it. That fine-looking, healthy, young English woman, with her bit of a house just as neat as wax, was often spoken of."

—Louis Legrand Noble, AFTER ICEBERGS WITH A PAINTER, 1862

Late night landing

The Stand, 1996

These days, with the exception of the Stand, most gathering takes place in the dark recesses of sheds.

St. George's Church

According to a Chafe family tradition, the first family members to settle Petty Harbour built a small chapel. In 1742, the Rev. Thomas Walbank reported that he was conducting services in Petty Harbour because a "poor fisherman" there had donated "a decent silver paten and chalice with gold." Margaret Williams of Bay Bulls brought an Elizabethan communion cup to Petty Harbour when she married John Chafe's grandson, John, in 1778. Around 1960, this cup was discovered in the possession of Angus Chafe, sawn into two pieces, the cup a dipper for his well, and the base awaiting employment in one of Angus's tool boxes.

Bishop John Inglis (1777-1850) of Nova Scotia consecrated St. David's Church and churchyard in 1827. It is not known how old the church was at the

Williams communion cup

A BISHOP VISITS, JULY 12, 1827

"This is one of the neatest fishing villages in Newfoundland. The Romanists are all on one side of the harbour, and the Protestants, who are all members of the Church, on the other. Like Torbay, it has communication with St. John's by land; but the path is only fit for foot-passengers. Mr. Langhorne was here to receive me, and I was again attended by Colonel Dunscomb, who had been with me at Torbay, and presented handsome flags to the churches at both places. Flags are used throughout Newfoundland, to give notice of service, and every church has its flagstaff. The flag is hoisted to the top at an early hour, lowered half-mast half an hour before service, and entirely when the service commences. St. David's church and burial-ground were consecrated, and 78 persons were confirmed. The church is a very neat building and the congregation attentive and interesting; so that I had great satisfaction in addressing them."

—Bishop John Inglis, *Society for the Propagation of the Gospel Annual Report*, 1827

St. Andrew's with churchyard and Island Rooms, c. 1890

Rev. Thomas Martin Wood

time, though some think it was erected in the 1780s, around the time the churchyard was opened. The church's foundation stones are piled in the extreme southeast corner of the churchyard. For many years, the Anglicans, like the Catholics, made do with itinerant ministers. In 1832, Petty Harbour was included in the dauntingly large district assigned to Deacon Thomas Martin Wood (1807-81). On May 23, 1835, two months before Bishop Fleming arrived with the lumber for St. Joseph's, Deacon Wood convened a parish committee, which voted to construct a new and larger Anglican church on a more prominent site. When Deacon Wood was transferred to Greenspond in 1836, Bishop Fleming accused him of fleeing the pox. It took 11 years for the congregation to donate enough labour and fish to pay for St. Andrew's Church, which was consecrated in September of 1846.

Fire destroyed the roof of St. Andrew's in 1934 and, shortly after, the congregation decided to turn this misfortune into an opportunity to build a larger church.

School theatrical

Both the church and churchyard were extended westward and several old graves and gravestones were covered by the new foundation. The church cornerstone was laid in 1937 and the first services were held in 1939. The new church was named St. George's. The English baptismal font in the church survived the 1934 fire unscathed, and dates to the first chapel.

The Old Anglican Churchyard

Some say it was the custom in the early days to bury people under flakes and stages. Until 1835, both denominations buried their dead close to shore. Graves in the old Anglican churchyard were for the most part dug wherever room could be found, and by 1899, the year the churchyard was declared full, the graves furthest up the hill were at a 45° pitch. A new Anglican cemetery was located a kilometre outside the community on a hill overlooking First Pond and Second Pond.

Though the churchyard is thought to date to the 1780s, no 18th-century gravestone survives. A landslide in 1895 buried the easternmost section of the churchyard and more graves were lost when the road was widened and the church extended. About

BUILDING A NEW CHURCH, 1938

"Reverend Frank Severn got busy right away getting the men of the parish to rebuild. They were listed in groups and notified when they were expected to show up for free labour. The women did knitting, sewing and cooking, and held sales and suppers in the parish hall. The teachers organized children's concerts and the adults 'put off' concerts, too. 'Tickets' were another fundraiser. Older children were sent door-to-door all over the community, selling tickets on items donated.

The school next door was used as a temporary church. Every Friday the older pupils set up the place for Sunday service. As pupils, we had a first-hand education in building construction; especially the boys as they watched the new church grow day by day. The older ones were called now and then to pick up or move things as the building progressed. They were glad to get an hour off school. The girls were called on sometimes to gather stones to help with the concrete foundation. That meant time off, too. The new pulpit was donated by the children. The boys collected a salt fish from each fisherman. The girls held concerts in the summer in sheds, boathouses, fish stages, wherever we could get permission. We charged admission—adults 10¢, children 5¢.

"We sang the songs we knew, recited poetry and made up our own plays. One memorable concert was held by our group of girls in Bob and Lou Wescott's house on Pynns Hill. A corner of the living-room was used for a stage, with a bed sheet for a screen. The room was filled with people, some sitting, some standing. The lights failed so we carried on by lamplight. My cousin Florence and I were in the middle of a homemade dialogue when we forgot our lines. We couldn't find the script, couldn't improvise—we just stood there, two 11-year-olds, very embarrassed. Someone came to our rescue. They took the only lamp to the kitchen and found the script. The play was over in a minute. We got some sympathetic applause. Probably it was from our mothers. One teenaged boy asked for his five cents back. But otherwise, the rest of the concert went off without a hitch."

—Sarah Pack, *ECTA Guidebook Project*, 2003

Girls in pinafores seated by the Long Run, 1886

Ruby Church

50 stones remain. The oldest commemorates Henry Chafe (1723-1801) and his wife Ann (Efford) Chafe (1733-1813). This stone stands immediately south of the pile of rubble left from St. David's Church. Another early stone commemorates William Merry, 28, and William Wills, 20, two fishing servants who drowned in December of 1817. Their outstanding wages likely went to the erection of the stone. Those in the churchyard who are not Chafes are often related to Chafes, such as five-year-old Suzanna Daspher (1806-11) whose father rented a fisherman's room from Henry Chafe, and who was married to Ann, Henry's daughter.

Several Rubys are buried in the churchyard, including Ann Ruby (1814-88), a blacksmith's daughter from Abbottskerswell, Devon, who married William Ruby and homesteaded on Ruby Line in the Goulds. Matilda (née Chafe) Ruby (1844-97) married their son, George. In 1913, George Ruby insisted on a new church location near Ruby Line, a dispute that resulted in the construction of two Anglican churches in the Goulds: Presentation and St. Matthew's. As only the Rubys supported St. Matthew's, it was commonly called "Ruby Church." On August 2, 1986, 11 members of the Goulds vestry attempted to demolish this "spitey church" and 44 friends of St. Matthew's rallied to the abandoned church's defense. A singular

Petty Harbour hearse

compromise was reached that allowed the exterior of Ruby Church to be restored and registered as a heritage structure; however no restoration work or heritage activity is permitted inside.

The Rarest Fruit Drops Soonest

Stones commemorating victims of the diphtheria epidemics of the late 1870s are found in most old Newfoundland graveyards. In Petty Harbour, there is a stone for Emmeline Chafe, who died of diphtheria on June 23, 1875. By the end of the year, two of her children had also succumbed to the disease. In January of 1877, three-year-old Theodore White and his five-year-old stepbrother Edward died within three days of each other. Fanny Chafe, 16, died of the disease in May of 1878. Sophie Chafe, 22, and her brother Phillip, 20, died within two days of each other, the same month. Their father, Phillip Chafe Sr., died of diphtheria a year later. By the time the stone in the graveyard was erected to Phillip and his two children in 1880, a third child, Sarah Ann, 26, had fallen to the disease.

Consumption (tuberculosis) was another devastating killer of the young. Like diphtheria, the disease seemed all the more dreadful for running in families.

SUZANNA DASPHER
(1806-11)

Death from my parents
 snatched me soon away
Twas God's decree that
 I should no longer stay
Therefore lament me
 not, tis often found
That rarest fruit drops
 soonest to the ground.

Solomon Chafe's cottage with Mrs. Chafe, 1886

In the churchyard, there is a stone for Annette Chafe (1804-23). Her brief life is typical of the disease. We know consumption took her sister, Elizabeth Chafe (1815-38), for when Elizabeth was in the last throes of the disease, she said would die happy if she could marry Matthew Morry. The obliging Matthew travelled from Calvert (then Caplin Bay) to Petty Harbour and married Elizabeth on July 18. She died four days later. Matthew went on to marry Eliza Colman in Ferryland in 1844.

Boones Head

Boones Head is most likely named for John Boon who, in 1675, was one of five planters in Petty Harbour, and the only one residing with a family (a wife and child). A planter named John Boon—possibly John Boon's son—was taken prisoner in St. John's by the French in 1706.

Due to the rain-catching alignment of its joints and fractures, Boones Head is highly susceptible to frost-splitting, erosion and rockfalls. There is nearly always a fresh scar on the cliff face. In the early 1990s, a stone rolling down the cliff stopped a half-metre short of the south wall of the nave of St. George's Church. The hill's first and so far only recorded fatality is Amelia Chafe, the four-year-old daughter of Samuel and Mary Chafe. Her gravestone in the churchyard declares she "was unfortunately killed by a rock which fell from the cliff as she was walking, on the 18th of September 1812." In former times, families took seriously the bestowing of favourite first names on a new generation, so Samuel and Mary christened a second

Three women piling faggots on a flake, c. 1955

child Amelia in 1813. When the second Amelia died within the year, they christened a third Amelia in 1817. This daughter lived until 1840.

The disorderly, ever-increasing piles of debris on the west, east and north slopes of Boones Head are prone to *earth flow*, a sudden slope movement triggered by heavy rain. On October 7, 1895, half an hour after midnight, during one of the wettest and windiest nights of the year, the north face of Boones Head collapsed. The slide buried 100 metres of the Southside Road and destroyed Jacob Chafe's cod liver oil factory, Solomon Chafe's house and 50 quintals (2,500 kilos) of dried fish. Solomon and his wife, who were inside their house, survived. An exceptionally heavy rain on October 12 and 13, 1934, resulted in three modest slides, two on the north face, and one on the east. The largest of the three carried Jacob "Joey" Chafe's abandoned saltbox partway into the harbour.

PETTY HARBOUR FISHERMEN WORKING TOGETHER

- In **1923**, form a Fishermen's Committee to manage the local trap fishery.

- In **1955**, successfully lobby to extend their fishing grounds to Long Point, south of Shoal Bay.

- In **1961**, unanimously vote to create a Protected Fishing Area, within which long lines (1961) and gill nets (1963) are prohibited.

- In **1964**, take over the management of the annual trap berth draw.

- In **1983**, respond to repeated cod gluts by creating the Petty Harbour Fisherman's Co-operative Society, giving fishermen control over the production and marketing of their own fish.

- In **1998**, support the Petty Harbour Model Fishing Village concept as a way to both maintain the fishery and realize the community's tourism potential.

Big Hill, 1886

The Fisherman's Co-op

In the early 1980s, Petty Harbour's 95 fishermen maintained as many as 90 traps and, in good years, landed over three million kilos of cod. Excess catches were handled by an informal arrangement that allocated each day's landings at a plant to different trap crews. If the price of cod fell, and plant operators decided they could make more by processing caplin and squid, the arrangement collapsed, and fishermen had nowhere to sell their fish. By 1983, the harbour's fishermen had had enough and 84 contributed $500 each to form the Petty Harbour Fisherman's Co-operative Society, so that co-op members controlled the buying and processing of the day's catch. The co-op began buying fish in 1984, and began processing fish in 1986 with the opening of the present processing plant, which was built largely by the volunteer labour of members. At its peak, the plant employed 150 workers and processed cod, caplin and squid. In 2003, the plant lay idle, but the co-op still had 48 members, engaged for the most part in the crab fishery.

Tom Best in front of the Fisherman's Co-op, 1986

The Groundfish Moratorium, 1992

"Ten years ago there was so much work here, and they still had to truck out some fish. Long before the moratorium was called, the federal and provincial governments did not do what they should've done—and they are still not doing it today—listen to fishermen saying that the stocks were going and the fish were getting smaller. We were totally, totally against the caplin fishery because we don't think that it should ever have been opened up. Caplin are the main source of food for the cod. If they take that away, the cod are not going to McDonald's to get something to eat.

When the moratorium was called, yes, most of the noise came from Petty Harbour. That was us, out there, beating at the door the night John Crosbie was down at the hotel announcing what they were going to give us. Indeed, it was! Petty Harbour sticks together when it comes to something like that. Now the younger crowd benefited from this, I would say. They got an opportunity to get educated, and get a trade and find work outside the fishery. Right now, the kids have nothing. Only for the bit of crab landed, this place would be a ghost town. The crab is all trucked out of the harbour. At the time the government was giving out crab processing licenses, crab wasn't an issue. To tell you the truth, some people didn't know what a crab pot was."

—Richard Clements, *ECTA Interview*, 1999

Fishing shed

Big Hill

In 1895, 70 families lived on the south side of Petty Harbour east of Boones Head. Big Hill is still Petty Harbour's steepest, most densely populated quarter. The fish plant below the hill, just inside of the breakwater, has changed its name and ownership, on average, every five years. A partnership led by Hannif Madakia opened the plant as Newfoundland Processors in 1976 and re-incorporated as Newfoundland Food Processors in 1979. The plant briefly operated as Cape Spear Fisheries under Quinlan & Daley, then in the early 1980s Dave Maloney of Bay Bulls bought the plant at auction and renamed it Petty Harbour Fisheries. Maloney received $900,000 to extend and modernize the plant in 1984. Gary Hearn of Petty Harbour bought the plant in the early 1990s, again changing the name, this time to Peerless Fisheries.

Petty Harbour street scene, 1886

Motion Path

> "In the winter, the planters employ themselves in getting fish, sawing deal boards, making oars, catching beaver, and fowling. They have innumerable ducks, several geese, wild pigeons, partridge, hares, etc."
>
> —The Journal of James Yonge, 1664

Motion Path

0.0 km & 0.6 km: Big Hill

There are several traditional routes up Big Hill. To find the East Coast Trail, hikers should not go to the end of the road, but follow a steep, narrow gravel lane tucked between two houses, half-way between the Fisherman's Co-op and the breakwater. This lane, called Big Hill Lane, runs for 15 metres up the hill, then turns sharply east and becomes Cavelles Lane, named for Cavelle Chafe, a former resident. The trailhead is immediately past the last house on Cavelles Lane.

Old pictures of Petty Harbour show barren hillsides and a surprising number of fields. In former times, any piece of ground not too steeply sloped or stony was turned into a garden or paddock. The lower part of the path up Big Hill still passes open patches of meadow and stone piles that once bordered fields. Children were sent out to cut alder boughs and other kindling for the stove, so no tree or shrub within hauling distance of a community grew past the sapling

Shore Names

There is no secure anchorage for a large ship in Petty Harbour. In the days of the migratory fishery, it is said, Council Cove was where captains hauled in to do business and exchange news. The name "Otterbury Point" is most likely a corruption of "otter burrow." River otters still frequent the Dial, a steeply dipping, clock-shaped ledge nearby that makes an ideal otter run.

Exchange at sea, 1887

Plants 101

Angiosperms (flowering plants) are the largest and most recently evolved group in the plant kingdom. Within this group are two sub-groups, the monocots (*monocotyledons*) and dicots (*eudicotyledons*). Monocots have a single seed leaf or *cotyledon*—the first leaf that develops in embryo. Dicots contain two cotyledons or seed leaves.

It is easy to distinguish between monocots and dicots in the wild. Monocot leaf veins run parallel to each other (e.g., Canada mayflower); dicot leaf veins fan out from a main vein in a complex network

Monocot (pitcher plant)

stage. Since all growth was scotched, no single canopy species could gain ground over the rest; the vegetation that has returned to the slope is a dense, leggy scrub of fir, mountain alder, white birch, mountain holly, northern wild raisin, pin-cherry, chuckley-pear and dogberry. There is an equally mixed understory of blueberry, sheep laurel, wild roses, bunchberry, Canada mayflower and wild sarsaparilla. Wear and washouts over the years have turned sections of the old path into a streambed. At the crest of Big Hill, the route follows a hunting trail that keeps to the seaward edge of the high, backcountry plateau. An abundance of berrypicking and hunting paths crisscross the plateau, which extends inland to Hare Hill and Watch Hill. One of the most defined paths leads to Cow Pond (also called Bathers Pond), a popular swimming hole.

◎ 1.0 km: Council Cove

In the summer of 1986, a 14-year-old boy, helping a girl set up a tent in a Big Hill meadow, started a fire to get rid of a bothersome anthill. The fire burned for a week and denuded the country southwards to Shoal Bay, a distance of 6 km. The fire missed small patches of wood at Council Cove, Freshwater River, Siles Cove and Fortune Gullies, but was otherwise thorough in its destruction. Most likely the flames travelled quickly and did not burn past the *duff* (surface litter), for by the late 1980s hectare upon hectare of blueberry bushes had taken over the landscape. Gradually, the blueberry is being supplanted by sheep laurel, Labrador tea and mountain alder. However, judging from the high berry content in fox scats seen along the path, blueberries are still an important food source on the plateau.

THE AVALON IS CREATED

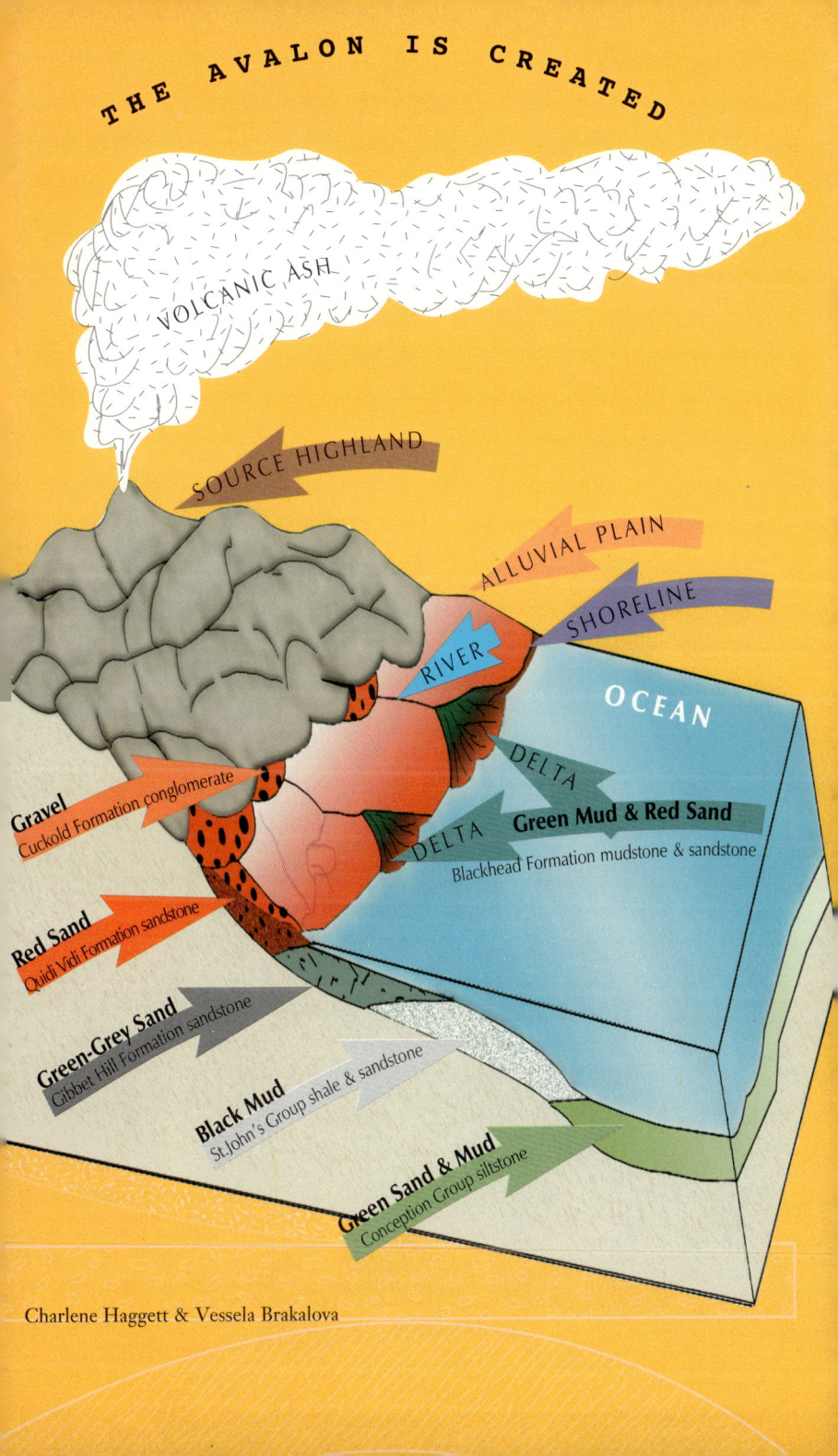

VOLCANIC ASH

SOURCE HIGHLAND

ALLUVIAL PLAIN

SHORELINE

RIVER

OCEAN

DELTA

DELTA

Gravel
Cuckold Formation conglomerate

Red Sand
Quidi Vidi Formation sandstone

Green Mud & Red Sand
Blackhead Formation mudstone & sandstone

Green-Grey Sand
Gibbet Hill Formation sandstone

Black Mud
St. John's Group shale & sandstone

Green Sand & Mud
Conception Group siltstone

Charlene Haggett & Vessela Brakalova

Peter Gard *Boones Head*

◎ Motion Path

Scott Chafe *Petty Harbour stage heads* c. 1970

Scott Chafe *Petty Harbour fish flakes* c. 1970

Peter Gard *Oyster leaf*

Darlene Scott *Kettles Cove*

Peter Gard *Starrigans*

Red-osier dogwood

Bunchberry

Rhodora

Agnes Marion Ayre,
Courtesy of the Agnes Marion Ayre Herbarium, Memorial University

Peter Gard *Motion Head erratics*

Peter Gard *Miner Point felsenmeer*

Peter Gard *Near Doubloon Pool*

Sedge (Carex flava)

Yellow pond lily

Agnes Marion Ayre,
Courtesy of the Agnes Marion Ayre Herbarium, Memorial University

Above Council Cove, 1988

Hikers are indebted to the fire for the unimpeded view of Motion Bay. Big Hill's denuded ledges and hollows look stark and exaggerated, as if the land's bones were showing. It takes decades for vegetation in an exposed environment to recover following a fire. Exposure to wind and desiccation on slopes and rock outcrops increases, and hollows collect extra water and eroded material. The first plants to return are those that thrive in conditions that are rocky, open or wet. Common juniper, blueberry, partridgeberry, three-toothed cinquefoil, bracken fern and caribou lichen spread over the drier areas. Round-leaved sundew, bog rosemary, bog myrtle, bog laurel, cotton grass, cinnamon fern, heath moss, larch and sedges thrive in the wet patches.

Two decades after the conflagration, many—possibly most—of the tree skeletons left by the flames are still standing. Using the skeletons as a measure, the vegetation above Council Cove has almost reached its former height. A high cliff face, like the one facing the cove, creates an updraft that cuts down on biting

(e.g., alder, roses). Also, the flower parts of monocots are arranged in threes, or multiples of three (e.g., irises and orchids). In dicots, the flower parts occur in fours, fives or multiples of four or five (e.g., roses, bunchberries). Although far fewer in number, the monocots include many important food species, such as corn, wheat, rice, sorghum, millet and sugarcane.

Dicot (Virginia rose)

Huckleberry

Two species of huckleberry occur on the Avalon Peninsula: dwarf huckleberry (*Gaylussacia dumosa*) and black huckleberry (*G. baccata*). Both bear the bell-shaped flowers typical of the heath family (Ericaceae). Shiny black huckleberries ripen in the late summer and early fall, the same time as blueberries. Unlike blueberries, which have numerous tiny, scarcely noticeable seeds, huckleberries contain 10 larger seeds, or nutlets. Although seedier, huckleberries can be eaten raw, and are usually mixed in with blueberries and prepared in the same manner. Black huckleberry prefers moist, dense soil and is generally found in inland bogs and fens. As it grows in richer ground, it produces a larger, tastier berry. Dwarf huckleberry is more tolerant of poor conditions and inhabits **barrens** (open country) and coastal areas.

Motion Bay excursion

Dwarf huckleberry

winds. Additional snow lands on the slope above the cliff and new growth is better protected than elsewhere.

◎ 1.7 km: Merrymeeting Point

Fishermen had favourite haul-in spots where they could enjoy a sociable noonday "boil-up" without being troubled by the ocean swell. Merrymeeting Point was one such place. Many Newfoundland settlements also have spots for trysts, usually a short distance outside the community. Merrymeeting Point is ideally situated for romantic meetings, for it is off the path and hidden by a low rise, and is below Cow Pond, a popular bathing spot.

For 350 years, hunters in search of seabirds and other game have crossed Big Hill to the Motion, creating a trail that, in many spots, is etched half a metre into the hillside. Elsewhere, the path runs along a half-metre-high dike, built from sediment that has washed down the trail over the years. Generations of blueberry bushes and other heath plants kept the sediment in place and contributed their leaves to the build-up. The old path took the shortest feasible route down the hill; a new zigzag route has been introduced to lessen erosion. The new route leads

Returned hunters, 1858

onto a ledge, from which there is a sweeping view. In the years since the fire, the already thin soil cover on Big Hill's south-facing slope has been further exposed and eroded, and it is chiefly species adapted to poor or disturbed soils, such as larch and mountain alder, that are flourishing. Caribou lichen and impoverished-looking sheep laurel cover the driest, most nutrient-poor places. The conifers on the slope have yellow needles and are stunted in growth—both signs of stress.

A short distance below the ledge (at **1.9 km**) the path skirts a bog. Everything generally found in a Newfoundland bog can be found in this one: red and brown peat moss, rusty-coloured and one-head cotton grass, pitcher plant, bog rosemary, bog laurel, sweetgale and leatherleaf—a plant with leaves arranged like the spine of a stegosaurus dinosaur. Before the fire, larch tuck (dwarfish, wind-shaped trees, also called tuckamore) ringed the bog and black spruce grew in the shelter of Big Hill. Only the skeletons of these hardy, distinctively shaped trees remain. Past the bog, the slope lessens and dwarf huckleberry is more common than sheep laurel. Plants on the lower part of a slope generally benefit from additional nutrients, moisture and shelter. The shrub cover becomes taller as the descent continues and there is more mountain alder and white birch

Leatherleaf

PETTY HARBOUR MEMBER

Between 635 and 545 million years ago, the Avalonian *Orogeny* (a major mountain building episode) created a Himalayan-like mountain system north of the present Avalon Peninsula. Over a period of about 20 million years, numerous southward flowing streams eroded this mountain system, creating a river plain and coastal delta composed of a 3.5-km thickness of sand, silt and pebble known as the Signal Hill Group. The group has four *formations* (separable, mappable units) between Petty Harbour and Witless Bay. From the lowest in position—and therefore oldest—to the youngest and highest layers, these are the Gibbett Hill, Quidi Vidi, Cuckold and Blackhead formations.

The youngest of the four, the Blackhead Formation, has been further demarcated into five *members* (subdivisions of a formation). Rock outcrops between Petty Harbour and Motion Head have the streaky, red-and-white sandy appearance typical of the Petty Harbour Member, a lower (older) unit of the Blackhead Formation. (This member is encountered elsewhere on the trail at Gunners Cove, Spear Bay, Staffordside and Maddox Cove.)

If the Blackhead Formation is that portion of the eroding mountain that once formed a river delta, the Petty Harbour Member is the part of the delta where river material was deposited in thickly *braided* (many-channelled) strata near the sea's edge, often during flood events. These ancient sand and gravel deposits *lithified* (hardened) into *beds* (rock layers) of red pebble conglomerate, sandstone and mudstone. The member is composed of about 30 per cent red sandstone and 70 per cent granule-to-pebble conglomerate, deposited in no fixed pattern, for river deposits by nature are variable. The diameter of the fragments depends on the fluctuating strength and carrying capacity of the river's flow.

Between 400 and 353 million years ago, a second major Earth movement—the Acadian Orogeny—folded and fractured the Signal Hill Group, tilting or upending the originally horizontal rock beds.

mixed with the huckleberry, as well as robust, mixed patches of chuckley-pear, blueberry, rhodora and dogberry. Reaching the coast, the height and mix of plants changes dramatically, to a low-growing community of common juniper, crowberry, three-toothed cinquefoil, grasses and partridgeberry, all plants that can tolerate the abrasive ice, salt and wind conditions occurring within an ocean spray zone.

◎ 2.6 km: Freshwater River

Freshwater River has dug a substantial channel through the disorderly glacial till at the bottom of Big Hill. The 1986 fire missed a stand of fir on the bank. Elsewhere on the bank, the vegetation is a green, robust mix of mountain alder, sweetgale, bracken and cinnamon fern, well watered and protected. There is no bridge across the river but, generally, it is possible to cross using streambed boulders as stepping-stones. Strong spring run-offs occasionally flood the channel, making crossing difficult.

Newfoundland's small rivers vary considerably in flow, particularly downstream from an expanse of wetland with its meandering watercourses. Streams flow high during the spring snowmelt, and again once autumn rains set in. During the dry summer months, there is usually a lag between rainfall and run-off, as the dry ground absorbs water. A heavy rainfall over a short period will cause streams to overflow, resulting in the flash flooding of low-lying areas. Such events are common on the Avalon Peninsula. Cape Race on the Avalon holds the official Newfoundland record of 157 mm for the maximum amount of rainfall in a 24-hour period. Unofficially, more than 200 mm fell on some slopes near St. John's during tropical storm Gabrielle in 2001.

Freshwater?

Like many small streams, Freshwater River appears to be swift flowing and clean near the coast. Further inland, however, a convoluted drainage route has slowed run-off, creating Fortune Gullies, an ideal breeding and feeding habitat for many aquatic and semi-aquatic creatures, and the surrounding tracts of bog and fen are welcome staging, feeding and breeding areas for migrating waterfowl. Out of sight of the coast, near their headwaters, small streams often run through *drokes* (narrow, wooded valleys) that offer attractive habitat for beavers, muskrat, mink and river otters. Numerous beaver dams, for example, below Watch Hill Pond, block a droke draining into Freshwater River.

Due to their greater diversity of habitat, small water systems are usually biologically more productive than larger systems, per unit of area. All manner of suspended organic particles supply nutrients to small creatures that, in turn, become food for carnivorous plants and larger animals. Particularly after rain, small streams carry a considerable load of dissolved organic matter and register coliform counts that render them problematic as a source of drinking water. Increased animal and human activity has raised the likelihood of fecal coliform contamination along the trail. The risk may be low, but drinking untreated water is not advised.

Siles Cove starrigans

◎ 3.2 km: The Flats

The name "the Flats" was likely inspired by the extensive sea ledges along the coast; or possibly by the level heath behind. Inland from the spray zone of crowberry and common juniper, the lush patches of cinnamon fern on a grassy slope indicate moist ground. As the path climbs towards Siles Cove, plants increase in height and variety. Colourful rhodora thrives, as do knee-high patches of sheep laurel and blueberry, and wind-dwarfed thickets of mountain alder, chuckley-pear, fireweed, mountain holly and purple chokeberry. Blue-bead lilies grow in the shelter of bracken ferns and tufts of deer grass border the path.

Trees grow fastest in the summer and produce softer wood; on the coast, however, cool weather retards tree growth. Summer growth is particularly affected, and coastal trees are made of a much denser wood than their inland brethren. The 1986 fire burned to the coast near Siles Cove, leaving behind photogenic stands of *starrigans* (or *crunnicks*, wind-killed or fire-killed trees) bleached white but otherwise intact. The

Collecting Starrigans

Ambrose Hearn, one of the old-time eccentrics of Petty Harbour, by preference, harvested only recently burned starrigans for firewood, and would be black with soot by the time he got home from cutting wood. He went up country with a butter tub and a loaf of bread and was not too concerned where and when he came out. One time he came out on Topsail Road in St. John's, and was seen driving his dog team and a sleigh full of starrigans down Road De Luxe.

MOTION BAY SHIPWRECKS

On January 1, 1853, the schooner *Lima*, en route from Liverpool, Lancashire, to St. John's with a crew of five, was lost near the Motion. The bodies were recovered and buried in the Anglican churchyard. On April 15, 1861, the *Prospero*, also en route from Liverpool to St. John's, struck an iceberg in Motion Bay. The first mate and five crewmen, all badly frostbitten, were pulled from their lifeboat by the French brig *France* and brought to St. John's. The captain and the rest of the crew escaped in a second lifeboat. Their fate is unknown. On March 28, 1863, the barque *Spirit of the Times*, owned by Ridley & Co. of Harbour Grace, on a return voyage from Liverpool with a cargo of salt and dry goods, was wrecked in Motion Bay. On May 7, 1875, the brigantine *Dora* was wrecked near Petty Harbour. On January 22, 1892, the schooner *Avenger*, on its way from Boston, Massachusetts, to St. John's to its new owners, Clift, Wood & Co., ran ashore near Petty Harbour. The crew was saved but the ship was declared a total loss. On August 10, 1912, the *Mayflower* from Western Bay was lost near Petty Harbour. The schooner *Huntley* was wrecked in Motion Bay in 1921.

Siles Cove rocks and the Bight

smallest twigs are sound on these coastal skeletons after two decades of exposure to ice, wind and salt spray. The starrigans on the outside of the expired stands are the most wind shaped and twisted; the ones at the centre have much straighter lines. Whatever their shape, starrigans make ideal look-outs for birds nesting in the area.

◎ 3.4 km: Siles Cove

Fire missed a patch of trees on the small headland (at **3.3 km**) just before Siles Cove. The fir-dominated grove is a welcome haven for birds and hikers seeking shelter. The trees also host a flourishing understory of wild sarsaparilla, blue-bead lily, starflower, bunchberry, goldenrod and woodland herbs. Between the conifers, patches of mountain alder let in more light, enough for sheep laurel and blueberry to grow. As the path descends, it edges around Siles Cove. The cove's north rim has formed into a steep, frost-shattered rock face. The cove's south side opens out into a series of gently sloping ledges. In heavy seas, the ledges receive a spectacular pounding.

Harp seal

Paddy Root

"Sile" is a pronunciation variant of "seal." The ledges are easily accessible from both land and sea and likely became, for many seals, both a good resting spot and last resting-place. Northeast winds drive sea ice as well as small cod and other bottom feeding fish into Motion Bay. The seals follow. Wherever there are beaches or gently sloped ledges, it is worth looking for seals, particularly during the winter months when seals often rest immobile for days. Most winters, one or more inexperienced seals haul out for a few days on "ledges" in front of the Petty Harbour Post Office and the community boat launch.

◎ 3.8 km: Paddy Root

Paddy Root (also called Patty Ruth) is a trap berth named for a man who, years ago, took advantage of a spring at the spot to keep a garden. It is still possible to see the faint outline of the garden next to the path. Look for a rectangular-shaped green area between the path and the coast where you can just make out the faint undulations of *lazy beds* (potato rows). The extensive wetlands between Siles Cove and the Bight support pitcher plant, red and brown peat moss, deer grass, cranberry, round-leaved sundew, hummocks of caribou lichen and, most years, an impressive patch of dragon's mouth orchid, one of the most beautiful native orchids. Slightly drier areas host crowberry, Canada mayflower, Labrador tea, bog rosemary,

Dragon's Mouth Orchid

The flamboyant, pink-to-magenta flower of the dragon's mouth orchid (*Arethusa bulbosa*) has three erect sepals, two side petals forming a small hood, and a conspicuous lower lip that has a scalloped margin and prominent yellow ridges down its centre. Nectar secreted by the lip attracts insects. A single, grass-like leaf matures after flowering and remains on the stem until the following year. The leaf carries on photosynthesis and produces the sugars necessary for bulb regeneration. Dragon's mouth orchids were once used as a home remedy for toothache.

Dragon's mouth orchid

purple chokeberry, bunchberry, bog laurel and bakeapple.

◎4.1 km: The Bight

Waves are gradually widening the Bight and deepening its reach. Cinnamon fern and wind-dwarfed larch and fir cling to the edges of the many wet patches. The extra measure of exposure plants receive at the Bight shortens their growing season, and delays flowering. Canada mayflower, for example, blooms at the same time as blue flag, rather than a month earlier. At the Bottom of the Bight, the northeast storms of winter—the same ones that bring seals ashore at Siles Cove—have carried driftwood well inland. Boardwalks near the Bight differ from boardwalks elsewhere along the trail in that the larch planks rest, not on fresh-cut spruce, but on scavenged logs.

Spotted sandpiper

The Bight is a good place to look for plants that favour exposed, peaty seaside conditions, such as thin-petalled or beachhead iris (*Iris setosa var. canadensis*), sea-lyme grass (*Leymus mollis*) and oysterleaf (*Mertensia maritima*), also called blue bonnet or ice plant. Coastal mist offers as good a shelter as a forest canopy, and plants associated with woodlands are often found on the seaside. In addition to the Canada mayflower, look for three-leaved false Solomon's seal (*Maienthemum trifolium*) and starry false Solomon's seal (*M. stellatum*).

Loons, terns, gulls and even the occasional gannet frequent the Bottom of the Bight. Greater yellowlegs and other shorebirds are often seen poking around shoreline rock pools and seaweed for small fish, periwinkles and other delicacies. Shorebirds poke around the nearby bogland as well, and there are often bird footprints in the mud of dried-out *flashets*—the local term for the open water areas found in wetlands. Flashets are not really ponds, for they fill with *flash*, i.e., sudden rushes of water, and do not collect and hold water like ponds. Between rainfalls, flashets are often dry. East of the Bight, the hiker crosses the gently northward plunging *hinge* (fold axis) of the Blackhead Syncline. Small veins of quartz in the area contain copper minerals that have weathered green.

BUMP AND GRIND

Only the occasional erratic between Petty Harbour and Witless Bay is of "foreign" provenance, i.e., is a fragment of granite, volcanic rock, sandstone or siliceous siltstone transported from an area near Mobile Big Pond, 20 to 30 km to the west. Generally, the further rocks were carried, the more they were subjected to the rough conditions of glacial travel, and the smaller and rounder they became.

◎ 4.3 km: Big Rocks

As glaciers pass over frost-shattered rock, boulders are plucked up and embedded in the ice. Because they have been transported from their original site and strewn across a new location, such boulders are called *erratics*. Most of the erratics between Big Rocks and

LONG POINT SHIPWRECKS

On February 6, 1882, the brigantine *Lizette*, (or *Isette*) from Hamburg-Blankenese, Germany, on its way from New York to St. John's with a cargo of provisions, caught in slob ice near Bay Bulls. The vessel drifted north into Motion Bay. Several Petty Harbour fishermen approached the *Lizette* to advise Captain J. Buttner that he should abandon ship at Long Point. Buttner, thinking the men were **wreckers** (men who lured boats to shore) waved his rescuers away. The brigantine struck Dick Frenchs Rock. Several unsuccessful attempts were made to attach a line to the ship by means of a ramrod shot from a musket. The first three men swept from the rigging were rescued by David Chafe's expert throw of a jigger. The mate grabbed the line, and two of the crew grabbed the mate. The captain and three other crewmen were less fortunate. The captain's body was later recovered. Much of the *Lizette's* cargo of pork was salvaged and the numerous, robust children born in Petty Harbour the following year were known as "pork babies."

Motion Head did not travel far. The ones showing alternate sandstone and fine conglomerate bedding were likely sheared or scraped from the cliffs of Lower Cove Head, a little over a kilometre away (at **6.9 km**). As they travelled only a short distance, they look much as they began. The glacial debris on the beach is about 30 per cent red sandstone and 70 per cent granule-to-pebble conglomerate, a ratio that closely matches the composition of the Petty Harbour Member, so it, too, is mostly of local origin.

◎4.5 km: Long Point

During breeding season there is often considerable tern activity on Long Point. The extended rock ledges at the point make good perching spots for seabirds,

A "dog cat" to the rescue

Recovering a body, 1877

but it is unlikely that nesting takes place, for the point offers no protection against foxes or other predators. The streams crossed between Big Rocks and Long Point are tea-like in colour. Typically, water drawn from a peatland source is tannic brown, highly acidic and unappetizing in taste. Water drawn from a fen tends to be clearer and more potable, but also more productive of organisms. The flashets nearest the trail

On February 8, 1905, the 206-ton barquentine *Vidonia*, commanded by Captain Job Vine, left Petty Harbour loaded with 3,596 quintals (183 tonnes) of salt cod destined for Bahia, Brazil. The captain set a course near the shore to avoid the offshore ice pack. With a change in wind, the coastal slob compacted, trapping the *Vidonia*, 2.5 km offshore. One crewman walked to land to report the situation. Seas and currents carried the *Vidonia* to within 100 metres of shore, near Long Point. After the vessel struck rock and began to leak, the captain and six crewmen scrambled to land. They spent a stormy night sheltering behind rocks in their overcoats, sustained by a small amount of food. The next day they went astray on Motion Head and contended for eight hours with snowdrifts and tuck; they were rescued by two Petty Harbour men, who had set out with a dog-slide to see what had become of the vessel. Although the *Vidonia* stayed afloat for some time, the bottom of the vessel was torn out and the cargo lost.

Yellow Pond Lily

The water-lily family (Nymphaceae) consists of about 70 aquatic pond species native to both temperate and tropical regions, three of which are found in Newfoundland. The yellow pond lily (*Nuphar variegatum*), also called the bull-head lily, inhabits quiet, muddy-bottomed ponds and lakes. Each plant produces a single flower, and numerous leaves shaped like drooping hearts. The long leaf stalks curve to allow the leaves to rise and fall with changes in water level. In this way, the leaves continually float on the surface and are exposed to the maximum possible light. Flower stalks rise several centimetres above the surface of the water and bear yellow cup-like flowers, which are composed of six stiff, fleshy sepals that surround the smaller petals, numerous stamens and a disk-like stigma. Lily tubers were widely used by native Americans for medicine and food. Moose and beaver also seek out the starchy roots, leaving behind broken pieces of plant that often drift to the pond edge.

Yellow pond lily

Niche habitat, pond near Long Point

are habitat for yellow pond lily and pond weed, and sport little islands of blue flag. Flashet water looks black, not brown, due to the peat substrate of the pools.

◎4.7 km: The Hole

Leaving Long Point, the path follows a flat stretch of coast, then climbs a broad knoll. The knoll's seaward-facing slope is thickly carpeted with beach pea, and loose glacial till from the slope has accumulated on the ledges below. In this more open, rocky habitat, the beach pea is mixed with Scotch lovage. The knoll's extensive summit is dry, gravelly and exposed, and the species found there are ones that do well on dry sites: crowberry, trailing and common juniper, three-toothed cinquefoil, gall-of-the-earth and partridgeberry. Patches of caribou lichen thrive where storm winds have eroded the heath. This occupation is likely temporary; an area of sun-warmed, light-exposed soil is a prime location and heath plants such as crowberry will reclaim the land quickly, for they are well adapted to the sheltered habitat and warmer microclimate that extends about a hand's width above the ground. The trail dips into a narrow valley that runs inland from a deep-water gulch. The gulch is called "the Hole" and the valley "the Gully." The trap berth at this spot goes by both names. The Gully is a moister, more sheltered environment than the knoll, with more accumulated organic material. In it, moisture-loving plants thrive, such as sweetgale, bog rosemary, bog laurel, blue flag, cranberry, bakeapple, cotton grass, sedges and Labrador tea.

5.0 km: Alexander Pond

Wind-lapped, lily pad-shaped Alexander Pond is dotted with yellow pond lilies and bordered with trailing juniper, blue flag, wild roses and sweetgale. The trickle flowing in and out of the pond bears the unlikely name of Queens River. (A second, larger Queens River runs into Shoal Bay, at **0.7 km** on Spout Path.) The pond's shore makes an attractive camping spot. The pond water is too tannic for most tastes, but there is potable water east of the pond, near the remains of a hunter's shack. Past Dick Frenchs Rock (at **5.2 km**) there is a second rise, overlooking a jumble of oddly angled ridges and hollows. Hodgepodge deposits of till typically occur where a *moraine* (debris banked by the edge or foot of a glacier) has been reworked by meltwater. It was landscapes of this type, in Scotland, that inspired the game of golf. The shore end of the rise has eroded, revealing a mishmash of unsorted gravel and boulders, the latter rounded by their grinding, glacial journey. Chaotically churned and ground-up rock of no fixed order or size is typical of glacial till.

MOTION SHIPWRECKS

On January 18, 1834, the ***Rover*** wrecked off the Motion. On November 8, 1850, the barquentine ***Wasp***, owned by Joseph Dingwell and captained by Andrew Coffin, carrying lumber, cattle and produce from Grand River, Prince Edward Island, to St. John's, encountered strong northerly winds as it attempted to round Cape Spear. The weather worsened. The vessel was blown south and the crew lost sight of Cape Spear Light. The vessel struck the coast immediately south of the Motion, a half-hour after sighting land. Only one of the six on board survived. The owner's 16-year-old son was among those who drowned. On October 3, 1860, the brigantine ***Caroline Schenk***, owned by, and under the command of, Captain Bond, was wrecked at Motion Head. The barquentine ***Salina*** was lost at Motion Head in December of 1899.

◎ 5.5 km: Motion Head

Cod migrating to the northeast coast in the spring usually show up earliest around Cape Spear. Portuguese fishermen likely first discovered this phenomenon for, as early as 1508 (a decade after John Cabot and the Corte-Reals) and as late as 1736, Motion Head appears on maps as *cao de portogesi* or *cap des portugaise*. Portugal's fleet of approximately 50 ships was neither large nor well defended. In 1580, the Portuguese and Spanish crowns were united under Phillip II (1527-98) and the English, who were at war with Spain, took advantage of the union to seize Portuguese vessels, fish, and oil in Newfoundland. Sir Bernard Drake, brother of Sir Francis, captured five Portuguese ships in 1580 and 16 more in 1585. In 1588, most of what remained of the Portuguese fleet was deployed—and destroyed—during an attempted invasion of England by the Spanish Armada.

It is likely that the Portuguese clung on in *petit abra* (Petty Harbour) for another generation, for in 1618 there was "a great combat between some insolent English and certain Portuguese at Petyte Harbour, and one of the English [was] dangerously hurt with a pike."

17th-century pikeman

Cod fishing on shoal ground

(Richard Whitbourne, *A Discourse and Discovery of New-found-land*, 1622) The Portuguese moved on, and Petty Harbour was added to the "English Shore."

The "Easter Island" effect of the solitary, standing stones at Motion Head is most likely a consequence of a strong flow of glacial meltwater running through the till at the terminus of a glacier. The flow washed away all but the largest blocks. The monoliths seemingly increase in size and prominence as the path approaches the Motion, an impression created, in part, by a decrease in the height of vegetation and—south of Motion Head—the absence of soil. The largest rocks so resemble the bedrock on which they sit that they likely shifted only a short distance.

Sandstone splits and weathers into interesting shapes. Approaching the head, the wind shaping of the boulders gains extra depth and detail, for headland winds are strong and abrasive, and no tree cover provides protection from the elements. At the head itself, a low-lying ledge is littered with large red conglomerate and sandstone boulders. The ledge continues for some distance under the sea, past Motion Rock. In the winter, lines of three, sometimes four, great breakers ride up the ledge, one of the most impressive wave shows on the East Coast Trail. It is this "motion" that gives the head its name. Gulls perch on Motion Rock in the summer, cormorants in the fall. Sometimes a river otter will haul onto the rock, scattering the birds.

Motion Head is particularly eerie and exciting in the fog. Even in thick mist one can hear and smell the black-legged kittiwakes, which breed on the cliffs. On a calm day, it is relatively easy to land a boat on the low, sloping shore and the landscape is hunter-friendly, for hunters have ample cover, but their prey have none. Seabirds swoop close and often over the

Polar Bears

The polar bear (*Ursus maritimus*) is the world's largest land predator. Adult males weigh 500 to 600 kilos and females about half that. They are not pure white, but lemony-coloured, especially when seen against their Arctic habitat. Polar bears are protected from cold by a thick layer of fat, and by a dense coat of translucent hair that reflects solar heat inward to the base of the coat, where it is absorbed by the bear's black skin. Polar bears rely mainly on their keen sense of smell for hunting. It is believed they can locate seal breathing holes that are as much as one kilometre away and covered by up to 90 cm of ice and snow. Their eyesight and hearing are believed to be similar to a human's. Polar bears are strong swimmers, using their large front paws as powerful oars while their rear paws trail behind and act as rudders. Small bumps and cavities on the soles of the feet act as suction cups, preventing the polar bear from slipping while chasing prey on ice.

The Polar Bear

John Winsor Chafe, and Jacob Chafe, and Howard, Jacob's son
Went down to the Motion with dog-slide and gun.
When they reached the Motion, the birds did not fly
Jacob said to Howard, "Go boil the kettle, boy,

I'll go to the Pulpit, to take a look around."
Right there upon the ice floes, a polar bear he found.
The bear stood on his hind legs, ready to make a start.
When Jacob quickly fired, and pierced him through the heart.

John Winsor Chafe and Howard, they were thunderstruck.
Jacob said to Howard, "Give him another shot!"
Howard quickly fired, and put him in his gore.
They put him on the dog-slide and hauled him up the shore.

Dan Winsor Chafe, the skinner, he gave the flesh away.
Some said it was good eating. Others threw it away.
They went to town the next day, the flesh it sold quite good.
Each one that put their dollar down just took it as it stood.

—collected from Frank Chafe, Howard Chafe's step-son

Slaying white bear, c. 1605

THE CUCKOLD FORMATION

The rock on the trail between Motion Head and Hearts Point Cove Ridge is Cuckold Formation red sandstone and conglomerate. The flood events that laid down the conglomerate component of this formation took place earlier than the flood events depositing Petty Harbour Member sediment. The river ran a steeper course and carried larger-diameter material from higher reaches. Cuckold Formation conglomerate contains noticeably larger *clasts* (pebbles) composed of *felsic* (light-coloured) volcanic lava and ash eroded from a volcanic highland.

Flat ass kettle

wind-whipped, strange looking cliffs, not bothering to keep their usual distance. The occasional bald-headed eagle patrols the coast. Further inland, northern harriers cruise the foggy barrens, hoping to startle a hare or rodent. Bright orange lichen grows on rocks where avian predators habitually perch and wait.

One winter in the 1910s, Jacob Chafe and his son Howard went to the Motion to hunt duck. Around 9:00 a.m., Jacob told his son to boil the kettle for tea and walked on to check for birds at the Pulpit, a large rock mass on the eastern shore of Pulpit Cove. Rounding Pulpit Cove, Jacob walked into a polar bear. The incident inspired a mock-heroic ballad.

⊚6.1 km: The Island

Leaving Motion Head, the path keeps close to the coastal bluffs and the terrain rises slowly to Pulpit Pond. The pond is a popular bathing spot for black-legged kittiwakes. The birds are "flighty," meaning they are likely to fly off at a hiker's approach. From a distance, the plateau's vegetation looks uniform, but there are small-scale variations in height and species composition. Areas of exposed gravel and extended patches of crowberry and caribou lichen show where growing conditions are most severe. Mountain alder and clumps of bilberry grow in the scattered spots that are more wind sheltered. The alder has been heavily *browsed* (chewed) by moose and often there are moose prints and moose droppings on the path. The Island is a long, moderately high rock ridge attached to the coast, for in Newfoundland any coastal rock that "stands out" can be an island. The cliffs of the Island are on the east limb of the Blackhead Syncline, so they dip 20° west.

Hunter shooting birds in a flyway

◎ 6.9 km: Kettles Cove

Before the Groundfish Moratorium, there were no trap berths on the stretch of coast between Motion Head and Hayes Point. The shore was reserved for hand-lining, which took place on offshore grounds called Island Rock, Old Terry, Bantam and Shango. The path follows a descending, table-like ledge at the base of Lower Cove Head Ridge, passing numerous patches of bakeapple and two small ponds. The ponds are in a low valley that runs between Lower Cove Head and Pulpit Pond. Over-wintering and migrating seafowl often choose the valley as a flyway, so it is well known to hunters. Pigeon Gulch is a deep, narrow wedge of a place and Kettles Cove is even narrower. At Kettles Cove, there is a choice of trail route. An inland path climbs Lower Cove Head Ridge (also called Tinkers Hill or Old Terry Hill) to Lower Cove Pond. A less trodden coastal route descends the seaside ledge through heath to Piccos Gulch. West of

Flyway, Lower Cove Head

Kettles Cove

Lower Cove cliffs

Niche habitat, Piccos Gulch

Piccos Gulch, the hiker must scramble up a bluff to bypass Big Gulch.

Kettles Cove is named for Kettles Rock, a kettle-shaped, 100-tonne rock that once perched on a three-metre-square rock islet not far from shore. Fishermen jigging or hand-lining on the underwater ledges of Island Rock or Old Terry used Kettles Rock as a landmark. If the sea was calm, they also hopped onto the islet to "boil a kettle at Kettles Rock." The rock withstood pounding seas for untold years. Then, in January of 1977, two duck hunters noticed the "kettle" was gone, most likely washed off its perch by the preceding week's storm. Even without Kettles Rock to help, Kettles Cove and Pigeon Gulch frequently "steam" with choppy or breaking waves, and the cliff tops nearby have been swept clean of soil and vegetation, so constant is the battering from wind and spray.

◎ 7.3 km: Piccos Gulch / Lower Cove Pond

Piccos Gulch is named for Captain Picco of Portugal Cove, the captain of the *True Blue*, which was lost in the cove in 1830. River otters, sometimes seen fishing from the step-like rocks of Piccos Gulch, travel the stream connecting Lower Cove Pond to the sea. Their rub weaves in and out of the thick, dark green sweetgale that engulfs the streambed. The narrow valley of the stream is abundant with cinnamon fern, pitcher plant, Labrador tea, bog rosemary, tall meadow-rue, cranberry and bakeapple. Down by the gulch, Scotch lovage and beach pea grow in sea-worn cracks, and wild roses, bakeapple, mosses and sedges flourish wherever water collects. The gulch is the fourth and last place where the path crosses the *hinge* (fold axis) of the Blackhead Syncline. Both the landscape and syncline dip to the north.

The Wreck of the "True Blue"

"Picco was out in the "True Blue." He was a great 'swoil' killer and had 5,500 that year. On March 29, the wind ceased and the vessels made sail to work to land. There was no light on Cape Spear in those days, the ice was loose, and that night it snowed and blew dreadfully. About daybreak it was worse, and the vessels were anxious... 'Pat' Mackey was in the "Devonport," and after running for a good while, he hove her off to sea. There was no braver man than Mackey, but he knew when to stop. Picco was coming behind him and shouted, 'Aren't you going to run in, Pat?' 'No,' replied Mackey, 'I don't think it's safe.' ''Tis safe enough for me,' shouted Picco. 'Good luck to you,' returned Mackey. Picco missed the Cape, ran in, and took the land near Petty Harbor Motion. A blinding snowstorm was raging and not a soul was saved. He had 30 of a crew, men and boys, for men were scarcer then and a boy of 15 could get a berth as easy as a grown man can now."

—James Murphy, Murphy's Old Sealing Days, 1916

River Otters

River otters (*Lutra canadensis*) seldom wander far from water. They are primarily nocturnal, but often can be glimpsed in early morning or late afternoon near their rubs. They swim with a distinctive undulating, serpentine movement. Their streamlined body, broad, flattened head, muscular neck, webbed toes and long, tapered tail, suit them to an amphibious way of life. Otters are skilled fishers, but those inhabiting seacoasts (such as the ones along the trail) also rely heavily on mussels, whelks, sea urchins and other marine invertebrates. Otters also will take insects, and the occasional bird and small mammal.

Overgrown otter rub, Piccos Gulch

River otter

Lower Cove Head was a good spot to hunt partridge. The hill's exposed summit hosts a fragile cover of mountain alder, Labrador tea, bakeapple, caribou lichen, trailing juniper and low-growing sheep laurel. Taller wind-pruned conifers and mountain alder grow on the north bank of Lower Cove Head Pond. The goldenrod, raspberry and fireweed on the south side of the pond seem out of place. Human feet or perhaps otters' bellies have opened a niche for these plants, which typically appear where there has been a disturbance.

7.7 km: Big Gulch

Big Gulch is the most dramatic and exposed of several large openings facing Lower Cove. A small stream runs into the ocean on the gulch's western side. There are dense pockets of woodland in the more protected, southeast facing valleys between Big Gulch and Hearts Point Cove. Crossing the valley above White Rock (a trap berth named for its white ledge) the trail passes first through a shrub zone, then through a forested zone where the trees grow progressively taller. Briefly, in the narrow heart of the valley (at **8.1 km**) there is a miniature wood, perfect even to the moss-covered rocks. Most days, the hiker can feel the higher temperature and humidity of the hollow's microclimate, which supports white birch, dogberry, maple and other deciduous growth.

8.6 km: Burkes Head

Approaching the southeast-facing notch above Rocky Cove (at **8.3 km**) the heath rises to waist height and the conifers grow taller, too. In the hollow, there is a flourishing glade of fir, with some alder and birch, the understory mostly spinulose wood fern and

Otter Rubs

Otters are known for their sliding. They use sliding to cover ground quickly and will travel over snow with a series of graceful jumps followed by a slide that can carry them several metres. They evidently enjoy the activity and will slide repeatedly, especially on inclines. In winter, they toboggan down snowy banks on their bellies, their front legs extended and back legs trailing. In summer, they use grassy or muddy slopes in similar fashion. Otters create paths alongside streams or ponds, called **rubs** or **slides**, which can be detected by how the vegetation is flattened or destroyed. In winter, look for a ploughed passage through the snow.

Iceberg east of Cape Spear, 1882

LOWER COVE SHIPWRECKS

Nineteenth-century sources call Lower Cove "Leeward Cove" or "Lord Cove." Possibly, the name "Lower Cove" was misheard. Captain Picco of the sealing schooner ***True Blue*** was lost in the cove with his crew on March 30, 1830. On January 1, 1865, the brigantine ***Nautilus*** came to grief, most likely at Burkes Head. Owned by Lawrence O'Brien & Co., the brigantine was carrying coal from Sydney, Nova Scotia, to St. John's. Three men who were on deck survived and were brought to St. John's the next day. The bodies of Captain John Burke, his 14-year-old son William and four others, wedged in the rocks, were retrieved by men lowered over the cliff with ropes. On June 23, 1932, the 147-ton schooner ***Cote Nord***, owned by Angus Genge of Flower's Cove, carrying tar in steel drums, was wrecked near Kettles Rock. For many years thereafter, salvaged tar was used to seal Petty Harbour roofs. A decade earlier, the schooner had run rum along the New England coast.

bunchberry. Rocky Cove is named for the amount of fallen rock in its waters; Smooth Cove, in contrast, is uncluttered. Split the Gulch (or Split Gulch) is named for a large rock outcrop dividing the gulch.

An old trail ascends the glacier-scraped expanse of Burkes Head to the summit of Hearts Point Ridge. Monolithic erratics are scattered everywhere, some crisscrossed with thick quartz veins, others containing large clasts, still others perched delicately on smaller rocks. One perch rock appears to be hovering. Heath moss flourishes in the cracks of the *scrape* (a slope of exposed rock) and in the lee of boulders, along with cranberry and three-toothed cinquefoil. Where water collects, there are patches of cinnamon fern, sweetgale, Labrador tea and leatherleaf.

Burkes Head (at **8.6 km**), like Piccos Gulch, is named for a respected sealing captain who perished nearby. During his 35 years hunting seals, Captain John Burke commanded 15 vessels, including the *Kingaloch*, a ship that entered the annals of maritime law in 1844 when Burke ordered a contingent of his crew to board the *Dash*, which, like the *Kingaloch*, was passing through an iced-over tickle. The *Dash* was temporarily without a crew as its men were running before their vessel on the ice. Burke claimed the "abandoned" *Dash* as salvage and after a fierce court battle was awarded one-sixth of the *Dash*'s value. Johnny Burke (1851-1930), the eldest of Captain Burke's three surviving children, became Newfoundland's most famous balladeer.

Recovering bodies from a gulch, 1877

89

Motion Path

French soldier, c. 1705

Canadian soldier on raquets

◎ 9.1 km: Hearts Point Ridge

According to local tradition, the English kept a lookout for French raiders on Watch Hill, northwest of Hearts Point Ridge. A French force is said to have rested for three nights at "Three Nights Lodging" in the valley of Queens River (the larger of the two rivers bearing this name, running into Shoal Bay at **0.7 km** on Spout Path.) The two sides reportedly fought, then buried the fallen on Hearts Point Ridge, presumably at a place (so far, undiscovered) with enough soil to cover a body. Some say the name derives from a surname, possibly that of the Cornish mine captain Thomas Halse. It is likely Halse explored the many thin copper-bearing quartz veins running through the ridge and point, hoping to find a better vein than the one at Miner Point. Copper is scarce on the ridge, but not *hurts* or *whorts* (blueberries). That so remote a place would be named for its harvest of berries, however, is another mystery.

No recorded military action matches the tradition of a battle on Hearts Point Ridge. The event that comes closest is Daniel d'Auger de Subercase's raid of 1705. On January 15, Governor de Subercase left Placentia with 370 French regulars and 80 irregulars from Quebec, of whom 40 were Abenaqui warriors. Temperatures were mild for the first part of the march and 80 per cent of the men threw away their snowshoes. The weather turned bitter and 60 cm of snow fell. The governor rested his exhausted force for two days before attacking and capturing Bay Bulls, then pushed on to St. John's and took the city, with the exception of Fort William and the South Castle. He then withdrew to Petty Harbour, which, like St. John's, was sacked and burned. A detachment of raiders manned three captured vessels and sailed south, destroying structures and settlements along the coast.

Jigging: May 23, 1839

"On our return we saw many fishing boats, and passed one that was anchored under a headland, jigging codfish. A jigger is a plummet of lead, with two or three hooks stuck at the bottom, projecting on every side, and quite bare. This is let down by the line to the proper depth, and then a man, taking a hitch of the line in his hand, jerks it smartly in, the full length of his arm, then lets it down slowly and jerks it in again. The fish are attracted by seeing something moving in the water, and every now and then one is caught by one of the hooks. As soon as the man feels he has struck one, he hauls in upon the line, taking care to keep it tight till he heaves the fish into the boat. In this way several were caught while we were in sight by the two men in the fishing-boat, and they tossed us three or four fine fish as we went by, at the request of the owner of our punt."

—Joseph Beete Jukes, *Excursions in and about Newfoundland*, 1842

Northern harrier

Northern Harrier

The northern harrier (*Circus cyaneus*) inhabits open country, where it glides languidly over bogs and barrens, its wings slowly flapping or held in a shallow V-shape. The male is pale grey and the female brown. Both sexes have a distinctive white rump patch. Northern harriers feed primarily on small rodents, such as voles, although they also take small birds, frogs, insects and carrion. They typically fly low, sometimes grazing the tops of vegetation when hunting. This habit of harrying—i.e., startling or flushing—prey gives the hawk its name. In Newfoundland, the startled prey was sometimes domestic, hence the name "hen hawk" or "hen harrier." In addition to excellent vision, harriers have a sound-reflecting facial disc, similar to, but less complete than an owl's, that helps the bird detect creatures.

The broad summit of the ridge is crisscrossed with low crests and depressions where sheltered heath plants grow to knee, and sometimes waist height. Where the ridge is most exposed, plant growth is suppressed to the point that plants that usually reach shrub size such as blueberry, purple chokeberry, sheep laurel, northern fly honeysuckle, mountain holly and northern wild raisin, barely grow higher than the ground-hugging crowberry and partridgeberry. Like other highlands scorched by the 1986 fire, the ridge has exaggerated wet and dry environments. On the ridge's broad summit, the heath is a checkerboard of moisture loving and drought tolerant plant communities. At **9.4 km**, hikers can detour off the path for a few metres and look down into Hearts Point Cove. To the north and east, there is a panoramic view of Motion Head and its cover of erratics; there are plenty of erratics even on the summit of the ridge. To the south, the view extends to Ferryland, with the easternmost tip of each cape visible.

◎ 9.7 km: Hearts Point

The south face of Hearts Point Ridge is broken into a great sweep of steps and terraces, a terrain at odds with the smooth scrape of the northwestern face, crossed by the trail a kilometre earlier. The terraces follow the dip of the bedding, 20° to the northeast. The path zigzags down the seaward edge of this natural step pyramid. Each terrace collects and releases water, like a rice paddy on a mountain slope; the plants on the terraces are species that thrive in wet environments. In addition to shrubs like sweetgale and mountain alder, there are ferns, peat moss, pitcher plant, cotton grasses, sedges and, on at least one ledge, a patch of club-spur orchid (*Platanthera clavellata*). Only when the valley has been reached can the hiker look back and see the full extent of the terraced slope.

Hearts Cove Ridge from the air

Northern harriers have an elaborate courtship display, with the male performing spectacular aerobatics over his territory. He may dive down in mock attack, while the female flips over onto her back in mid-air and presents her talons. Harriers also indulge in food passing in the air, especially when they have young to feed. The clutch size ranges from four to six eggs. A flimsy nest is usually built on the ground, and the female alone incubates, while the male does all the hunting. After hatching, the young scatter into surrounding vegetation and the female returns to hunting.

It was at Hearts Point that the saga of the *Regulus* reached its tragic conclusion. The *Regulus*'s grounding at Staffordside in 1908 (described at 5.9 km on Cape Spear Path) was followed, in the same year, by a collision with the *Ocland* of Norway. Although it was widely believed the Norwegian captain was at fault, the owners of the *Regulus* lost the damage suit and paid out $15,000. On July 22, 1909, the *Regulus*, loaded with 1,360 tonnes of coal from North Sydney, Nova Scotia, and with machinery from the dismantled whale factory in St. Lawrence, collided with an iceberg in dense fog off Cape Race. The crew saved the ship by jettisoning cargo, flooding the rear tanks and raising the damaged bow out of the water.

The *Regulus* limped into St. John's and was repaired and returned to its regular run. The misfortunes continued. In July 1910, the *Regulus* collided with the British steamer *Karema* off Nantucket. To pay for the damages, A. Harvey & Co. auctioned the *Regulus* off, only to buy the ship back, a move decried in the press as an insurance scam. On October 23, 1910, the

Lower Cove from Burkes Head

Armies of newsboys regularly patrolled St. John's streets selling topical Johnny Burke ballads at two cents a copy. "The Loss of the SS *Regulus*" likely circulated in broadsheet form at the time of the tragedy. The ballad was collected in *Burke's Ballads* of 1912. No tune is indicated, possibly because one dirge-like melody, that of the "Petty Harbour Bait Skiff," fits all. The SS *Regulus* went down close to where the *Nautilus* had wrecked 45 years earlier. The earlier tragedy claimed Burke's father and older brother. Considering this, the line, "The widows left in grief; / The husband, son and those they loved," is particularly poignant.

Loss of the "SS Regulus"

Ye daring sons of Newfoundland, that fear not storm or sea
Please hearken for a moment and attention give to me,
While I explain in language plain, that filled hearts with dismay,
Of how the "Regulus" got lost in Petty Harbor Bay.

On Sunday morn, with happy hearts with glad and cheery smile,
She cast her lines and got up steam and sailed from old Bell Isle;
And as she steamed up near Cape Race, it blew a heavy breeze,
Her main shaft broke and left her disabled on the seas.

SS Regulus

Word from the Cape was soon despatched, to send without delay
Some help to shipwrecked mariners, disabled in the Bay.
The tug "John Green" then got up steam and to the ship did go,
And got on board a hawser the "Regulus" to tow.

She towed her for about a mile, while wind and seas did roar,
When soon the tow-line parted and she drifted toward the shore;
The look out on the tug "John Green" to those on board did shout:
The port lights on the "Regulus" did suddenly go out.

The tug-boat's crew from that they knew the steam boat was no more,
They knew that she had foundered on the breakers near the shore;
The tug-boat then for many hours the Bay did cruise around,
But no sign of the "Regulus" could anywhere be found.

The tug "John Green" bore up for home, they saw it was no use;
The danger of the tug being swamped, she then gave up the cruise;
And brought the sad and gloomy news to friends in St. John's town,
How Capt. Taylor and his crew that Sunday night went down.

May God, the Ruler of the land, the tempests and the deep,
Make light the sorrows of the poor, the widows left in grief;
The husband, son and those they loved, most fervently we pray
For those poor souls who lost their lives in Petty Harbor Bay.

—Johnny Burke, BURKE'S BALLADS, 1912

HEARTS POINT SHIPWRECKS

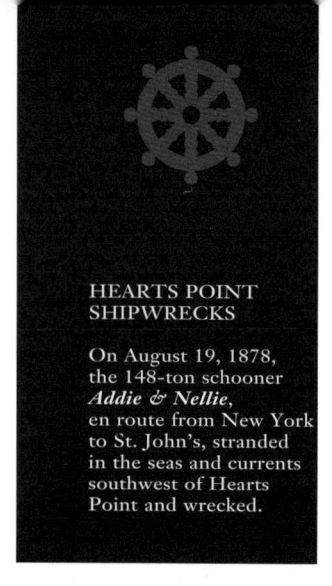

On August 19, 1878, the 148-ton schooner *Addie & Nellie*, en route from New York to St. John's, stranded in the seas and currents southwest of Hearts Point and wrecked.

Hearts Point Cove Ridge

Regulus left Bell Island, having failed to pick up a cargo of iron ore: the shipper, seeing the *Regulus*, demanded a better vessel. Captain Taylor set a southward course "up" the southern shore, some say to pick up a cargo of fishmeal from the whale factory at Cape Broyle. The empty ship, riding high in the water, was vulnerable to heavy seas and winds. As the *Regulus* rounded Cape Spear, the wind increased in force and a thick fog blew in. Five kilometres off Bull Head (North Head), the *Regulus* broke its tail shaft and Captain Taylor dropped anchor and requested assistance. The tugs *John Green* and *D.P. Ingraham* responded, but only the *John Green* was successful in locating the distressed vessel in dense fog. During the hour or more it took to attach a towline, the southeast gale carried the tug and the *Regulus* north. Around 2:30 a.m., after two hours of towing, the *John Green's* straining towline broke and the *Regulus* with its crew of 20 disappeared into the fog off the unforgiving cliffs of Lower Cove. The ship's hull—split fore and aft—was located by divers at Hearts Point. An extensive search failed to recover any bodies.

◎ **10.0 km: Hearts Point Cove**

The path briefly follows a ridge inland, then turns seaward and descends the precipitous north side of a narrow, U-shaped valley. The pocket stand of fir at the western end of the valley escaped the 1986 fire,

Hearts Point

as did the tangle of wind-twisted conifers at the eastern end of the cliff edge. Climbing the next ridge, the trail runs parallel to a deep fissure that splits the headland above Hearts Point Cove (at **10.1 km**). This cleft runs 10 metres east of the trail, but is invisible from the route. On a scale many orders of magnitude greater, the crevice resembles the abrupt frost splits that occur in sandstone boulders. Frost wedging likely attacked an up-angled joint or weakened bed. Once the wedging started, the sea removed disconnected fragments from below. The fissure is not unique, for the wedge-shaped island off Hearts Point and a smaller island near Brian Doyles Landing Place are separated from the mainland by similarly aligned fractures.

The trail crosses a confusion of hollows and ridges. Hearts Point, a high cliff face composed of sheared-off, reddish-coloured Quidi Vidi Formation sandstone, is seen from several angles. In the hollows, white birch, mountain alder, dogberry and mountain holly compete with the returning conifer growth, including some sizeable larch. The canopy is open enough to allow the plants beneath to grow knee- to waist-high. After crossing a ridge called the Tolt (at **10.3 km**) the path switchbacks down a steep slope through a flourishing stand of white birch. The route continues over a series of gently rolling red sandstone ridges to the coast, through waist-high sheep laurel heath and bracken fern.

QUIDI VIDI FORMATION

Crossing the ridge, there is a gradual change from the conglomerate and red sandstone of the Cuckold Formation to the older, paler red sandstones of the Quidi Vidi Formation. There is no obvious point of transition between the two formations, which look similar. The ancient river carrying sediment first spilled over onto a flood plain, laying down thick beds of fine-grained Quidi Vidi Formation material. As material accumulated, the river established a more efficient channel and carried periodic floods of coarser, Cuckold Formation sediment down from higher reaches. The path will stay with the Quidi Vidi Formation until Queens River on Spout Path (at **0.7 km**).

Ferns

Ferns are vascular plants found throughout the world; estimates of the number of species range from 6,000 to 15,000 worldwide. Although most grow in damp, shady places, some thrive in dry, open areas. Ferns vary in height from a few centimetres to tree size in tropical regions. Fossilized ferns found in rocks of the Lower Devonian Period (about 410 million years ago) predate seed-bearing plants. During the Carboniferous Period (350 to 275 million years ago), before the evolution of flowering plants, ferns were the dominant vegetation and formed dense forests of unbroken green. More than 40 species of ferns occur in Newfoundland. Spinulose wood fern, cinnamon fern and bracken fern are commonly found all along the East Coast Trail; sensitive fern, New York fern and interrupted fern are less common.

Common Ferns

Several difficult-to-distinguish species go under the inclusive name of Spinulose wood fern (*Dryopteris spinulosa sensulato*). This widely distributed woodland fern group grows up to a metre in height in moist or wet forest habitats, along stream banks and in fens. Lacy, solitary **fronds** (blades or stalks) sprout asymmetrically from a creeping **rhizome**

◉ 11.0 km: Bottom Gully

In Newfoundland, a "gully" is a leisurely watercourse, usually one that broadens out into a series of pools or ponds in its upper reaches. Bottom Gully, called Bay Bulls Gully on 19th-century maps, receives most of its flow from Hearts Point Ridge. Where the gully meets the coast, species normally found in an open, wet environment, such as wild roses, plumboy, sweetgale, tall meadow-rue and violets, are joined by species characteristic of disturbance, such as raspberry, birdfoot trefoil, dandelion, wild strawberry, clover, yarrow, fireweed, hawkweed, pearly everlasting, aster and goldenrod. The disturbance, in this case, is the sewage line running under Pipeline Road, which has served the Goulds since the late 1980s. Tests have shown that the gully is no cleaner or more contaminated than other small streams along the trail. The keen-eyed will note the abundant guano left by gulls foraging at the outfall. (Hikers who choose Pipeline Road as their means of exit to Shoal Bay Road and the Goulds shorten Motion Path by 3 km.)

Leaving the gully, the path follows the cliff edge, zigzagging over rough outcrops and through boulder fields and heath vegetation. Walking from north to south, the landscape appears gentle and rolling. Turn around, and the land transforms into a crazy quilt of upturned cliffs and ledges. The ledges regularly split

Spinulose wood fern

(rootstock). The fern stem is green, with light brown scales, and the thrice-divided frond is light green to yellowish-green. Spores are on the underside of the frond.

Cinnamon fern (*Osmunda cinnamomea*) inhabits open to semi-open moist areas. A cluster of tall, upright green fronds appears in the spring. The spore-bearing fronds that emerge in the middle of the cluster are covered in cinnamon-coloured hairs. These fronds wither and die following the release of spores. Cinnamon fern fronds turn orange-brown in late summer. The fern's crisp, carrot-like rhizome—about the size and shape of a brazil nut—was sometimes eaten by children in the late fall and early winter. This treat went under a variety of names, including "butter plant," "butternut," "butter root" and "banana."

Bracken fern (*Pteridium aquilinum*) occurs worldwide. Its rhizomes spread rapidly underground and the fern forms extensive colonies. Its blades grow singly rather than in clusters. The large olive-green frond of the fern is coarse in texture and divided into three nearly equal parts, creating a triangle. Bracken fern prefers open, water-saturated environments and often invades burned areas where it grows in association with sheep laurel.

Cinnamon fern

Bracken fern

Uncommon Ferns

Sensitive fern (*Onoclea sensibilis*) prefers wet soil and is usually found near water, generally in environments that are periodically flooded and nutrient-rich. It has coarse, pale green, broad-leaved fronds that are stained pink when young. Note the wavy margins on the lower **pinnae** (primary leaflets) and **pinnules** (secondary leaflets), and the wing-shaped frond. The fern is "sensitive" because it is easily killed by frost. Look for this fern where the trail crosses Bottom Gully on Motion Path (at **11.0 km**).

In Newfoundland, the New York fern (*Thelypteria noveboracensis*) is at the northern extremity of its range. Elsewhere, it grows in moist forests, or along stream or pond margins, particularly in acidic soil. In Newfoundland's cooler climate, it is more likely to be found in open areas where there is lots of moisture. The fern's delicate light green fronds taper towards both the tip and base.

Sensitive fern

into square fragments, some of which are now stepping-stones along the trail. There are often fox prints, in addition to the usual fox scats, imprinted in the soft peat of the pathway. The area was logged off, most likely shortly after the construction of Pipeline Road. In the fall, blueberry and wild roses contribute vivid reds and yellows to a colourful landscape of lichen-covered boulders and patches of fern, peat and sedges.

Newfoundland's First Mine

Early explorers and colonizers regularly noted mineral deposits as they charted the coast. Then, as now, investing in a mine could lead to fabulous wealth—or ruin. Perhaps a wily captain traded his knowledge of a deposit to settle a customs dispute, for, in 1773, the St. John's customs collector Alexander Dunn wrote to two influential Scottish friends that he knew of a valuable copper deposit in Shoal Bay. The bay has numerous copper-bearing quartz veins visible from the sea. Eager to be first with a claim, George Stewart, Earl of Galloway, and John Vans Agnew of Barnbarroch approached King George III of England for a mining grant. They must have caught King George on an exuberant day, for on February 22, 1775, the monarch granted Vans Agnew and Stewart mining rights to the entire island of Newfoundland—and the coast of Labrador—for 999 years.

In May of 1776 the Cornish mine captain Thomas Halse gamely landed a dozen Cornish miners at Shoal Bay and ordered them to sink a shaft, drive out a level and remove ore. Two shafts were eventually attempted, one directly into the side of the cliff, the other immediately inland of the cliff, about 20 metres above sea level. A refined sample of ore containing 80 per cent copper was shipped to England in October of

1777. Unfortunately, the two-metre-wide vein the miners uncovered with their shaft soon dipped below sea level, and pinched out further inland. Furthermore, it was impossible to keep the mine dry. The Scottish partners lost £9,000, and King George failed to earn his 10 per cent. Halse shut down the mine in the fall of 1778.

The mine and its workings were still evident when William Epps Cormack (1796-1868) visited the site in 1822. He reported numerous quartz veins containing copper in the vicinity. In 1839, Joseph Beete Jukes, the colony's first geologic surveyor, visited the site and was much less impressed. Captain Sir James Pearl (1790-1840) obtained rights to the mine in October of 1839. Pearl likely learned of the mine from Jukes, when he invited the geologist to Mount Pearl, his estate, to identify a shale deposit mistakenly thought to be coal. The captain's death in January of 1840 ended whatever initiative he had planned. (Pearl's name lives on in the City of Mount Pearl.)

◎11.5 km: Shoal Bay Mine

The path reaches a small valley and stream. In season, hikers interested in sampling some tasty, but less commonly eaten, Newfoundland berries can search the stream bank and the birch grove for plumboy, squashberry, creeping snowberry ("ants eggs"), bunchberry, northern wild raisin, chuckley-pear and skunk currant. The stream runs down a Quidi Vidi Formation sandstone bed that dips 25° to the northeast, straight into the ocean.

The white birch grove on the south bank of the stream sits on an impressive pile of tailings from the old mine. The path first cuts up the tailing pile, then across the mine vein. The shallow cut to the west is where the

Look for this fern beside streams at Long Point Cove, at **3.4 km** on Spout Path; and in large patches beside a braided stream, south of the sea stack below Little Bald Head, at **5.7 km** on Spout Path.

Interrupted fern (*Osmunda claytoniana*) is a large fern that grows up to 120 cm high. It is closely related to and looks much like cinnamon fern; however, its spores are not born on a specialized frond, but on pinnae in the middle part of the frond. Fertile pinnae are smaller than those above or below, giving the frond an "interrupted" appearance. The fern grows in medium-rich soil in mixed or deciduous woods, where there is ample light, often on stream banks. Look for this fern mixed with cinnamon fern in the sheltered hollow at Landing Place of Bald Head, at **10.2 km** on Spout Path.

New York fern

Joseph Beete Jukes

Mine at Shoal Bay

Plumboys

The plumboy (*Rubus pubescens*) goes by a variety of names, such as dewberry, eyeberry, dwarf raspberry and ground raspberry. Blackberries, too, are sometimes called plumboys in Newfoundland, adding to the confusion. The trailing stems of the plumboy are distinct from blackberry brambles and raspberry canes; they trail along the ground, sending up low-growing shoots with shiny, red-tinged three-part leaves. Pinkish-white flowers appear on these stems in June, followed by one or two shiny-skinned, wine-red to purple-black (when ripe) berries. The trailing stems occur in damp, grassy habitats and shady, open woods. The fruit must be hunted for with a skilled eye, for it is rare to find these delicate, juicy berries in abundance. However, even small handfuls are a treat.

vein pinches out inland. East of the trail there is a narrow gulch, the chief source of ore. It is possible, with care, to scramble into the gulch, where there are meagre remnants of quartz containing chalcopyrite (bronze-yellow), covellite (purple) and bornite (blue-green). Digging through the tailing pile in 1839, Joseph Beete Jukes noted chalcocite ("grey sulpheret of copper"), a mineral common in copper deposits. Remnants of copper-bearing quartz veins can also be found in the tailings.

Copper deposited by hot fluids is normally intermingled with quartz, for the materials are deposited simultaneously. The copper minerals occur as small stringers in the quartz veins. If the mined veins resembled other veins nearby, they were likely narrow and fragmented; this would explain the impressive but worthless pile of chipped sandstone next to the mine. The miners likely extracted the copper before shipment. So far no pile of slag has been located, or evidence of a wood-fired retort. The site has been thoroughly dug over by treasure hunters, and a small crucible, possibly used to melt copper out of ore, was among the items found. In 1839, Joseph

Plumboy

A Mine Visit: May 24, 1839

"At 6 a.m. I started in a four-oared punt for Shoal Bay, about five miles down the coast. The morning was cool, but beautiful, with a light air offshore; and the bare lofty precipices of hard red sandstone, which here form the coast, produced magnificent cliff scenery. There was of course a swell, as we were on the margin of the wide Atlantic, and the manner in which we effected a landing was by rowing on the crest of a wave into a crevice just wide enough to admit the boat, and which shortly turned round at right angles behind a broad mass of rock, forming thus a snug shelter for our little craft. After some search we found the place where the mine had formerly been, and where some iron staples and bolts still remained in the rocks. There was, however, no appearance of a shaft, nor could I find anything which could lead me to guess as to the size or importance of the vein. Some pieces of vein stuff, apparently old refuse, lay about, containing small patches and strings of ore, which proved to be grey sulphuret of copper. After a delay of an hour or two the wind gradually rose, and, seeming inclined to shift towards the east, warned us to be off, which warning it was lucky we obeyed, as the sea was rising, and by the time we returned to Petty Harbour it was blowing pretty strong."

—Joseph Beete Jukes, Excursions in and about Newfoundland, 1842

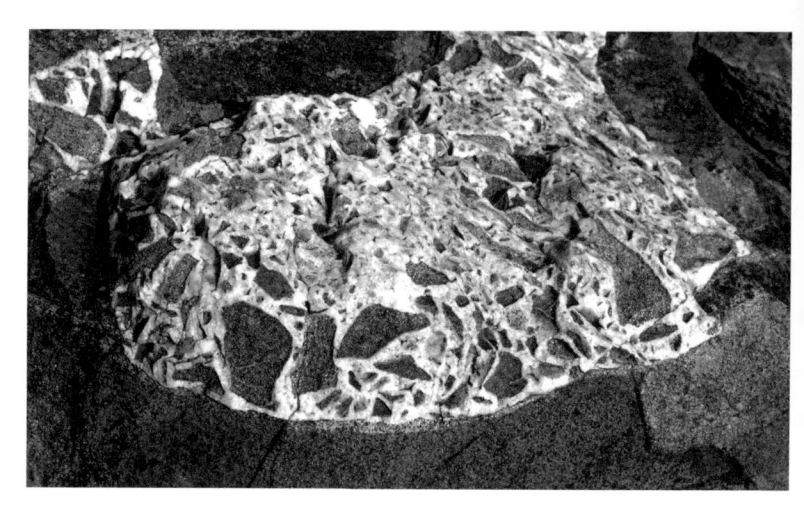

Salmon Head quartz breccia

Beete Jukes found no evidence of ore processing; indeed, he found little more than can be seen today.

The Miner Point Campsite is situated a little inland from the trail, in an idyllic grove of white birch. This was probably the location of the miners' camp. Fishery activity and forest fires likely had a greater impact on the area's vegetation than one short-lived mine. If birch is symptomatic of recent disturbance, and the mine has been inactive for 225 years, why have conifers not encroached upon the birch stand? Possibly loose tailings provide a poor foothold for conifers exposed to the fierce storms that periodically drive in from the northeast. A century's worth of treasure-hunting may have played a role, too. The outer margin of the grove has died back but trees in the centre of the stand are healthy and well spaced, creating a pleasant area of open wood and dappled shade. In a deciduous forest, moss cannot grow on the forest floor because of the accumulation of leaf litter. Hence, moss is found only on protruding rocks, and at the base of tree trunks.

Miner Point felsenmeer

◎ 11.8 km: Miner Point

Leaving the wood surrounding the mine, the path again enters heath. Whitened stumps point to recent woodcutting. Seasonal fishermen maintained stages and sheds in the area until the 1960s; the cut zone that resulted extends only a short distance inland. The fishermen left a "weed footprint" along the trail of clover, pearly everlasting, dandelion and buttercup. Native plants that colonize disturbed areas, such as hawkweed, yarrow, flat-topped white aster, goldenrod, raspberry, wild strawberry and fireweed, also have found a niche. A large quartz vein crosses the near-horizontal beds on the south side of Miner Point. The vein contains both green calcite and well-developed blue-green bornite crystals—the mineral extracted from the mine. Joseph Beete Jukes landed at the point in 1839. The L-shaped opening he describes is most likely a gulch called Quidi Vidi (at **11.7 km**), the only place to pull in near the point. In later years, fishermen attached a metal ladder to the gulch cliffs.

Salmon Head quartz veins

⊚ 12.0 km: Salmon Head

The *felsenmeer* (sea of boulders) that begins at Miner Point extends to Nippers Cove. The blocks and boulders are mostly red sandstone of local origin. Quidi Vidi formation sandstones and mudstones are brittle and contain numerous micro-joints, which are continually shattered by surface frost. Deeper fracturing occurred between 400 and 353 million years ago, during the Acadian Orogeny and the closure of the Iapetus Ocean. Silica-rich fluids present at about a 10-kilometre depth in the Earth's crust rose along zones of weakness in the rock, precipitated, and formed crystals in the fractures. Some rocks in the area are so crosshatched by veins that they look like parcels held in a string bag. The quartz breccia also found in the area formed where rock—shattered by a network of fractures—infilled with quartz crystals.

The Shoal Bay Treasure

By the late 19th century, it was widely believed that the mine at Shoal Bay had been a cover for treasure-hunting. This belief was bolstered by the popularity of Robert Louis Stevenson's *Treasure Island*, published in 1883. Possibly inspired by Stevenson, the Newfoundland antiquarian Henry Francis Shortis (1855-1935) published a Shoal Bay treasure story in the 1880s. In Shortis's wild tale, a dastardly pirate pair—a merciless captain and his bloodthirsty first mate—offload 14 boxes of gold and silver into a longboat, row to shore, blow up their ship and all on board, and behead the four porters they trap in the treasure pit. The mate perishes from exposure, and so does the captain, but not before he leaves a treasure map with a man from Holyrood, who carries the map to the United States in a sea chest. His grandson turns up one day in Petty Harbour and tells his story to

Red Fox Dens

Past Salmon Head, a little before Nippers Cove, there are two red fox burrows dug into turf hummocks at the coast. Hikers often see the kits in the spring. Fox dens most commonly occur in rocky crevices, but sometimes foxes dig underground burrows in soft ground. Foxes sleep outside during the winter. Solitary male and female foxes inhabit the same territory, but pair up to breed in dens in the spring. Pairs use the same den year after year, but frequently have one or two alternative dens. Litter size depends on prey abundance and ranges from two to 10 kits, with an average of five. Kits reach adult size at six months and by autumn leave the family group to be on their own.

Newfoundland red fox

Shoal Bay Treasure, 1897

"The men, who had regarded both me and my Spout with sulky ill-concealed aversion, did not fail to point out a pebbly cove where, in the days of yore, treasure is said to have been secreted by some roving buccaneer; and in search of which, one of my guides, with a company of other like-minded persons had misspent much precious time. They urged me to descend, see their excavations, and say whether I thought there was any use in their groping longer for the hidden gold. But that contempt which they had felt for me and my Spout, I felt for them and their treasure; and quite declined to turn aside from the homeward track. It was well done; for the darkness of night was far advanced ere we reached a safe footing, and the cottage was still to seek."

—James Lawson, Temple Bar, 1897

Pirate captain

Michael Monahan, then promptly slips through a stage hatchway and drowns. Monahan gamely attempts to find the treasure with three friends, only to be chased away by ghostly shrieks and fearsome apparitions. All four treasure-hunters die by the year's end.

Monahan's fate did not discourage others from seeking out the Shoal Bay treasure. Some of the countless hummocks around Miner Point supposedly belong to the murdered pirates. As you dig, will you uncover treasure or the bones of a vengeful ghost? Some claim there is just one ghost, a black man who, when asked to look after the treasure, foolishly volunteered. If you try to land by boat, it is said, rocks will tumble on you from above, thrown by pirate ghosts. A visiting Englishman once saw a treasure box wedged into a crevice. Alas! The more he reached for it, the more it slid past his grasp.

◎12.3 km: Nippers Cove

The charm of Nippers Cove (also called Nippers Harbour) as a fishing berth is summed up by its name: the cove is an ideal place to fish from if you do not mind being tormented by black flies, mosquitoes and stouts. Shoal Bay is open to the sea and lacks a secure anchorage; it has only the odd crevice and gulch—like Quidi Vidi—where an experienced fisherman might moor a small boat on a good day. Catches had to be hoisted up cliffs to stages. If the weather was rough, the men landed their fish in Petty Harbour.

In spite of these obstacles, in 1869, 17 men fished out of Shoal Bay and the total population of the shore was 103. Surnames associated with Shoal Bay, such as Raymond, Doyle, Heffernan, Frizzell, Clark, Finn and Hearn, are still commonly encountered in the Goulds and Petty Harbour. In addition to fishing for cod and

Old Shoal Bay Road

Johnny Burke was famous for his minstrel shows, in which he would get up in black face and play a character called "Bones." Judging from internal evidence, this ballad was likely played as a Bones piece. A crackie is a small dog, loud and useless.

Come boys while I tell ye, a place ye know well,
Where they buried a fortune, a very long spell;
It's a place they call Shoal Bay, on the Southern Shore,
Where gold it is buried, they say, in galore,

Some say 'twas a pirate they call Captain Kidd.
In Shoal Bay this wonderful fortune he hid;
And for years they were digging this fortune to raise,
Till the boys in the village got near in a craze.

Now, this money that's buried—a great many went
With pickaxe and shovels, and put up a tent.
And just as they stuck the first pick in the ground,
The ghost of a darkie did hover around.

They rushed from the spot on that terrible night,
And a crackie got turned inside out from the fright;
And a man from Cape Broyle who did watch the queer sight,
His whiskers turned foxy, that always were white.

Now a crew from Burin, at least so we're told,
They started a' digging and struck on the gold;
And the load was so heavy to bring down the track,
That a hump like a butter tub grew on their back.

—Johnny Burke, SONGSTER, 1903

WRECK OF THE HMS *TWEED*

On October 3, 1813, the 18-gun naval sloop HMS *Tweed*, under the command of Captain William Mather, left Cork, Ireland, as escort to a 52-ship convoy headed for Newfoundland. On November 4, in the face of worsening weather, Captain Mather ordered his fleet to stand to and wait out the night. The captain believed he was 60 km offshore. The wind increased to gale force, accompanied by driving rain. Shortly after midnight, on November 5, the *Tweed* and one of the convoy ships, the *Southampton* (see the Thoroughfare, at **2.4 km** on Spout Path), drifted into unforgiving cliffs and breaking seas near Nippers Cove.

The quick-thinking lieutenant on watch, rope in hand, leapt to a cleft in the rocks with a fellow seaman. Reaching the top of the cliffs, the two men secured a rescue line. Of the 60 who attempted the crossing, 40 lacerated and battered seamen survived, including the captain and most of the officers. Before the rescue could be completed, however, a heavier-than-usual swell lifted the sloop off the rocks, and the *Tweed* sank with the ship's purser, surgeon and 65 of the crew. The survivors spent

Royal Navy sloop of war

salmon, Shoal Bay's settlers raised pigs and goats and harvested wood. It is not known how many stayed the year round. Signs of past settlement can be found near Nippers Cove and Raymonds Gulch. Eyebolts used to secure traps are drilled into the ledges in many places. Up until the 1920s, fishermen from Bay Bulls regularly rowed to Shoal Bay in nine-man skiffs (eight men rowed, one steered). In 1955, Petty Harbour fishermen successfully petitioned the government for the fishing rights to the Shoal Bay grounds, as far south as Long Point.

Shoal Bay Road began as a 19th-century cart track linking Shoal Bay to the Goulds. The track is still used regularly by woodcutters, hunters, cabin owners, hikers, bikers and skiers, and has branches leading from Nippers Cove and Raymond Head. Near the sea, a canopy of mountain alder arches over the path. Where the tracks join, about a kilometre up the road, there is a mysterious etching of a schooner cut into a boulder. At the Nippers Cove end of the track, immediately south of the stream, it is still possible to see where the route widened to allow a horse to back a cart off the path. In this way, a cart could be turned around and loaded with fish without unhitching the horse.

Gulch near Doubloon Pool

◎12.5 km: Shoal Bay

The path follows Shoal Bay Road up the hill to by-pass a cabin. Leaving the road after 100 metres, the path quickly reaches a heath-covered bluff overlooking the sea. Descending into a small valley full of leggy, flourishing birch, pin-cherry and northern wild raisin, the path continues over rough ground through waist-high sheep laurel. There is considerable evidence of conifer grow-back. Nearing Doubloon Pool (at **12.8 km**) a side trail leads seaward onto a broad, gently sloping rock ledge. More than 550 million years ago, flowing streams created the ripple marks preserved in the sandstone. Ancient flood events ripped up flakes of desiccated mud (called "rip-up clasts" by geologists)

Rip-up clasts

a miserable night in freezing rain, huddled in a rock crevice. The next day, they walked to Petty Harbour where they were cared for by local families until transported to St. John's.

SHOAL BAY SHIPWRECKS

On May 14, 1835, the 698-ton barquentine ***Thomson***, commanded by Archibald Henry and transporting timber from Saint John, New Brunswick to Cork, Ireland, was stranded and wrecked in Shoal Bay. In 1909, a schooner owned and commanded by Captain Dicks, having picked up supplies in St. John's, was crushed in the ice off Shoal Bay. Six men and one woman spent the night on the ice on a "shelving rock," as turbulent seas prevented their crossing to shore. They were picked up the next day by the tugboat ***Ingraham***. On January 26, 1915, the ***Earshall*** was lost in Shoal Bay.

Garnippers, Gallinippers, Nippers, Nips and Nipperkins

In the 18th century, Newfoundland's biggest, meanest biting insects were called "garnippers" or "yellow nippers." Both the deerfly and larger, less common horsefly gall their victim—they take a bite out of the flesh, causing their prey to jump. Regular "nippers" seem always to have been mosquitoes. A "nip" is a tight place to get into and a "nipper," short for "nipperkin," is the distressingly small container used to measure out the morning "nip" of rum, usually brought to the men by a boy, affectionately known as the "young nipper."

Waterfalls at Raymonds Gulch

and carried them downstream, depositing them in different-coloured sand.

Fishermen and hunters who, year after year, gather resources along a shore, constitute an informal nomenclature board. In most cases, a feature that is of no use, however impressive it may look from a trail, is unlikely to be named. The striking bowl-shaped gulch north of Burnt Point is a case in point—for, scenic though it may be, it is jammed with rocks. Brittle Quidi Vidi formation sandstones and mudstones in both this gulch and the next—Raymonds Gulch—were fractured by the collision of continents during the Acadian Orogeny. However, no silica-bearing fluid travelled through the joints to create quartz veins.

The trap berth off the gulch, called Doubloon Pool or Upper Side of Burnt Head, is named for a Spanish wreck, said to be visible still on a fine day, along with its cargo of gold doubloons. There were 23 first-rate berths, picked on first draw. Doubloon Pool, like the similarly named Fortune Cove (near Petty Harbour), was one of 20 second-rate berths drawn for by crews possessing a second trap. (There also were nine third-rate draws.) The gold doubloons in the pool were no doubt welcome compensation for the added work and absent fish.

◎13.3 km: Raymonds Gulch

A tall conifer forest presses against the coast at Burnt Point. There is no evidence of the fire that gave the point its name. Merlins sometimes perch in the grove and direct high-pitched protests at intruding hikers. The rusted fastenings driven into the ledges on the north side of Raymonds Gulch likely were used to secure a winch and *derrick* (a mast with a boom), for the trap berth nearby is called "the Derrick." Not just the day's catch, but skiffs were likely hauled up, for neither the ledges nor the angle of the gulch protected boats from storms blowing in from the east or southeast. Above the ledges, on the north rim, the stunted, spray-blasted trees have mostly died back and there is a lush understory of green moss, bunchberry, partridgeberry, starflower and twinflower. The gulch's depths do a better job of protecting trees; at the head of the gulch, the trees grow straight and tall to the cliff edge, and tumble into the opening when their time has come. The tree-lined forest track up the west rim still looks the way it must have in days when horse carts were used to haul fish up the path. Two waterfalls pour from a single stream on the south rim. The stream is full of flat boulders that make perfect stepping-stones. These, too, likely date to the days of cart traffic. The small pool next to the path, half-hidden by trees, is an idyllic place for cooling feet or paddling. The path crosses an abandoned field just before Shoal Bay Road and there is another cleared area at the end of the road.

WRECK OF THE *FLATHOLM*

On November 17, 1950, the 133-ton trawler ***Flatholm***, newly purchased by National Sea Products and on its way from the United Kingdom to St. John's and Halifax, lost its bearings in thick fog. Captain R. A. Winn proceeded with caution but the trawler nosed between two flat rock outcrops and was unable to reverse out of the trap. As heavy seas washed over the vessel, it "rose and fell like a cork" and one of two lifeboats was swept away. Captain Winn radioed in his position incorrectly, sending the rescue ship ***Blue Foam*** northeast of St. John's. The captain and his Nova Scotia crew of 13 rowed all night in the surviving lifeboat before fishermen came to their rescue near Bay Bulls. Over time, local fishermen salvaged the wreck, selling the ship off piecemeal. The trap berth "Steamer," nearby, is named for the wreck.

Six Men and One Woman taken off the Ice

Come all you hardy fishermen, and hark to what I say,
And hear how six were rescued, boys, near Petty Harbor Bay.
And one lone woman with the rest upon the ice all night.
Till early Sunday morning, when the "Ingraham" hove in sight.

A schooner owned by Captain Dicks set sail about sunrise,
Bound home before a pleasant breeze, with fishery supplies.
When near Shoal Bay they met the ice, that forced her near the land.
The crew was forced to take the ice, the strain she could not stand.

All night upon the open ice these poor men had to stay,
Until they spied the tug boat, just about the break of day,
While some got on a shelving rock, from boisterous seas run high,
Not to remain upon the ice, on that cold night to die.

But soon the news spread round, boy, and very soon reached town.
When soon the "Ingraham" left St. John's, and on the crew bore down.
When six men and one woman, they landed safe on shore,
Picked up near Petty Harbor Bay, kind friends to see once more.

—Johnny Burke, HARBOUR GRACE STANDARD, 1908

Swell among ice

Spout Path

Spout in winter

Spout Path

◎ 0.0 km: Shoal Bay Road

In 1998, the Spout Path trailhead was shifted inland to avoid a cabin on the coast. The new route cuts through a dense stand of matchstick fir. Before the cut, the ground was moss covered and only the tip of each tree was green; the dead lower branches were ghostly and lichen-covered. The cut introduced bright light into a low light environment. The plants now bordering the trail were the first to respond to the new opening: bunchberry, blueberry, partridgeberry and haircap moss (*Polytrichium commune*), a light-loving moss commonly seen in association with blueberry. Other plants no doubt will colonize this section in coming years.

Shoal Bay Road is an important avenue of access to desirable stands of timber and firewood. Recently harvested *cut blocks* (cut areas) are covered with sheep laurel and stumps. Older cut blocks are occupied by dense stands of young fir. The path quickly moves beyond the cutting into an aging wood where many trees are leaning or fallen. Here, too, the fir regeneration is dense, blanketing the forest floor and crowding the path's margins. Larch, sheep laurel and mountain alder occupy spots where there is wet or thin soil.

Haircap moss

◎ 0.4 km: Raymond Head

After climbing to Raymond Head, the path follows a ridge and descends sharply into a *droke* (or *drook*, a sheltered, wooded valley). There is a junction near two large boulders. Homeward-bound hikers seeking a short cut to Shoal Bay Road often use the

Droke near Raymond Head

Having left the ancient river environment of the Quidi Vidi Formation at Queens River, hikers will stay with the older shallow marine environment of the Gibbett Hill Formation until North Head.

Quidi Vidi Formation sandstone ledges near Raymond Head

unmaintained access trail that leads west. Reaching the heart of the valley on the main path, a small stream is bordered by a marshy area. Drokes offer shelter, warmth and varied light and moisture conditions, and consequently are dynamic, species-rich places. Below the mixed canopy of fir, pin-cherry, white birch, mountain alder, northern wild raisin, chuckley-pear and larch, there is a flourishing understory of blueberry, wild roses, common juniper, cinnamon fern, mouse-eared hawkweed and creeping snowberry. Thriving streamside plants include a diversity of rushes, sedges and grasses, as well as sweetgale, tall meadow-rue, flat-topped white aster, Labrador tea, cinnamon and bracken fern, goldenrod and black knapweed. Leaving the stream, the trail enters a stand of wildly wind-shaped conifers and tall white birch. There is a turn downhill to Queens River, through a funnel-shaped growth of tuck and wild roses.

Queens River bridge

◎0.7 km: Queens River

Queens River falls into a round, steeply walled cove, which in heavy seas transforms into a punchbowl of churning, seething waves. On calm days, milky green siltstone ledges loom under the water. Along the cliff there are comfortable areas of crowberry heath where hikers can lunch and wave-watch. On calm days, river otters pick through the mussel beds, or play on the rocks and ledges. The open, stony environment bordering Queens River is dominated by ferns, but numerous other interesting plants grow along the banks, including flat-topped white, purple-stemmed, and New York asters, goldenrod, horsetail, marshberry, meadowsweet, sweetgale, bog myrtle, mouse-eared hawkweed, fireweed and tall meadow-rue.

◎1.0 km: Queens River Flats

South of Queens River, the trail passes through alternate areas of enclosed and open wood. The thicker groves are mostly white spruce, with an understory of moss, ferns, horsetail and bunchberry. A mix of spruce and fir is found in the open areas, with a dense understory of shrubs and sheep laurel. After 200 metres, the trail turns east onto an extensive rock ledge called Queens River Flats. Here, the hiker will find no fixed route, but must walk up the ledge to

Composites: Asters and Goldenrods

The aster family (Compositae) is one of the largest plant families, containing more than 20,000 species worldwide, or about 10 per cent of all flowering plants. The family includes a number of edibles, such as lettuce, endive, chicory and artichoke, as well as species cultivated for their flowers, such as marigold, daisy, sunflower and chrysanthemum. Each flowerhead—and there are often many flowerheads per plant—houses dozens of tiny flowers, each containing both pistils and stamens. By grouping small flowers together, Compositae species reduce the energy invested in making flowers visible to pollinators, thus bettering their reproductive odds in adverse environments. Over the long haul, the strategy results in greater genetic variability and adaptation to habitat, for an insect will make contact with, and cross-pollinate, dozens of flowers while visiting a single plant.

Within the Compositae family, goldenrods and asters are the most diverse and widespread genera. Goldenrods number over 100 species, of which 90 are North American natives, and a half-dozen are found in Newfoundland. Goldenrod flowerheads are usually bright yellow and occur in clusters at the top of the stem.

Site-specific adaptation has allowed goldenrod to invade a wide range of habitats. In Newfoundland, for example, the bog goldenrod (*Solidago uliginosa*) is restricted to crowberry barrens and peatlands, while the hairy goldenrod (*S. hispida*) is found only on limestone barrens. Seaside goldenrod

Rough-stemmed goldenrod

Bog aster

(*S. sempervirens*) prefers beaches and salt marshes. Large-leaved goldenrod (*S. macrophylla*) inhabits shady woods. Rough-stemmed goldenrod (*S. rugosa*) is a large plant that occurs abundantly in open, disturbed areas, as does the equally rough-stemmed but more narrow-leaved Canada goldenrod (*S. canadensis*).

Aster flowers are daisy-like in appearance and can be white, pink, blue or purple. There are more than 600 species of asters worldwide, of which about 150 are native to North America and more than two dozen are common in Newfoundland. Like goldenrod, aster species have adapted to a wide range of habitats. The New York aster (*Aster novi-belgii*) is typically found in fens, meadows, shorelines and wet spots. Purple-stemmed aster (*A. puniceus*) is found in black spruce fens, along flooded river banks and in freshwater marshes. Bog aster (*A. nemoralis*) grows in acid bogs and fens. Rough-leaved aster (*A. radula*) prefers floodplains and wet woods. The flat-topped white aster (*A. umbellatus*) prefers moist woodland clearings.

Spout Path

Queens River discontinuity

where the path reenters the woods. The ledge's beds dip about 10° to the northwest, an ideal angle for frost wedging and waves to plane off successive layers of material. The water running down the ledge collects in crevices. Wetland species, such as cranberry, bog aster, bog rosemary, blue flag, sweetgale, St. John's-wort, round-leaved sundew and even horned bladderwort—growing in a small patch of black moss—thrive where the seepage is steady. Heath species, such as purple chokeberry, bilberry, crowberry and trailing juniper, as well as stunted mountain alder, spruce and larch, occupy the drier hollows and cracks. Here and there are meadow plants, such as wild strawberry and aster. There are pockets, too, of seashore plants, notably harebell and seaside plantain.

From Queens River Flats, hikers can look back to the exact spot, called a *boundary* or *contact*, five metres below Queens River Bridge, where pinkish-red Quidi Vidi Formation sandstone sits directly on top of older greyish-green Gibbett Hill Formation sandstone and siltstone. This is one of the few sharp geologic boundaries visible on the trail. More than 550 million years ago, sand and silt from a river delta settled southward onto a shallow marine shore or estuary. In most places the river and sea deposited alternate layers of material, and the shift from a marine environment to a river delta was gradual. At Queens River, however, a sharp transition occurred, resulting

Coastal heath

n the permanent emergence of the delta top. The nature of the event is uncertain. A major flood may have extended the shore, depositing large quantities of material; or a fall in sea level or uplift of the Earth's crust may have caused the ocean to retreat, oxidizing the topmost layer of exposed marine sediment.

⊚1.4 km: Red Rocks

After leaving Queens River Flats the trail keeps to the rocky edge of a coastal plateau, passing through both flourishing heath and open wood. In shady areas, there are lush carpets of bunchberry; in damper areas, plumboy, squashberry, skunk currant and ferns flourish. The rivulets intersecting the trail are so cluttered with stone that they resemble rock gardens. A few venerable conifers, their trunks white with lichen, hold on in sheltered spots, but elsewhere dead and wind-thrown trees are numerous. Scattered conifers grow amid the sheep laurel, their needles yellow-tinged, indicating depleted soil conditions. The coastal heath here is likely maintained by a combination of factors: stony ground, repeated fire-damage and, inland from the heath, a steeply rising ridge that likely directs strong, irregular gusts against weakened and exposed trees.

The trap berth Red Rocks is named for a fisherman's mark: several red sandstone erratics near the shore-

Red Rocks

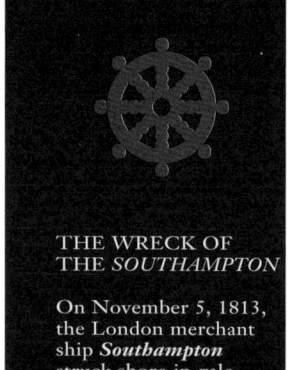

THE WRECK OF THE *SOUTHAMPTON*

On November 5, 1813, the London merchant ship *Southampton* struck shore in gale force winds and fog, 3 km south of its escort, the HMS *Tweed*. Captain Henry Lee and all on board scrambled to the top of Island of Long Point. Without food or shelter, they were exposed to freezing wind and rain for two days: it took one day for survivors from the HMS *Tweed* to walk to Petty Harbour, and a second day for a search party from Petty Harbour to reach Long Point. By the time the rescue party arrived, four on the island had died from exposure. The survivors of the ordeal were brought back to Petty Harbour and cared for until they recovered strength, then delivered to St. John's where they were returned to their home port.

Island of Long Point from the sea

line that stand out from the greyish-green rock on which they sit. Near Red Rocks, the path circles a narrow gulch, visible from its south side. The trail then follows the coastal plateau for some time before dipping again, this time into a dry gulch full of fireweed. Stone steps are set into a bluff slope on the landward end of Hauling Gulch (at **1.9 km**). This steep-sided gulch is ideally shaped to amplify wave action. Crews that drew this berth held their lines firmly against the gunwale of their trap skiff and let the rising swell do the work of hauling the trap. On the down swell, the line's slack was hauled in, and a trap was out of the water in no time. The open woodland south of the gulch is home to a greater mix of species than the heath to the north. Sheep laurel, fir and spruce are joined by larch, mountain alder, chuckley-pear, northern wild raisin, wild roses, Labrador tea, common juniper, crowberry, bunchberry, partridge-berry and ferns.

⊚ 2.4 km: Long Point

Nearing Long Point, the trail passes through a wind-shaped, lichen-whitened coastal wood. At **2.2 km**, there is a lookout over a steep gulch. The trail briefly continues through woods, then skirts the same gulch at its head. The pockets of straight-growing conifers

Heath at Long Point

tucked into the depths point to a protected environment. The fissure's rock walls echo with the cries of gulls and black-legged kittiwakes. Waterways such as this offer refuge to injured or fatigued birds, and make good hunting spots. This is true for foxes as well as humans; there is a fox den on the isolated spit of land on the eastern side of the gulch.

The broad heath at Long Point is dotted with red sandstone boulders split by frost. Blue flag, bakeapple, rushes and wild roses flourish in the small pools and wet areas. Foot traffic has introduced pearly everlasting, goldenrod, wild strawberry and clover. Beach pea, Scotch lovage, harebell, seaside plantain, grass and hawkweed have taken over slopes close to the ocean that are too steep for crowberry heath. On the steepest of these slopes, the mossy ground has slid into crescent-shaped hummocks, a phenomenon known as "moss creep."

It is highly recommended that hikers detour eastward across the heath to the Thoroughfare, a channel separating Long Point and Island of Long Point. Small boats can navigate the Thoroughfare in calm weather, hence the name. Island of Long Point is an aircraft carrier-shaped offshore rock with narrow cliff ledges that offer secure nesting for black-legged kittiwakes. Alert, discretely spaced herring gulls assess the foraging scene from the "carrier's" broad, slightly tilted deck. Greater black-backed gulls, being larger and more aggressive, take the best viewing spots. The Spout is a kilometre away by sea, but still a two-kilometre walk along the trail.

The two gulches passed on the way to the Thoroughfare align with two gulches on the south side of Long Point Cove. The Thoroughfare itself aligns with the sea cavern powering the Spout. Joints and faults often occur as sets of fractures. As fractures erode they thus form into sets of related features, which run either parallel, or at a consistent angle to each other.

Of the more than 20 major caves, tunnels and channels that occur between Queens River and North Head, approximately half trend 45° northwest. The other half are at a right angle to the first, trending 45° southwest. Closely spaced sets of shallow cave openings occur at Long Cove and Drop Cove; sets of close-spaced, parallel-running gulches occur at Long Point and Miner Point.

◎ 2.7 km: Long Point Cove

A climb of 300 metres through sheep laurel heath is rewarded by an unencumbered view of fortress-like Long Point Cove. Below, on stormy days, waves rage over broad sea ledges, and nesting black-legged kittiwakes cling to the crevices above. Since 1955, the trap berth called East Side of Long Point Cove has marked the beginning of the Bay Bulls fishing grounds. The trail enters a wood that arches over a lush bunchberry carpet. It takes only a slight change of location and a small drop in available light for bunchberries to fail to produce berries. In one spot,

---

COASTAL MORPHOLOGY

Many processes contribute to coastal erosion. The movement and folding of the Earth's crust creates joints and faults. Glaciers scrape or push against surface rock and, more substantively, press their colossal weight down on, or against, fractures. Groundwater percolates into a myriad of cracks. Seepage freezes, often many times each winter, each time expanding nine per cent in volume, wedging apart cracks. Waves, ice and currents selectively pound, loosen and shift weakened rock.

The varied cliff features along the Gibbett Hill Formation coast—from Queens River to North Head—are similar in one sense: they all have

Alan Kenworthy

Peter Gard

Alan Kenworthy

Spout Path

Peter Gard *Queens River droke*

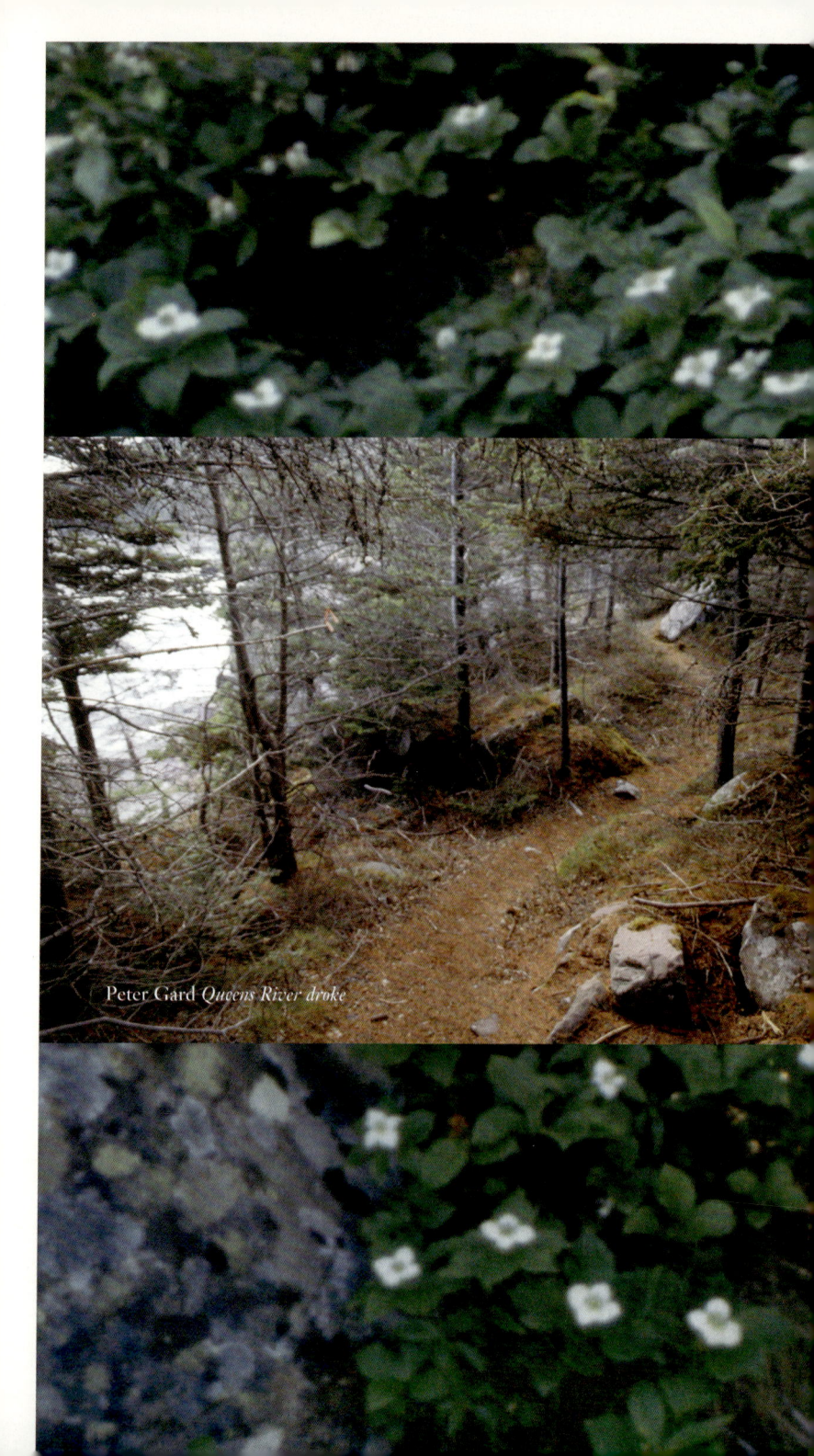

Roger Tory Peterson *Raptors* Courtesy of Newfoundland Museum, Catalogue No.984.13.7

Peter Gard Pierced Point sea stack and eagle

Labrador tea

Joyce Etsuko Cho

Sheep laurel

Peter Gard *White birch wood—fall, winter and spring*

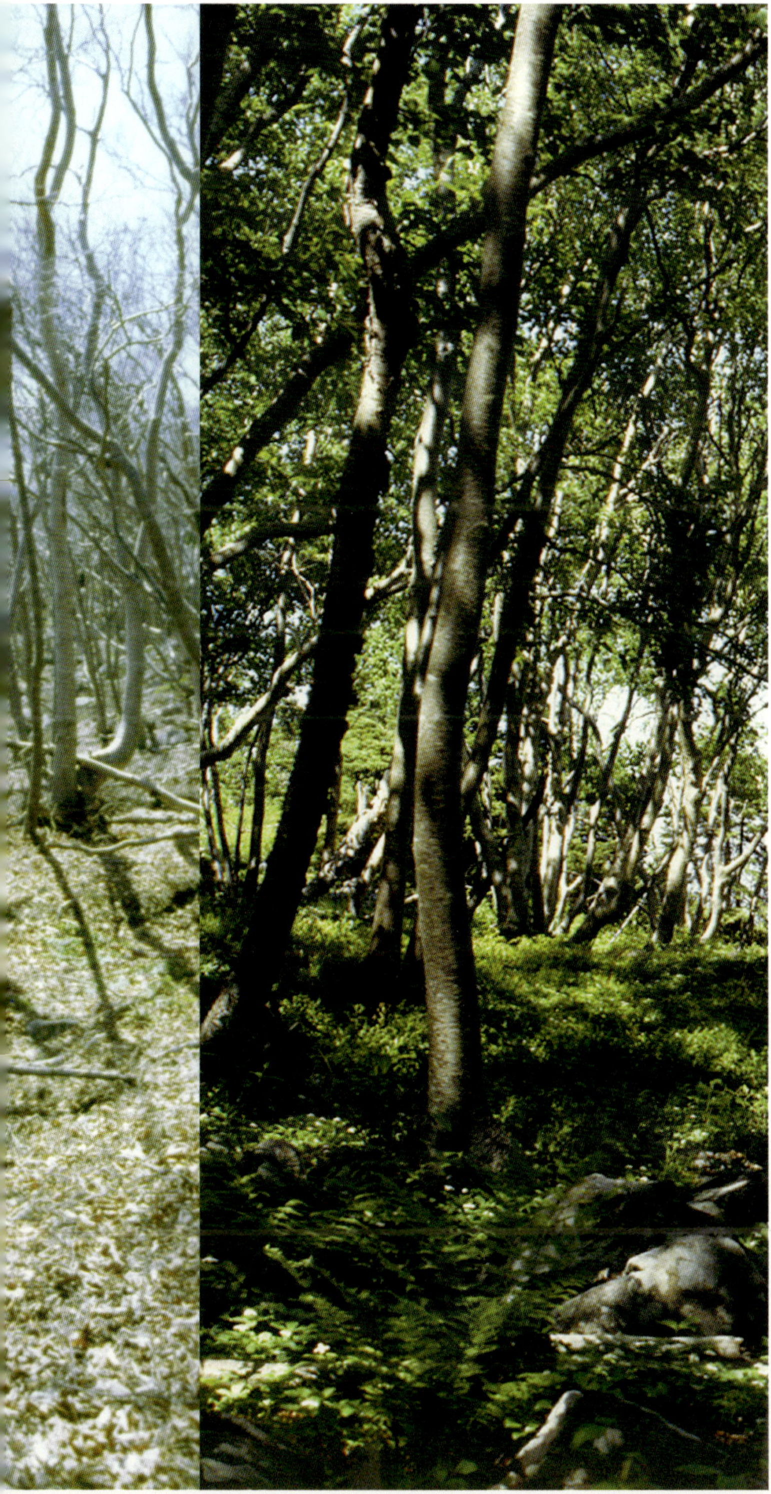

Peter Gard *Pulpit Rock*

Peter Gard *Queens River hiker*

Alignment of the Thoroughfare with the Spout

every plant will have bright red berries; in the next spot along, not a single plant will have borne fruit.

Near the deepest part of the cove, prevailing winds regularly blow a cliff waterfall back up the cliff face into the woods, creating a skyward flowing "blow-back" stream, surrounded by rotting black vegetation. Circling Long Point Cove, the trail climbs again, this time through a birch wood, and enters a mixed forest with numerous downed trees. Many of the conifers still standing are dead, or look like they soon will be. Reaching Middle of Long Point Cove (at **3.2 km**) the trail passes two narrow crevices that align with two crevices on East Side of Long Point Cove. A recent cliff collapse on East Side is best seen from these crevices.

Blow-back stream

been fractured from above, then excavated from below. The greenish-grey sandstones of the formation are brittle and crack easily, and the formation's thick-bedded units—five to six metres thick—favour the breaking off of large blocks. At the Thoroughfare, a probable fault line, exposed to heavy seas, has been carved into a broad channel. At the Spout, in an environment that is more protected, waves and frost have excavated the same fracture, carving only a low, narrow cavern. Here, as elsewhere along the coast, the greater the exposure to waves and freezing spray, the more advanced the erosion.

Conifer Regeneration and Fire

Although black spruce (*Picea mariana*) is a slower growing tree than balsam fir, spruce seeds are better adapted to fire. Not only can spruce cones withstand high temperatures, the heat from fire helps open cones and release seeds. Commonly, after fire, black spruce replaces fir, the least fire resistant conifer in the area, and repeated fires do severe damage to the fir seed supply.

Fire is part of the natural life cycle of the boreal forest. Long, cold winters and cool summers slow bacterial and fungal action in northern forests. Soil acidity also inhibits decomposition. Fallen trees, branches, needles and leaves pile up faster than they can decay. This accumulating **duff** (surface litter) limits light and retards growth. Fire burns off built-up organic matter, leaving behind mineral-rich ash. New, fire-created openings let in light, and a succession of species begin their return.

With so many trees down, the cove is a good place to observe the effect of wind-throw on ground cover. In subdued light, mosses predominate. In areas with partial light, bunchberry covers the ground. Heath takes over where the light is bright. A mix of sheep laurel, blueberry, northern wild raisin, Labrador tea, raspberry and goldenrod is found in areas recently opened by wind-throw. Older open areas tend towards a monoculture of either sheep laurel or dense spruce regeneration. There are patches of squashberry, skunk currant and New York fern where the ground is damp, such as by the stream at **3.4 km**.

◎ 3.5 km: Two Gulches

Passing inland of West Side of Long Point Cove, the trail traverses a dense tangle of standing and fallen fir. The thick undergrowth of white birch, fir, sheep laurel and northern wild raisin adds to the confusion. The path breaks out half-way along the first of two deep, steep-walled gulches. The trail circles the first gulch, cuts over to the second (at **3.8 km**) and then turns east and proceeds along the south side of the second at a height that affords a good view of both, and the spit of land in between. The gulches run parallel to each other, but at a 45° angle to the coast. In spring and summer, rank, clamorous colonies of black-legged kittiwakes nest on narrow ledges within the dark walls. The largest nesting group is near the mouth of the first gulch.

There is a large patch of thistle at the head of the first gulch, and pearly everlasting is present, too. Bird or human activity likely brought in the seed. Young conifers, especially white spruce, grow on the cliff edges, slopes and ledges, but nowhere is there an older stand of trees that has not been thrown into confusion by wind and ice. Some trees have just their tips bent, a hint that they will soon lose branches or

Aerial view of Two Gulches

be blown over. Conifers do not easily recover from weather damage. Birch and alder do much better, for they respond to disaster by shooting out a new branch or trunk.

◎ 4.1 km: Miner Point

In 1946, Joe Crockwell of Bay Bulls prospected for copper by blowing the top off a headland, thereafter dubbed Miner Point. A hidden cavern runs under the point, parallel to the two long gulches just passed. Preliminary exploration suggests that the cavern extends as deeply into the cliff, and that the two gulches, too, were once caverns. There are places where the cavern walls are the same height, or higher, than the gulch walls, but the elevation of Miner Point is greater than the elevation of the coast north of the point, so the roof of the cavern has not yet foundered.

The cavern cannot be seen from the trail but must be visited by chartered boat. The strong current and deadly undertow pulling into the cavern suggest why a nearby trap berth is called "the Spinner"; and why fishermen—or anyone in a small craft—would be unwise to explore the spot without a powerful boat and an experienced guide.

Cavern

Landing rock removal gear, 1995

Rock removal, 1995

◎ 4.5 km: The Spout

In 1995, three East Coast Trail volunteers, Nigel Groves, Joe Lee and Mike Fitzpatrick, shifted a large boulder that blocked the centre of the Spout blowhole, dividing the waterspout and reducing its historic height. The shifted boulder sits three metres to the seaward side of the hole. The 70 kilos of tackle used by the team was landed and hauled up the cliffs by hand. The small rocks still in the hole atomize the stream water blown up by the bellows action of the waves below.

The Spout blows highest in the spring and fall when the Spout River overflows into the blowhole. The Spout sometimes dries up in the summer when the river runs low. A southeast-facing subterranean cavern acts as the Spout's bellows. Waves push air into the cavern and river water flowing into the hole is sprayed back out in a great loud gush, just like a whale's spout, or a geyser. The spray is composed entirely of fresh water and during the winter freezes into a substantial ice cone.

Plants growing in the Spout's spray zone include seaside plantain, New York and bog aster, beach pea, wild roses, round-leaved sundew and pearlwort (*Sagina procumbens*), this last a well-known garden invader that thrives in over-saturated environments, including natural ones. Blue flag, tall meadow-rue and tall sedges grow in the larger crevices. The fir and spruce around the Spout have an abused, ragged appearance, which is not surprising since they spend most of the winter encased in ice.

The Spout in History

1664

"We intended for St. Johns but the wind not permitting us, we bore away for Bay Bulls, and past by Spout Cove, lying between Petty Harbour and Bay Bulls. It's a hollow rock, into which the sea squeezing in waves, the water and air spout out at a great hole that is over it, and make a noise, to be heard 2 or 3 mile and seen as many leagues. Here my father was cast away, about 20 years since. It was in the night, and the cliffs are steep and inaccessable. It pleased God that one nimble fellow climbed up, and carrying a line, drew up a rope, which he fastened to a tree, they all climbed up by it and were saved."

—THE JOURNAL OF JAMES YONGE, 1664

1689

"A hollow place which the Sea runs into, and having a vent on the top of the Land near the Water side, spouts up the Water in that manner that you may see it a great way off, especially if there be any Sea which causes the greater Violence."

—THE ENGLISH PILOT: THE FOURTH BOOK, 1689

JAMES YONGE

The Plymouth surgeon James Yonge (1647-1721) visited Newfoundland four times between 1663 and 1670. Yonge's journal contains the earliest known mention of the Spout, in an entry for June of 1664.

THE ENGLISH PILOT

The Spout was enthroned as a mariner's mark when it was described in the fourth book of *The English Pilot*, a widely circulated navigational guide. It appears on maps etched by John Seller (1671) and Henry Southwood (1675) that accompany the guide.

1754

The water spout described. A pro[bable] conjecture concerning the cause [of] this phenomenon. Beautiful prosp[ect] in Newfoundland.

THE FIRST MAGAZINE

The London editor Edward Cave (1691-1754) invented the idea of combining odd bits of news, literature and gossip into a monthly publication in 1731. He wanted his subscribers to think they were opening an arsenal of valuable ideas, so he called his publication a "magazine," borrowing the term for a military or ship storehouse. Under the *nom de plume* "Sylvanus Urban," Cave edited *The Gentleman's Magazine: or, Monthly Intelligencer* until his death. The magazine was the most popular of its day. An anonymous correspondent, most likely a naval officer, contributed a detailed description of the Spout to the July 2, 1754 number.

"Being upon the coast of Newfoundland, 5 or 6 leagues to the southward of St. John'[s] I was agreeably entertain'd with the sight o[f] a natural fountain, which the inhabitants c[all] the water-spout. It rises from the shore, whi[ch] is rocky, and 30 feet above the sea, to the height of 40 to 50 feet above the rock, in a column of water capable of being seen 5 o[r] miles. It is not a continued fountain, for the water rises from the rock, and gains its extreme height in a quarter of a minute; wh[en] failing of supply, it falls, and ceases for near[ly] the same space of time: But I observ'd the intermissions were not regular, neither were the jets always to the same height; being sometimes much higher, and of longer continuance, than at others; from which (as I had not an opportunity of being nearer tha[n] at the distance of a mile and half) I imagine it is occasioned by the motion, or what is commonly call'd the swell of the sea; for although there had not been much wind for several preceeding days, yet I observ'd, a considerable agitation near the shore, as indeed there generally is, which, where it is flat, creates a surf, but where steeper, breakers. This I observe, because I am told th[at] fountain never fails, even in a course of the most serene weather. Now, in this place, whi[ch] is rocky and steep, I concluded that there might be a large cavern, probably somewhat like an inverted hopper, the mouth of which might be upon a level with the surface of the water; under this, the sea rushing with impetuosity, and meeting with resistance, would consequently rise, and the higher it ros[e] being more confin'd on all sides, wou'd force itself with violence through the aperture on t[he] top of the rock; and accordingly as the swell o[f] the sea was greater or less, so wou'd the jets o[f] the fountain be higher, or lower, and of different duration.

Notwithstanding the wild and barren aspect this country wears, I must acknowledge the prospect is in this place beautiful; there is somewhat which strikes the spectator with pleasure and surprize. From the shore, the country rises irregularly to a great height, and is intirely cover'd with firs and spruce trees; and from the top of the mountains, through the woods, a river rapidly descends, over many falls and obstructions, which form beautiful cascades; at length it arrives at the rock, out of which the fountain issues, where the waters precipitate into the sea together."

—Anonymous, THE GENTLEMAN'S MAGAZINE, 1754

1794

"Between the Bay of Bulls and Petty Harbour is one of the most singular natural curiositys in Newfoundland. This is a natural fountain and is occasion'd by the following concuring circumstances. By the sea, under a chain of rocks, is a large cavern, which runs many yards underground. At the extremity of this cave there is an aperture or hole which runs up to the level or surface above. At the entrance to this cavern the water is very deep. When the winds blow strong on shore a very heavy swell is roll'd into the cave with amazing velocity, it is hemmed in on both sides, and when the waves meet with the resisting rocks at the further end it forceth the passage upwards with most extraordinary strength—so much so that the waters rise into a column into the air and is to all intents a grand and magnificent fountain. This fountain, view'd from the sea, has a fine effect. It appears to be inland about half a mile. In the distance there is a rise of land, and when ting'd with azure blue, which it generally is, makes a charming background to show off this column of water to the greatest advantage."

—THE NEWFOUNDLAND JOURNAL OF AARON THOMAS

AARON THOMAS

Aaron Thomas (1762-1822?) was born in Wigmore, Herefordshire. In 1794-95, he was one of 220 men aboard the 32-gun frigate HMS *Boston* assigned to the Newfoundland station under Captain James Nicholl Morris. Thomas's name appears on the ship's list as an able seaman but, judging from the many entries in his diary dealing with supply, he likely worked as an unlisted captain's steward or purser's assistant. His sketches and elaborate stories of shipboard and shore life were composed for a close friend. Thomas's manuscript remained in private hands until the 1960s, at which time it was edited and published by its owner. Thomas visited the Spout on July 18, 1794, while on patrol from Placentia to St. John's. His concluding words suggest that he, or one of his shipmates, made a sketch, now lost.

Spout Path

LIEUTENANT EDWARD CHAPPELL

A native of Kent, Edward Chappell (1792-1861) joined the navy at the age of twelve and saw service in the Mediterranean and the West Indies. He was promoted to lieutenant shortly before joining the navy sloop HMS *Rosamond*, which patrolled the Newfoundland and Labrador fisheries in the summer of 1813. Chappell's published account of this voyage mixes youthful enthusiasm with entertaining embellishments and the prejudices of the day. The Spout was revealed to Chappell and his companions, in most dramatic fashion, after the *Rosamond* had travelled for some time through thick fog.

1813

"We had not before obtained so near a view of Newfoundland; therefore the whole crew were extremely earnest in their contemplation of its naked rocks and frowning forests; and as the mist slowly cleared away, every point of land became the subject of their scrutiny. Immediately opposite to the ship, appeared a remarkable natural curiosity, called the Spout, which is visible at a great distance from the shore. We had no opportunity of examining this phænomenon minutely; but could easily perceive that the spout in question was occasioned by a column of water forcing itself through a fissure in the rock; and being impelled to an amazing height, it assumed the appearance of volcanic smoke. In this state it admirably answers the purpose of a landmark, for those who are otherwise unacquainted with the coast."

—Edward Chappell, VOYAGE OF HIS MAJESTY'S SHIP "ROSAMOND" TO NEWFOUNDLAND, 1818

1827

"We sailed in the Orestes for Ferryland, 40 miles, at a very early hour; but being baffled with light winds, we made but slow progress. An opportunity was afforded us for examining a natural curiosity on the shore, which is rarely visited, although it is a mark which guides all vessels on this part of the coast. It is called the Water-spout. It is formed by a small natural shaft, from the surface of the ground to a cave beneath. The sea is forced into the cave, and with such violence as to throw the water or vapour through the shaft, many feet into the air; sometimes to a great height, when the wind is violent and the sea rough. We approached it in a boat, and had a fine view of the cave; but the surf was so great, that Captain Jones was hurt in landing, and no one else attempted it. The aperture above is not twelve inches in diameter, but the rush of the vapour is violent, and the noise of the sea in the cave tremendous. In the evening a thick fog compelled us to stand out to sea, under easy sail, for the night."

—Bishop John Inglis, SOCIETY FOR THE PROPAGATION OF THE GOSPEL ANNUAL REPORT, 1827

BISHOP JOHN INGLIS

In 1825, Newfoundland was joined to the Anglican diocese of Nova Scotia, and in June of 1827, Bishop John Inglis (1777-1850) left Nova Scotia to visit the new addition. The bishop travelled to both the north and south coasts of the Island, visiting churches and schools, appointing new clergy and attending to church affairs. The bishop was the first to describe the Spout as a sightseeing destination, rather than a mariner's mark, and the first to describe the entrance to the sea cave. Captain Jones likely attempted what is still the safest landing place at the Spout, a set of seaward ledges at the entrance to the cave. The visit occurred on July 13.

Bishop John Inglis

Spout Path

1858

JOHN MULALLY

In 1858, the financier Cyrus W. Field (1819-92) was so certain of his ability to lay a cable linking Newfoundland and Cape Breton that he turned the venture into a pleasure excursion. Principle among the guests invited aboard the SS *James Adger* was Samuel F. B. Morse (1791-1872), the inventor of Morse code and the telegraph. The *Sarah L. Bryant*, the barque carrying the cable, failed to keep its appointment at Port-aux-Basques and, to pass the time, Field and his guests embarked on a 10-day sightseeing jaunt to St. John's, an interlude that included a visit to the Spout. John Mulally accompanied Field's 1857 and 1858 expeditions as a special correspondent for the *New York Herald*.

Cyrus W. Field

"Saturday, the 18th [of August] was the day fixed for our departure, but still we were unwilling to leave till we had made some return for the hospitality we had received from the people of St. John's. The Company, therefore, invited over two hundred of the principal inhabitants of the city on an excursion about 10 miles outside the harbor; and about twelve o'clock we set out with one of the most pleasant and sociable parties that was ever collected on the deck of a steamer. The day was as fine as could be desired, and the scenery of the coast magnificent. We saw the "Spouting Rock" as it is called, which is one of the greatest natural curiosities in the island, and, perhaps, in the world. The rock itself is not more than 30 feet above the surface of the water, and has a cavity in its centre which runs through it to the base, and which is from six to seven feet in diameter. A small stream of fresh water flows from an overhanging hill into this cavity, and when the tide is out finds its way through an opening in the rock into the sea. When the tide is coming in the waves rush with such force into this hole as to throw the fresh water in the cavity to a height of 20, and sometimes 40 feet. After a pleasant trip of two or three hours along the coast we returned with our guests to the harbor, where we parted with many mutual regrets. Cheer after cheer was given and returned, handkerchiefs were waved, and when we could hear each other no longer, the cannon thundered out our adieus."

—*John Mulally*, THE LAYING OF THE CABLE OR OCEAN TELEGRAPH, 1858

1897

"Being resolved not to quit Newfoundland without visiting a place which figures in charts as the Spout or Blowhole, and which is situated on the coast in this vicinity, I braved Mrs. Howlet and her associates for three nights more, and sent out for a man who could act as guide to the spot. For though he, with that contempt for nature which is a characteristic of most rustics, had never, during a lifetime passed in its immediate neighbourhood, once condescended to turn aside and see for himself this natural wonder, yet he knew where it lay, and had the true instinct of a savage in making his way through morasses and places of embarrassment. So we started at cockcrow; on foot, of course. In little over two hours we were come to a part of Shoal Bay, four miles from our starting-point; and taking into account the nature of the ground traversed—its rocks, hills, and swamps—we were pleased to think we had accomplished the distance in very creditable time.

On the shore of the bay, we enlisted a second man, to accompany us for the remaining three miles of travel. This short journey it took us an absurdly long while to perform. Every step was a struggle. At every step, the feet were to be watched, lest they should stumble amongst concealed or overgrown pitfalls; and the eyes, lest they should be torn out by the dense network of interlacing branches. For a mile or so we went through a "brûlée," which of all things in this world is the most odious to go through. Clouds of charcoal dust rise in suffocating gusts. Your clothes are blackened and rent by shreds of charred unyielding twigs, which retain none of the elasticity of life, but in their deaths are grim and sturdy, prodding the rash intruder, and goading him to oaths. Progress is retarded, well-nigh stopped. Force is useless, patience and gentle disentanglement alone avail.

Emerging from our "brûlée," and refreshed by a gurgling spring, we came on a giddy bluff. Picking our way in single file, and clutching at the bank with our hands, the black flies took a mean advantage of our plight, and attacked us with bloodthirsty fury.

JAMES LAWSON

Today, James Lawson (1855-1949) would be described as a freelance travel writer. In 1897, Lawson "took it in mind" to visit Newfoundland upon seeing a giant tortoise loaded onto a steamer in Halifax, destined for the governor in St. John's. Lawson visited a chain of lakes—most likely above Petty Harbour—where he spent several nights camping and fishing, filled his basket with trout and cranberries, listened to the loons and enjoyed the swirling fog and storm-tossed bush, until he got thoroughly soaked. By his own estimation he rambled 15 km across "blasted heath" to the house of a woman named Howlet—still a common name in Petty Harbour—where he was accommodated in a "closet" and eaten by vermin. His unsympathetic hostess noted he was a month ahead of the flies.

The Spout, 1855

Perhaps they had had dear proof of the truth of Dr. Watts' assertion that: 'Satan finds some mischief still / For idle hands to do.' Anyhow, now that our hands were fully occupied, they had us at their mercy, and small mercy they showed! Clambering on from point to point, from ledge to ledge, we heard at length the thunder of the Spout; and when we had weathered a jutting horn of cliff, the Spout itself came in view. With infinite toil we slid and scrambled down to its level, and were amply rewarded for all our pains.

A very fair view of this Spout may be had from the sea; but as, except on rare occasions, landing is impracticable, those who would claim closer acquaintance must not grudge the walk, and undergo no light fatigue. The men who were with me, finding themselves jaded, and (like the town ladies in Goldsmith's novel) 'all of a muck o'sweat,' said with an angry sneer: 'There aren't two people in all St. John's who would tramp these weary miles to see a thing like that.' 'I' (added one) 'was never here before, and for sartin sure I'll never be here again.' So saying, they turned their backs on the Spout, and assuaged their heat with cress and berries.

Glad to be rid of their ungracious company, I did my exploration in peace.

The vent of the Spout is but a couple of feet in diameter; and in the intervals that occur between the spoutings of the waters, it is an easy enough matter to approach and look down into the funnel. Thirty yards or so away, is a great yawning cave open to the Atlantic; and the swell, rushing heedlessly into this cavern, and suddenly finding itself inconveniently cramped, bursts in frenzy from the only orifice it can find. This orifice is not only some distance inland, but is also 30 feet at least above the level of the sea. Yet the column of spray, at the time of my visit, was being projected full 40 feet into the air. In days of storm, and gales from the east, its height is said to be almost doubled. I threw some sticks and stones in the hole, when the waters were heard beginning to rumble in their cave below, and they were instantly flung aloft, with force incredible. When the column had reached its height, I was touched by its resemblance to the noblest geysers of poor perished Terawera. [In 1886, New Zealand's Mt. Terawera erupted with great loss of life. Terawera is in the Taupo Volcanic Zone, an area noted for its geothermal geysers and mud pools.]

After sitting by this strange hole for a reasonable time, I fell back on where my guides lay stretched in sleep, and we gathered ourselves together for the return journey, being hard pressed for time."

—James Lawson, Temple Bar, 1897

Bald-Headed Eagle

Like the pie**bald** horse and **bald**-coot, the **bald**-headed eagle (*Haliaeetus leucocephalus*) is named for its show of white. Adults are dark brown with a white head and tail, and yellow beak, eyes and feet. Eagle feet, like osprey feet, have talons equipped with small spikes for capturing and handling prey, primarily fish. The eagle is Canada's largest bird of prey; two-metre wingspans and weights over 7 kilos are not uncommon. Females are larger than males.

Widely spaced pairs of eagles nest along the Newfoundland coast, on cliffs, sea stacks and the tops of trees. The nest, on average 1.5 to 2 metres across and about one metre tall, is the largest made by any North American bird. Long-established nests can be much larger, as each year new twigs and branches are added. In a small depression in the centre, lined with softer vegetation and feathers, the female lays two eggs (though sometimes one or three) two to four days apart.

During the first few weeks of life, eaglets are shielded from the sun, wind and rain by one of the parents, usually the female. At this time, the male brings most of the food to the nest, though eventually both parents contribute to feeding the

Top of the Spout

◎ 4.6 km: Top of the Spout

Immediately south of the Spout, during breeding season, the hiker can hear and smell (but not yet see) a colony of nesting black-legged kittiwakes. Kittiwake feathers are scattered over the heath, blown up the cliff face by gusts of wind. The path edges around massive cliffs, through white spruce and bunchberry, crosses two streams, then returns to the coast at the head of the cove, where the view is unimpeded. Herring gulls nest on the broad sea ledge below. Jagged, fallen rocks litter the ledge (a part of the cliff foundered in 1999). Some years, only a few kittiwake chicks from this colony survive to adulthood; perhaps the herring gulls have too easy a time spotting dinner.

High cliffs are often crowned with healthy growth, for cliff-top vegetation is protected from winter freezing by an updraft that settles snow on the top surface of the cliff. If trees near the cliff edge get too ambitious during mild years, they are downed during hard-wind years. Scattered white spruce, only, have survived this cyclic phenomenon. The plant growth surrounding the spruce is limited to what can shelter under snow. The trail route takes advantage of this open fringe of heath and widely spaced trees. Denser forest growth is never far back from the edge.

Eagle on a sea stack

◎ 5.1 km: Little Bald Head

After a climb up a steep ridge, the path reaches Little Bald Head Campsite. The ECTA camp is located beside a stream and has five developed sites with tent platforms, and six undeveloped sites. A short side trail leads to the "thunder box," an open, throne-like toilet with one of the most celebrated views on the trail.

Leaving the campground, the path continues up a series of short rises, then descends into an open wood of spruce and white birch. Depending on the level of shade, the understory shifts from heath to woodland plants. Clumps of half-sprawling, half-twisted birch trunks create an unusual effect. In exposed habitats, the main trunk of a birch sapling is often damaged. If this happens, the tree will become shrub-like as numerous replacement branches arise from the ground. White birch and mountain alder improve the soil through their yearly leaf fall; hence, the rich layer of plants beneath the trees.

◎ 5.7 km: Sea Stack

Ocean currents flowing beneath the cliffs of Spout Path create an undertow strong enough to trap and

young. The young have enormous appetites and grow rapidly; nonetheless, it takes from 10 to 12 weeks for an eaglet to fledge (develop feathers)—large gulls fledge in less than half that time. After fledging, the young show considerable aggression towards their parents, though they cannot fully fend for themselves for another two to three months.

Young eagles sometimes overheat, especially on a warm day, and if they become too hot will flop over on their side, perhaps with a leg or two stuck out in an effort to increase heat loss. The adult is most likely nearby, keeping half an eye on the nest. In order to reduce stress on the young and their parents, hikers are asked not to linger long near the nesting area.

Sea stack camouflage

Landing Place jump

Ledges at Landing Place

sink a small boat or kayak. Those who fished the shore generally stayed away from cliffs as much as they could. Seen from land, the sea stack at **5.7 km** is one of the most recognizable icons of the East Coast Trail. Seen from the sea, however, the stack is camouflaged by the cliffs behind, and its form is not evident to someone fishing offshore, hence the stack was never named. It "pops" into view only if a vessel draws near, an effect that has become a stock-in-trade of boats conducting tours of the Spout.

Bald-headed eagles nest on a second stack, which is behind the first, but—unlike the first—has only begun to separate from the cliff. The eagles are best viewed from the north side of the cove (at **5. 5 km**). The sea stack is best viewed from the cove's south side, near a salmon berth called Founder (at **5.7 km**). A nearby side trail leads to a waterfall. Here, too, the hiker can see the sea cave penetrating Little Bald Head— identified as "Pierced Head" on some nautical charts. Numerous black-legged kittiwakes and herring gulls nest on the cove's cliffs and sea ledges. The black guillemots in the water likely nest in nearby cliff crevices. Truly massive white spruce grow tall and straight along the cliff edge and, immediately inland, the ground beneath the spruce is covered in bunchberry. Larch trees grow where the ground is boggy. South of the waterfall, the trail traverses a *braided* (multi-channel) stream full of tall meadow-rue and ferns, including a patch of New York fern. South of this stream, the path crosses a blueberry heath where a stand of old, gnarly birch is losing ground to a robust growth of black spruce and sheep laurel.

◎5.9 km: Landing Place

Shortly after passing the sea stack, the hiker has a choice of paths. Some hikers choose the lower route, overgrown with sheep laurel, which runs close to the cliff edge above a massive rock ramp called the "Landing Place." To reach land from a boat at Landing Place, bird hunters must hop onto a small island near the lower end of the ramp and nimbly jump two narrow waterways. The ramp is littered with erratics and glacial till, and shelters conifers as well as seaside plants such as Scotch lovage, beach pea, blue flag, wild roses and harebell.

The more developed route keeps to the height of land and passes through a stand of tall, widely spaced birch. This mature grove is a peaceful place. The soothing sound of leafy branches in the wind combines with the song of robins and the occasional warbler. There is a small spring, bordered by squashberries and peat moss. Around the spring, the ground is dry and the undergrowth soft, making this an ideal place to rest before the challenging walk ahead.

Past Landing Place, the trail climbs up a boulder-strewn path through a mixed forest into an open area dotted with large trees, mostly black spruce. For a few hundred metres, the route passes through sheep

Hatching Asynchrony

Most birds do not sit on the nest until all their eggs have been laid, for they prefer to hatch their brood at one time. Birds of prey practice hatching asynchrony, hatching offspring in sequence. Ornithologists have long debated the significance of this adaptation. According to one theory, hatching asynchrony is the latest in a chain of evolutionary events. Prey species breed cyclically, an adaptation designed to reduce predator success in lean years, so there will be fewer predators around in years of chick abundance. Avian predators have responded by hatching chicks in sequence: in years of prey abundance, all offspring survive; in years when food is scarce, late-hatching offspring fail to compete with older, larger siblings. Brood reduction through starvation is seen in a number of bird species, including almost all Newfoundland gulls and birds of prey. In some species, including bald-headed eagles, the first-born is not only fed first, but may kill the smaller sibling.

Goowiddy

Sheep laurel (*Kalmia angustifolia*) contains andromedotoxin, a toxic substance that poisons cattle, sheep, goats and horses. Inexperienced animals such as lambs, or even experienced animals, freed from a winter in the barn, will often eat anything green, including sheep laurel. Hence another common name for the plant: lambkill. Bees that visit only sheep laurel and related rhododendron blooms—fortunately, a rare event—produce a honey that is poisonous when ingested by humans. Locally, **goowiddy** or **goldwithy** leaves were "boiled out" to create a noxious mixture that was used to rid the head of lice. An even more repellent remedy, sheep laurel boiled with tobacco, was used to cure dogs of mange. Sheep laurel alkaloids retard forest regeneration by inhibiting seed germination and stunting the root development of conifer seedlings. If sheep laurel has become established it may take hundreds of years for forests to return.

Sheep laurel

Drop Cove Rock

laurel heath mixed with solitary spruce and scattered clumps of white birch. A little inland from the path, rolling hills of sheep laurel stretch unbroken to the north and south as far as the eye can see.

7.1 km: Drop Cove

Proceeding south, mountain alder gradually supplants white birch along the trail. Eventually, the hiker reaches an alder thicket. In places, the alder is mixed with scattered spruce, fir, dogberry and pin-cherry. During breeding season, hikers will hear Drop Cove long before they see it. There are black-legged kittiwakes everywhere in the cove, as well as scattered greater black-backed gulls, perched on prominent viewing spots, from which they lunge for unguarded eggs and chicks. In the fall, the cove is unearthly quiet, the only sound the occasional echoing cry of a raven or crow. The blade-shaped sea stack in the centre of the cove is glimpsed from several angles though for the most part the view is blocked by straight white spruce. The high cliffs of the cove create an updraft that protects these tall trees from wind damage.

Iron Doors

There is certainly a startling drop at Drop Cove. Before the introduction of legislation governing trap berths, berths were considered to belong to a particular fisherman. For many years the O'Briens of Bay Bulls fished from Drop Cove, rearing several large families out of the proceeds. Both the sea stack in the cove, and the cliffs nearby, are stained with iron oxide. As the trail climbs the ridge on the south side of the cove, there is a glimpse of Iron Doors, a row of four square-shaped, rust-stained sea caves on the north side of the cove. Such staining occurs when small, iron-bearing minerals in the rock rust with exposure. A little south of the cove, an area of scrubby birch covers a steep, boulder-strewn slope, most likely the site of a recent slide.

◎ 7.7 km: Green Hill

A 1754 account in *The Gentleman's Magazine* describes the slope above the Spout as "entirely cover'd with firs and spruce trees." In other words, Green Hill is how the coast must have looked before fire repeatedly swept through the area. The fire of 1892—likely the most extensive to strike the region—

Which FIRE?

Since the arrival of European settlers, forest fires have swept over the same territory at intervals, permanently altering the Newfoundland landscape. It likely took more than one fire to create the birch forests, spruce groves and sheep laurel heath along Spout Path. Some likely candidates are:

A fire in 1850 destroyed numerous dwellings between Petty Harbour and Bay Bulls.

A fire in 1859 caused much timber destruction in the area.

A fire in 1870 burned north into Kilbride, and as far west as Salmonier.

A fire in 1887 burned in the area for more than five days.

A fire in 1892 burned the hamlet of Freshwater and the country north to Shoal Bay. The summer of 1892 was exceptionally hot and dry and fires were numerous throughout the Avalon Peninsula. In July, the "Great Fire of 1892" levelled half of St. John's.

White Birch

White birch (near the coast, generally *Betula cordifolia*—the heart-leaved variety—but sometimes *B. papyrifera*) is the most common hardwood tree on the Island. It is present in low numbers in stands of conifers, but forms pure stands on moist, well-drained slopes that have been extensively burned or logged. Birch leaves are wedge-like to round in shape, dark green above and paler below. However, the most characteristic feature of white birch is its bark. Young bark is reddish-brown and smooth with white horizontal markings called **lenticels**. These tiny openings allow for gas exchange. As the bark matures it turns creamy white, eventually peeling off in sheets.

White birch is fast growing and its winged, lightweight seeds are often carried a considerable distance by wind. The tree is highly variable in form. Birches growing in conifer forests are leggy and spindly, branching out only at the canopy level as they struggle for light. If the surrounding conifers are harvested, these birches generally lose vigour and die. In open areas, the tree develops one or more trunks and numerous widely spaced branches supporting a broad, leafy canopy.

The Chaver

must have missed Green Hill, for the name dates back to the 1920s when salmon berths were first listed—there's a salmon berth called Green Hill. The path proceeds for some time through fir forest, a protected environment, but one still affected by weather, for most trees have fewer branches on their seaward side. Where the forest stands intact, the ground is mossy and the fir trunks are lichen-covered. Where trees have fallen, the vegetation is mixed, and both spruce and fir are regenerating amid the plant debris. The vegetation on Green Hill changes with elevation; where the path drops the ground becomes wetter, and an open wood of mixed birch and black spruce replaces the fir. There is glacial debris in abundance no matter which part of the slope the path crosses. Irregular, ankle-threatening collections of round boulders fill every hollow.

◎ **8.6 km: The Chaver**

Upon reaching a dramatic gulch known as "the Chaver," the path descends steeply through a birch grove. At the bottom there is a view of the coastline to the south and hikers can look back into the entrance of the gulch. In former days, a dark gulch might indeed call to mind a "chafer," for chafing dishes were box-shaped and used charcoal or coal to heat water

Sea arch below the Chaver

or keep food warm. A "chavish" is also an English dialect term for a flock of noisy birds. Waves "chafe," as do people—and birds—if something is not to their satisfaction. In that all these meanings fit the Chaver, hikers are free to pick a favourite. The Chaver has the same orientation as several major fissures north of the Spout, but is unusual for being singular, not part of a conjugate set. A little south of Chaver Cove (at **8.9 km**) there is a high, imposing sea arch that leans into the cliff like a tired hiker.

◎9.1 km: Shag Rocks

In Newfoundland, "shags" are cormorants. Numerous offshore rocks are named for the bird, though not necessarily those where the birds perch now, for flocks of cormorants will pick any safe offshore rock for a perch, and are cautious in their habits, preferring to keep away from people. In the spring, bird hunters would sometimes haul their dories up onto the rocks. Blinded by dense fog and heavy swells, two Bay Bulls fishermen accidentally rowed over the Shag Rocks and drowned when their dory capsized. Another fisherman tending his traps found the bodies bobbing in the water, one with a hand still clenched to an oar.

Falling Leaves

Colourful foliage and falling leaves go with the shorter days and cooler night-time temperatures of fall. In preparation for winter, plants enter dormancy, a period of decreased metabolism. Chlorophyll is broken down, and food and water move out of leaves and into the branches. Leaf veins begin to close off, and a new cell layer, called the abcission layer, grows where the leaf stalk meets the branch. As the leaf's green chlorophyll decays, previously masked yellow (carotinoid) and brown (xanthophyll) pigments surface. In plants with a high sugar content, such as some maples, by-product sugars trapped in the leaf convert to a red pigment (anthocyanin). Once all available nutrients have been withdrawn through the leaf's veins, and the waxy abcission layer seals, only nutrient-depleted protoplasm and cell walls remain. Veins hold the leaf to the tree until, on a gusty day, they break and the leaves begin to fall.

Shag Rocks and cliffs at dusk

GLACIAL REBOUND

Many sea caves and sea ledges along the coast of the Avalon Peninsula are approximately five metres above present sea levels, strongly suggesting that the sea, too, must once have been higher, relative to the coast. But at what date? Over the past 12,000 years, sea levels have risen globally due to glacial melt and higher water temperatures. Simultaneously, land freed from the weight of glaciers has rebounded. In Newfoundland, the current thinking is that, because the heaviest ice loads were well to the west, the eastern half of the Avalon Peninsula tilted upward, and land elevations were actually higher during the last ice age. This "teeter totter" effect was only partly countered by the thin glacial sheets covering the peninsula.

If this theory is correct, there is no recent history of coastal gains and losses along the eastern Avalon; the shoreline has *only* risen as the sea has risen. As there has been no complicated rise and fall of the land, sea caves and sea ledges that are higher than current sea levels must therefore

For 500 metres the coastline is of no great height, and the path is a stone's throw from the ocean. For the most part, the route keeps to a coastal fringe of low heath and wind-pruned larch. The low cliffs create enough protective updraft for the heath, in places, to grow waist-high. Immediately inland, there is a seepage zone full of mountain alder, peat moss and sedges. In a few spots, the birch wood on the slope extends to the coast. Small streams periodically cross the trail, creating damp spots full of fen plants and lush with sweet-smelling ferns. There are numerous wild, yet agreeable, places to rest. Greater black-backed gulls perch on the cliff rocks, and the cry of black-legged kittiwakes mixes with the sound of waves.

◎9.8 km: Bald Head

At Turn of Bald Head the trail climbs into a grove of white birch, then descends stone steps to Bald Head. Looking north, there is a daunting view of the Shag Rocks and the unforgiving wall of cliffs stretching north to Motion Head. Bald Head is composed of ledges, stacked one upon another, tilting inland. Eroded rock outcrops separate three *breaches* (sea caves) on the north side—the headland is named "Breach Head" on some nautical charts. The head is indeed bald. Crowberry predominates; however, low-

The Oven

growing alder and common juniper shelter in the lee of the scattered boulders. A few sea-bleached tree skeletons and shrubs suggest there may once have been more cover. Winds funnelling up from the caves have shaped the tuck and heath clinging to the cliff ledges. Away from the cliffs, the plant growth is head-high.

South of Bald Head, the trail keeps to a string of ledges running half-way between a coastal ridge and the sea. Three-toothed cinquefoil, common and trailing juniper and tuck grow wherever the terrain is exposed. Periodically, the ledges create well-watered hollows where the vegetation is more luxuriant. Most days, hikers can feel the extra warmth in these protected microhabitats. In one, there is thriving cinnamon fern, in another, a rare patch of interrupted fern. Near Landing Place of Bald Head (at **10.2 km**) the trail crosses a small fen.

◎10.6 km: Sculpin Island

Reaching the Bluff, a little before Sculpin Island Cove, the trail enters an open wood of mixed larch and spruce. Sculpin Island is not actually an island but a bare rock promontory. Its jagged, tilted sea ledges do indeed bring to mind a sculpin, as do the multi-hued green, orange and grey lichens on the rocks. Water

date to an earlier, heavier, period of glaciation, one estimated to have occurred about 100,000 years ago. Like the Shag Rocks, the Oven, a square-shaped cave south of North Head, is about five metres above sea level. Fishermen say that the Oven runs under North Head to Dungeon Cove, a distance of 300 metres. If the Oven has weathered 100,000 years of erosion, perhaps it does run as far as is claimed.

Trap Berths and Salmon Berths

Before the Groundfish Moratorium of 1992, Bay Bulls fishermen drew lots for 33 trap berths and almost 70 salmon berths between Long Point and South Head. Most berth names, like "Upper End Shag Rocks" or "Water in Shag Rocks," relate the berth to a prominent coastal feature. If there were no prominence in sight, berths were located using a local coastal feature, such as an unusually shaped, or coloured rock or gulch. The salmon berths between Bald Head and Sculpin Island—Rust of Bald Head, Landing Place of Bald Head, Breaking Point, White Spot and Harbour House—are named by this second method.

Sculpin Island

from Bald Head River percolates across the ledges in a series of short waterfalls, creating pools concealed by jutting rocks, populated by the occasional small trout.

The area of exposed rock at Sculpin Island Cove is impressive. Ice crystallization creates forces that are roughly ten times stronger than the tensile strength of sandstone, so even unfractured sandstone cannot resist frost-wedging. The sandstone beds at Sculpin Island Cove lack uniformity, another weakening factor, and their landward tilt traps rain and sea spray, ensuring they are saturated with water. The Newfoundland climate guarantees frequent thawing and freezing. Sculpin Island Cove's southeast-facing orientation and its broad sea ledges and low cliffs create spectacular wave shows during the winter.

Sea spray contributes to frost-weathering chiefly by stripping away vegetation that might otherwise protect the ground from freezing. Rock outcrops on some parts of the Newfoundland coast erode by as much as six centimetres a year, though a rate of two centimetres is more typical. Once rock has loosened, storm waves carry the debris away. South of the cove, the substantial exposed ledges continue. Some are surfaced with ripple marks that look as fresh as the day they were formed on an alluvial flood plain, more than 550 million years ago.

ROCHE MOUTONNÉE

Small, asymmetric hills formed by the movement of glaciers are called *roches moutonnées* for their fanciful resemblance to a rounded sheep's back. As a glacier advances over a small hill, a smooth surface is formed by abrasion. There is a subtle increase in friction and sub-surface melt as the glacier proceeds uphill and water percolates into fractures. Friction lessens as a glacier reaches the terminus of the hill, and sub-surface meltwater re-freezes, wedging apart the rock below the extremity. The glacier carries away most of the resulting fragments. An otherwise rounded hill thus develops a fragmented face, which glaciologists use to chart the direction of ice movement.

Roche moutonnée

The bare hill immediately south of Sculpin Island Cove is a classic *roche moutonnée*. It looks like a knobby hill from some angles, but is actually the eroded eastern end of a ridge. Apart from a stand of white birch in the lee of the hill, the area has the denuded look associated with a recent burn, possibly the 1966 fire that burned north of Bay Bulls. Plant recovery has been slow in the most exposed places, and there are numerous damp areas with broad patches of fern. Away from the coast, in more protected areas, a mixed cover of conifers, mountain alder, dogberry, chuckley-pear and northern wild raisin has returned. Some firs have an unusual "hourglass" figure: their midsections have been nibbled away by Arctic hare. As snow builds in winter, hares dine on growth they cannot reach at other times of year.

◎ 11.7 km: Freshwater

An impressive stand of conifers (at **11.5 km**) occupies the northern rim of the cove at Freshwater. A hollow in the centre of the stand, roughly the size of a root cellar, is where Joe Crockwell of Bay Bulls dug for gold

Transfer Names

In Newfoundland, major coastal features were named first. Inland or lesser coastal features were identified later, frequently with names that connected them to the first-named feature. This phenomenon, called **transfer naming**, can sometimes occur twice. On Mickeleens Path, for example, a hiker leaving Chest Cove and walking west, rounds Chest Cove Point to reach Chest Cove Point Cove. Twin Pond is the only Freshwater area pond with a descriptive name. The others are transfer named according to where they come out at the coast: Bald Head Pond, Sculpin Island Pond, Freshwater Pond, Grass Cove Pond, Pulpit Pond, and even Bread and Cheese Pond, far in the interior.

Freshwater falls and cove

North Head sunset

At Freshwater, Bay Bulls, there is a transition upwards into younger beds within the rock sequence. Walking southwards, hikers gradually leave behind Gibbett Hill Formation rock, formed from ancient shallow marine and deltaic sediments, and again step onto Quidi Vidi Formation rock, formed from alluvial plain sediments.

in the 1940s. Perhaps he was guided by a compass carved—some say by pirates—into a washbasin-shaped cavity in the cliff below the waterfall. In the summer, the cliff ledges bloom yellow with hawkweed.

The trail proceeds along a substantial fieldstone structure that may once have been a stone cart track. Fieldstone foundations and rock walls are in evidence throughout the meadow. At one time, three families of Halls (Jim, John and Robert) lived in Freshwater. The Allens fished out of Allens Cove, on the south side of Broad Gully River. The Walshes lived between Allans Cove and the lighthouse. Nearer the lighthouse, the Furlongs cleared Furlongs Garden. The half-tumbled concrete foundation at Freshwater belonged to a root cellar constructed in 1911 by Robert Frampton, the husband of Imogene Hall. The Framptons' house and stable were nearby. Robert Frampton was a skilled builder of boats and mender of kettles and pots, and was one of the first people in the Bay Bulls area to own a phonograph. At Christmas time, people would send a horse and slide to

Frampton house, Freshwater

Freshwater to pick up Frampton and his novel musical contraption. Frampton and a companion stocked the ponds surrounding Freshwater with trout by transferring live trout from one pond to another. The experiment was a success, with the exception of tiny Grass Cove Pond, where it is said the nine trout put in were the same nine got out three years later. Since trapping has stopped, beavers have built dams and created ponds where there were no ponds before; one industrious beaver family has turned Twin Pond into a single pond.

As long as you had the skill to navigate a fish-filled skiff into a wave-washed cove, the patience to haul your catch up steep cliffs, and the strength at the end of the day to haul yourself up the cliff, too, it was possible to make a living at Freshwater. The cove offered ample water and land for pasture and gardens, and bordered dependable hunting and fishing grounds. The surrounding country was a good place for trapping beaver and muskrat. Should supplies be needed, there was a cart road to Bay Bulls. In addition, a rough path followed the coast north to Sculpin Island Cove,

Musk mallow in bloom

Lighthouse Road

Early in the 20th century, the path linking Freshwater and Gun Ridge along the shore—the route now followed by the East Coast Trail—was superceded by Lighthouse Road, an inland track branching to Freshwater and the lighthouse. The Freshwater branch of the road passes a memorial to Albert Yard, a Witless Bay native who left a Bay Bulls tavern on the night of November 11, 1968, lost his companions and bearings, and walked into the woods thinking he was walking home. It is thought he died of exposure when he slipped and fell, hitting his head on a rock.

On its way to Gun Ridge, Lighthouse Road passes Twin Pond and Pulpit Pond before reaching the bike-churned expanse of Pulpit Pond Marsh. Sticks and planks thrown onto the marsh often make the route passable for pedestrians. Otherwise, there is a by-pass trail, which swings north of the marsh. The by-pass intersects an old north-south path, and the junction can be confusing. Hikers who do not proceed directly ahead, but who accidentally turn onto the old path, will end up either back in Pulpit Pond Marsh, or risk being fairy-led to some remote spot to the north.

Freshwater cart track

then turned inland along Bald Head River to Bald Head Pond. From there, the path crossed the *barrens* (open country) to Bay Bulls Big Pond. John Hall set off one day, most likely on this path, and was never heard from again.

The settlement was destroyed by fire in 1892, rebuilt, then abandoned during the First World War. Annie Hall, a recluse, stayed on into the 1920s. Each Christmas, a horse-and-slide furnished with a barrel for flour and a biscuit box for other things, circulated through Bay Bulls, collecting life's necessities for the recluse. Although Freshwater has not been inhabited for 80 years, numerous plants associated with settlement thrive in its meadows: sheep sorrel, ox-eye daisy, stinging nettle, yellow and mouse-eared hawkweed, yarrow, red and white clover, old-field

Freshwater bridge

toadflax, blue toadflax, common dandelion and musk mallow. Where nature is reclaiming wet ground, there are extensive patches of fern, bog myrtle and meadowsweet. Mountain alder, conifers, wild roses, northern fly honeysuckle, goldenrod, raspberry and blueberry have taken over the drier areas of the clearing.

◎12.1 km: Monkey Cove

Small, long-handled containers used to store molasses at the table, or to melt glass or shot, were called "monkeys." Certainly, Monkey Cove has this shape and it is common for coves to be named for containers. Then again, perhaps you needed to be a monkey to think of fishing out of such a place; or perhaps seamen, sent to replenish their ship's water barrels at Freshwater, and feeling the sudden chill of the open coast, donned *monkey jackets* (a short jacket that allowed sailors to scamper up rigging unhindered). In the sea shanty "Banks of Newfoundland" (c. 1800) sailors thinking of working the Atlantic crossing on a *packet* (a ship run on a schedule) are advised to keep a "big monkey jacket" ready at hand to whip over their blue dungaree jumpers, "For there blows some cold nor'westers / On the banks of Newfoundland."

Riding out a storm

UNUSUAL

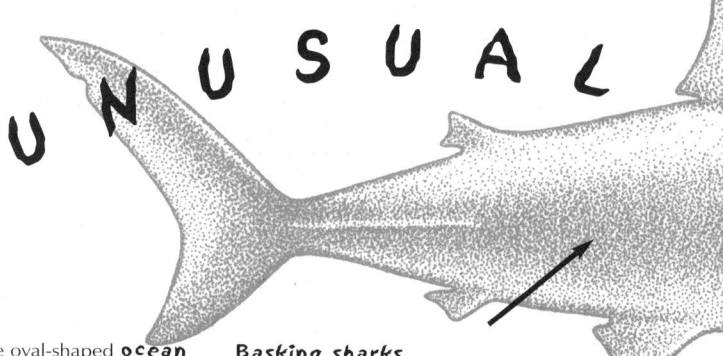

The oval-shaped **ocean sunfish** (*Mola mola*) is a summer visitor, feeding mostly on jellyfish, crustaceans, molluscs and starfish. Sunfish are grey to silver in colour, grow to more than three metres in length and can weigh in excess of 900 kilos. They are usually seen resting at the surface when the sea is calm. Sunfish have a small, beak-like mouth and large, triangular **dorsal** (back) and **ventral** (abdominal) fins. Their tails are no more than a small leathery fold. Their overall appearance is that of a tail-less head, wider than it is long. Other common names for the sunfish are headfish, moonfish and millstone.

Basking sharks (*Cetorhinus maximus*) are the second largest fish in the world, after whale sharks. They regularly visit the waters off the East Coast Trail in the spring and summer. The largest of these docile, slow-moving giants exceed 10 metres in length and weigh over three tonnes. Their appearance is typically shark-like, except for five large, collar-like gill slits behind the head, extending from the top to bottom surfaces of the body. The upper body is grey-brown to off-black while the underside is lighter. Basking sharks spend a large part of their time cruising the ocean surface with their mouth open, straining plankton from the water.

The **bluefin tuna** (*Thunnus thynnus*) is a powerful, exceptionally streamlined fish that can grow to more than four metres in length, weigh up to 675 kilos and swim at speeds in excess of 70 kph. The species is highly migratory and tagged fish have crossed the Atlantic in less than 60 days. Bluefin are coloured dark blue to black on the back, shading to a lighter blue on the sides and to silvery-grey on the belly. Fins and finlets to the fore of the tail are usually tinged yellow. Bluefin visit the waters off the East Coast Trail in early summer and remain until the fall. In former times, schools of tuna could be observed causing a commotion near the surface as they fed on squid, caplin and other small fish. However, Newfoundland tuna populations have been much reduced in recent years because of over-harvesting. In 2004, a single, prime quality giant bluefin sold in the Japanese market was worth about $60,000.

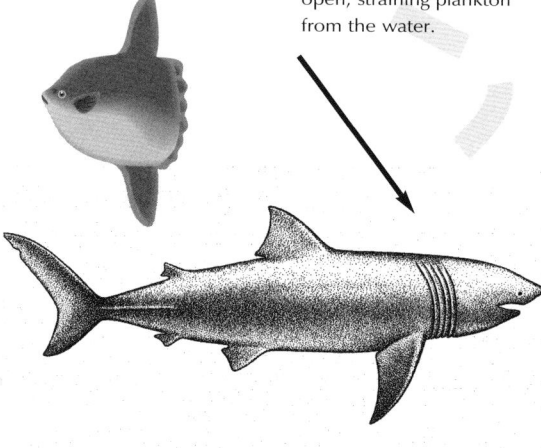

MARINE SIGHTINGS

On August 11, 1888, a 30-metre-long, lizard-like **sea serpent** with immense eyes, a brown-striped body and a huge fin attacked two dories sent out to check trawls by the schooner *Augusta*, off the southeastern coast of Newfoundland. It disappeared after being fired at from the schooner. As recently as 2000, similar serpents—possibly close relatives of the *Cadborosaurus willsi*, found on Canada's Pacific Coast—have been seen in Bonavista Bay. In 1971, two 1.5-metre-high, noseless, neckless, grey-furred creatures with monkey ears were spotted by two cousins who were hunting birds in the fog in Bonavista Bay. The boys may have happened upon a decomposing whale or shark. Neither monkey-like creatures nor sea serpents so far have been reported from the trail.

Spout Path

Fisherman's lunch box

Dungeon Cove

North Head light

Lighthouse door

◎ 12.5 km: Dungeon Cove

The trail skirts the edge of Dungeon Cove before turning south onto Lighthouse Road. In Newfoundland, a *dungeon* is a dark, semi-submerged sea cave. Or, by analogy, the lowest and filthiest part of a sealing vessel—generally where the cook and his helpers slept. Fishermen regularly hauled into Dungeon Cove and Freshwater to shelter from the wind, "boil up" a fish stew, or *take a spell* (rest). Lightkeepers used to descend partway into the depths, using a trail that is no longer evident, to buy fresh cod from the boats pulled in below.

◎ 12.7 km: Bull Head Light

Official records indicate that a cast iron lighthouse was installed in 1908 at North Head (also called Bull Head). Local tradition says 1912. The iron structure

North Head transition

on the site is the original. A covered walkway connected the light to a substantial residence, of which only the cement foundation remains. There were two lightkeepers, each of whom stayed a week at the light, returning to Bay Bulls when not on shift. Immediately east of the lighthouse, a derrick and winch were used to hoist up coal and other supplies from the Slat, a sloping sea ledge that sheltered a *tickle* (narrow run) where schooners could anchor. In the mid-1930s, a power line was installed connecting the lighthouse to Bay Bulls, and an electric light replaced the original kerosene lamps. The line was vulnerable to weather and vandalism and was not a success; in time it was replaced by batteries, brought to and from the lighthouse by horse and cart. With the coming of automation, the residence was no longer required and was sold off. The light presently operates using solar panels and is serviced by helicopter. There has never been a foghorn at Bull Head.

NORTH HEAD TRANSITION

At North Head, the lowest section of the cliff is composed of green-grey sandstone and siltstone of the Gibbett Hill Formation. Half-way up the cliff, these green-grey strata are overlain by red sandstone of the Quidi Vidi Formation. This transition is best seen from the sea, but can be glimpsed, too, from the top of the cliffs next to the lighthouse. As the hiker walks towards Bay Bulls the bedrock underfoot becomes redder—this is particularly noticeable on the bare ridges— until the deepest hued layers are reached at the Flats. A parallel change occurs across the bay and the shift to red sandstone is particularly evident if one scrutinizes South Head.

THREE FORMATIONS

More than 550 million years ago, a southward-flowing river filled in a large shallow marine environment over the course of about 20 million years. First, a delta was created; then land. Over time, the deposits compacted, de-watered and *lithified* (hardened) into solid rock. The river's currents left behind abundant sedimentary features preserved in the rock as ripples, cross-bedding and rip-up clasts.

Walking east to west, along the north shore of Bay Bulls Harbour, hikers mostly move "back in time" across three formations, each older than the preceding, each representing an earlier stage in the infill process. Firstly, from North Head to the Gun Ridge, hikers cross rocks of the Quidi Vidi Formation, red sandstones, siltstones and mudstones that were once ancient river deposits forming an extensive plain. Secondly, from Gun Ridge to Stanleys River, hikers cross rocks of the Gibbett Hill Formation, green-grey and locally red sandstones and siltstones that were once ancient stream and

NORTH HEAD SHIPWRECKS

On May 21, 1813, the brig *Integrity*, commanded by Captain Pearson, on its way from Liverpool, Lancashire, to Bay Bulls with a load of salt, struck ice and sank entering Bay Bulls Harbour. On November 22, 1814, the brig *Noddy*, under Captain Ferris, on its way from Sydney, Nova Scotia, to St. John's, was lost near Bay Bulls. On March 10, 1830, the schooner *Jane Hutton*, carrying a cargo of bread, flour, molasses and coal, was driven off course by rough seas, heavy ice and strong southwest winds. The vessel struck North Head three or four times before drifting 2 km offshore and sinking. The captain and crew took to the ice and with much effort repaired a damaged lifeboat. They came ashore at Petty Harbour.

On November 1, 1831, the brig *Ann*, on a voyage from Poole, Dorset, to Greenspond, was stranded and wrecked while beating into Bay Bulls Harbour. There was no loss of life. On December 24, 1831, the brig *Young Samuel*, under Captain Le Sieur, on its way from Quebec City to the island of Jersey, was stranded and wrecked off Bay Bulls. On August 6, 1836, the brig *Frances Russell*, commanded by Captain George, on a voyage from Grenada to St. John's, wrecked off North Head. On March 24, 1862, the sealing vessel *Eliza*, commanded by Captain Winsor of Aquaforte, lost its keel in ice and sank 8 km off Bay Bulls the following day. The crew escaped to safety. The brigantine was one of 40 Newfoundland sealing vessels crushed by ice that spring.

On May 7, 1875, the brig *Dora*, owned by Job Brothers, on a voyage from Liverpool to St. John's, struck ice off Bay Bulls. The brig went down almost immediately. All on board escaped over the ice. On June 10, 1886, the 39-ton, two-year-old schooner *Louis Dugan*, owned by Louis Dugan of Yarmouth, Nova Scotia, en route from St. John's to Lingan, Nova Scotia, foundered and sank in a squall. On April 30, 1892, the schooner *Annie A. Tell* of Harbour Grace was wrecked near Bay Bulls. On March 9, 1900, the 74-ton schooner *Sarah Jane*, recently purchased by the Harbour Grace merchant Dugald Dunn, was lost off Bay Bulls. On November 18, 1987, the fishing vessel *Marilyn Donald* caught fire off Bay Bulls. Arson was suspected.

Officially, lighthouses signal that a dangerous shore lies nearby, but they can also communicate other messages. From Bull Head Light, for example, it is possible to signal to a resident of the Keys, on the south side of Bay Bulls Harbour, that a cargo of liquor has arrived. It is said that Bull Head's chief lightkeeper Tom Maloney was on several occasions suspected of bootlegging. Some claim that Sir Michael Cashin (1864-1923) stonewalled the customs inspectors who sought to prosecute Maloney. Cashin was not only the MHA (Member of the House of Assembly) for the district of Ferryland but also, between 1909 and 1919, the Minister of Finance and Customs, a Wreck Commissioner, an influential merchant, and a widely suspected bootlegger himself. His district was one of the few that opposed prohibition in 1915.

In 1920, Cashin was out of power and Maloney and two other Bay Bulls bootleggers were caught red-handed. A few days before he was to be arraigned for trial, Maloney began his shift at the light. He persuaded assistant lightkeeper Harry Stone to join him and, reaching Gun Ridge, encountered a man with a horse and cart—some say a confederate—and asked for a lift. As the cart passed Dungeon Cove, Maloney stepped off and disappeared over the cliff without comment. Some claim Maloney was afraid he would implicate his friends at the upcoming trial. Others believe Maloney thought, if he went to his death unseen, his associates would be suspected of murder. Maloney's son found his father's body in the water, a few days after the tragic event.

⊚ 13.3 km: Top of the Head

Between North Head and Top of the Head (also called Columbine Point) the trail crosses several exposed ridges, separated by steep, sheltered hollows

deltaic deposits. Thirdly, from Stanleys River to Riverhead, Bay Bulls, hikers cross the Renews Head Formation, dark-coloured shales and thin sandstones that were once ancient tidal and shallow marine deposits, containing fossil Aspidella, part of the same rare Precambrian fossil assemblage found at Mistaken Point Ecological Reserve.

Aspidella fossil

Quidi Vidi Formation, the Beamer

Rosa Praed

Phantom Names

The utilitarian—but repetitive—names residents come up with to identify features in their area have occasionally challenged mapmakers to do better. Hikers who have encountered their twentieth "Freshwater" on the trail (there are two in Ferryland alone!) may well feel sympathy towards the common 19th-century British Admiralty practice of naming coastal features after ships, shipmates, politicians, flowers, girlfriends and fictional characters. As a former naval station, Bay Bulls has an abundance of such "phantoms." The most tenacious have appeared on maps for 150 years, but are still unrecognized by residents.

A noteworthy example of this phenomenon is the summit above Bay Bulls, called American Man by the people of Bay Bulls, but given the eponymous name "Captain Orlebars Cairn" by Commander John Orlebar. Orlebar surveyed the waters between Bay Bulls and Placentia for the British Admiralty between 1860 and 1863. In addition to adding his own name to the map—and giving himself a promotion—Commander Orlebar commemorated two (so-far-unidentified) friends or associates: Small Point (at **6.8 km** on Deadmans Bay Path) became Spriggs Point, and Hearts Cove Point Ridge (at **9.4 km** on Motion Path) became Vizzards Hill.

Locals also have never heard the spot they know of as "Top of the Head" called "Columbine Point," or "Chest Cove Point" called "Nùlma Head." In 1898, Lieutenant (later Captain) Hughes C. Lockyer, commander of the naval cruiser, third class, HMS **Cordelia**, took detailed soundings to determine the feasibility of turning Bay Bulls Harbour into a modern naval base. Earlier that spring, he had met Geraldine Stairs, the daughter of noted Halifax MP (Member of Parliament) and banker John F. Stairs (1848-1909). The commander of the **Cordelia** and Miss Stairs possibly compared favourite Shakespeare plays. "There's fennel for you, and columbines," says Ophelia to Hamlet, handing the melancholy Dane a flower that never grew on Columbine Point. Lockyer and Stairs must have discussed with some passion the popular Australian romance writer Rosa Praed (1851-1935), for Nùlma, the heroine of the latest Praed novel, published in 1897, graces a headland on Lockyer's chart. Published in 1899, the chart must have made a pretty present. Lockyer's engagement to Stairs was announced in 1901.

Existing names were sometimes misheard by mapmakers, or deemed insufficiently descriptive. In 1696, the Abbé Jean Baudoin transcribed Bay Bulls as "bayeboulle," a pronunciation remarkably similar to that heard by Commander Orlebar, 150 years later, when he put "Baboul Rocks" on the map, off South Head. Thinking that Joan Clays Hill was named for its daffodils, Orlebar changed the spelling to "Jonclay Hill." On Lockyer's charts, Little Bald Head became "Pierced Point," most likely because the sea cave running through it was a useful landmark for ships to note while navigating a dangerous coast. Bald Head was likely named "Breach Head" for the same reason.

HMS Cordelia *under full flag*

of varying depth. Foxes regularly patrol the ridge nearest the lighthouse, above the deepest of the hollows, for the abundant frost-split rock debris in the area shelters both predator and prey. The south-facing side of North Head slopes towards the water, ending in a series of seaward-sloping ledges, and southeasterly winds carrying sea air and spray are deflected by the ledges directly onto the land. Even in summer, hikers will likely feel the extra chill. The easternmost sea ledge is called the Beamer, most likely because of its resemblance to a ship *on its beams* (blown onto its side), something that might well happen to a vessel hit by southeasterly winds as it cleared Top of the Head.

A wall-like rock cliff extending out into the ocean protects Bull Cove (at **13.3 km**). Some say the cove is named for the *bull-bird* (dovekie); others claim that tides at the cove "pull like a bull," making it difficult to set or haul a trap. On stormy "southeasterly" days, hikers can watch waves "spout" from a crevice, 200 metres east of the cove. Grass Cove (at **13.5 km**) is punchbowl-shaped and more open. It is likely named for the distinctive "grassy" fen behind the cove. Apart from this one fen, there is little evidence of wetland build-up around Useless Bay. The steep slant of the shore and the abundant till underfoot likely promote

Quidi Vidi Formation, Bull Cove

TOP OF THE HEAD SHIPWRECKS

On January 12, 1866, the 130-ton brigantine ***Lavinia***, owned by J. & W. Stewart, carrying a cargo of salt, marble and wine from Cadiz, Spain, to St. John's, lost its position in driving sleet. The captain spotted land too late. Unable to manoeuvre against adverse winds through slob ice, he was driven ashore near Top of the Head. The brigantine's longboat had been smashed to pieces by an earlier storm. Captain, crew and passengers climbed into the brigantine's dangerously overloaded ***jolly-boat*** (a small boat hung over a ship's stern), which failed to clear the surf and slob and was broken in two by waves. Six crewmen scrambled ashore, but first mate Thomas Carroll and Captain Mercer, his wife and three-year-old child were lost. Only the captain's body was recovered.

Gull Nests

Joints, as they erode, form numerous ledges. Herring gulls (*Larus argentatus*) convert the most promising into nest sites. Gull nests, lined with grass, moss and seaweed, are as a rule sloppily constructed. During nesting season, they contain two to three bluish-grey to brownish eggs spotted with dark markings. As aggressive, confident egg raiders themselves, herring gulls pick spots that are widely separated from the nests of other gulls. Gull nests are often highly visible, for gulls look for places with good sight lines, so they can defend their young by relentless and persistent harrying. One partner protects the nest while the other drives off intruders. Nests are not easily approached. Gulls are undeterred by the size or form of the threat, be it a gull, raven, eagle, fox or hiker. They will energetically keep predators at bay, even after the young are long gone. Hikers who walk between North Head and Cape Boone during nesting season often become unwitting participants—each time they approach a gulch or cliff—in a series of tenacious harassment and dive-bombing attacks.

Useless Bay from the Flats

drainage. Near Grass Cove, the heath is dotted with venerable-looking tuck, both living and dead. Past the cove, an inland ridge provides increased shelter from wind and the tree line creeps closer to shore.

◎14.2 km: The Flats

At the Flats, the trail crosses the north-south *hinge* (fold axis) of the Bay Bulls Syncline. A five-kilometre section of this U-shaped fold runs the length of Bay Bulls Harbour. It should be noted that the two limbs of this syncline are unevenly represented along the shore. At North Head, east of the Flats, the syncline's eastern limb dips a shallow 20° to the west. At Riverhead, west of the Flats, the syncline's western limb dips a much sharper 65° to the east, and the rocks represented are much older. At the Flats itself, the hinge plunges southward, under Bay Bulls Harbour, and extends offshore past Baboul Rocks.

◎ 14.7 km: Pulpit Rock

The sharply tilted shoreline of Useless Bay offers no foothold for stages—or for trail boardwalks for that matter; the trail keeps to the scrubby heath slope above the ledges. The Acadian Orogeny, the 400- to 350-million-year-old mountain-building event that created the Bay Bulls Syncline, fractured the siltstone rock. Frost-wedging and wave action have knocked out the weakest spots, creating Seven Island Cove and Pulpit Cove, leaving artfully shaped sea stacks. Each cove has a spray zone of low-growing crowberry and common juniper. Chance clumps of blue flag cling to the crevices, along with trailing juniper and seaside plantain. Larch and spruce tuck have found a foothold on the roomier, more sheltered ledges. Halos of guano-enriched greenery surround active gulls' nests. One sea stack, the Pulpit (also called "Pulpit Rock") reminded hunters of a minister's podium. Good bird hunting spots were often christened with church names, possibly because dedicated bird hunters, like clergy, worked Sundays. The clergy had something to say about this, no doubt, for directly south of the Pulpit, on the other side of the bay (at **2.6 km** on Mickeleens Path), there is another good hunting spot—a red-faced rock ledge called "the Minister."

Seven Island Cove

Pulpit Rock with nesting gull

◎ 15.2 km: Raspberry Bottom

Considerable seepage and stream water runs down the tilted rock ledges at John Halls River (at **15.1 km**, also called "the Rivers," after a nearby trap berth). Hall (1821-1901) was one of the first settlers at Freshwater. Hikers are advised to take the re-route inland, through a wooded area, rather than do further damage to the boggy, slippery ground close to shore. White spruce grows on the drier ground of the wood, intermixed with northern wild raisin, mountain alder,

Raspberry Bottom

Witches' Broom

Bushy balls of twig that appear on the branches of spruce and fir are commonly called "witches' broom." A number of different organisms, all host-specific, give rise to these structures. Spruce broom rust (*Chrysomyxa arctostaphyli*) infects black and white spruce, while fir broom rust (*Melampsorella caryophyllacearum*) infects balsam fir. Both rusts are fungal diseases that stimulate an abnormal growth, sometimes called "Peter Pan tissue" because, like Peter Pan, it is eternally young.

Large numbers of upright shoots, thick and short, with yellowish-green needles, form broom-like structures on infected branches. In late summer, the needles are covered with orange-to-yellow spores. In both rusts, infected needles drop off at the end of the growing season. However, the disease remains in the woody tissue of the broom and new shoots are infected as soon as they emerge the following year. Brooms start off small, but can reach two metres in diameter.

Witches' broom

rhodora, wild roses, purple chokeberry, sheep laurel, Labrador tea and blueberry. Marshberry, cranberry, blue flag, horsetail and bog myrtle grow in boggy areas alongside the river. Reaching Raspberry Bottom, the trail crosses the base of a glacier-scraped slope that, more recently, has been assaulted by wood harvesting and fire. The returning growth is patchy, which on a steep slope is a recipe for soil erosion and seepage. The route passes through pockets of impoverished heath and wood. Bracken fern and raspberry indicate the drier areas; larch and cinnamon fern the wetter ones.

◎ 15.6 km: Cape Boone

The White sisters, who married two Pack brothers, must have served Commander Orlebar a particularly fine cup of tea, for on his 1864 chart of Bay Bulls he recorded—immediately east of Gun Ridge—a community of "Whites" living below "Whites Hill," fishing off "Whites Rock." The Packs settled these places in the 1840s, and a hill was never—as far as the Packs are concerned—called "Whites Hill." It became Cape Boone after Bill Pack married Mary Boone of

Cape Boone steps

Bareneed, and several of Mary Boone's relatives moved to Gun Ridge. Like Raspberry Bottom, the cape's rocky crown has been slow to recover from wood harvesting and fire. What was formerly woodland has turned into a hard-to-classify area that is not quite heath or fen, but a mix of sedges and such typical heath shrubs as sheep laurel and Labrador tea.

Approaching Gun Ridge, the trail runs close to the cliff edge and there is much broken rock, wedged by frost from the cliff above. Many of the substantial trees sheltered by the high cliffs and rubble are deformed by witches' broom. In places, the gnarled and twisted trees create a dense canopy, limiting ground cover to a few splashes of chuckley-pear, mountain alder and pin-cherry, underlain by bunchberry and moss. Nearing Gun Ridge, the path skirts the edge of Packs Meadow and rounds a small wooded point.

Eastern dwarf mistletoe (*Arceuthobium pusillum*) is a parasitic seed plant that mainly attacks black spruce. It also gives rise to distorted, compact masses of branches and twigs. Mistletoe roots embed themselves in a tree's bark and absorb nutrients from the host's tissue. The aerial shoots growing from the host are green to brown and have scale-like leaves and no branches. Although the shoots contain chlorophyll, mistletoe obtains most of its carbohydrates from the host tree. Often, shoots occur along the entire branch length. Each fruit contains a single sticky seed that is explosively expelled when mature, usually in late summer. Seeds are propelled as far as 15 metres and readily adhere to the objects they strike. Unlike brooms caused by rusts, mistletoe brooms retain their needles over winter.

Eastern dwarf mistletoe

◎ 15.8 km: Gun Ridge

Some say Gun Ridge was once a British battery. It is more likely the ridge was a prime hunting spot back in the days of *guns* (muskets). The settlement was often called "the Packs" for short, after its chief residents. Thomas Pack (1810-76), a native of Ipplepen, Devon, arrived in Gun Ridge in the 1840s. At its peak, the settlement had five dwellings, three occupied by Thomas Pack's sons. The family had a reputation for industry, particularly when it came to harvesting wood and working the land. There are numerous fields in the area, some pitched at improbable angles. Almost everywhere you look, you will find signs of house foundations, fieldstone walls, potato rows and root cellars. In 1917, the Packs erected a sawmill. A waterwheel drove the mill during the summer, a stationary engine during the winter. The engine was reassigned during the summer to hoist fish out of boats. Gun Ridge was abandoned in the mid-1950s, its inhabitants moving to Bread and Cheese and beyond.

Nothing happened in Gun Ridge that did not involve climbing of some sort, whether it was hauling wood, tending to livestock, hauling fish over the rocks up to stages or *spelling* (carrying) fish to flakes. The only obliging feature in the cove was Front Door, a trap berth named for being across from the front door of Bill Pack's house. In his time, Bert Pack (1897-1983) was the most popular fiddler in the area. Christmas *fools* (mummers) usually left Bert Pack's house until last, in order to finish their celebrations in grand style.

Gun Ridge is still sometimes used as a grazing area for horses and cattle. Plants observed in the meadow include sheep sorrel, ox-eye daisy, buttercup, raspberry, stitchwort, clover, thistle, yarrow and tall meadow-rue. Pack's Meadow is a good spot for both common and bird's-eye speedwell. On the steeper

---

AT BERT PACK'S

"Then came St. Stephen's Day or Boxing Day as it was known. People dropped in; some dressed out in the fools as it was called then. It's now known as mummering or jannying. They visited people's homes and left the fiddlers for last, which always brought us to Bert Pack's. You were treated in every house to homebrew or blueberry or ginger wine. Bert played while some stepped it out and another sang or recited."

—Queen Maloney, "Auld Lang Syne," *The Seniors' News*, December 1987

Bert Pack

fields, nutrients have washed to the bottom of slopes. The impoverished meadowland at the top chiefly hosts hawkweed and finer grasses. The house in the woods next to Gun Ridge River (in 2004, the easternmost house in Bay Bulls) was built in the 1930s by Andrew Proctor, a Scottish technician working at the Marine Biological Research and Fishing Station at Stanleys River.

GUN RIDGE IN 1950

"The road rises and falls with the hills, ending in a thick growth of sturdy pine and a few houses and gardens overlooking the harbour far below, the silence broken only by the chatter of children and the occasional noisy passing of motor boats going to or from the nets at sea. Here, again, is an English group, whose forebears were more or less thrown up by the sea, and still as English as were the first arrivals three or five generations back."

—J. Harry Smith, *Newfoundland Holiday*, 1952

Gun Ridge, 1998

Gun Ridge, c. 1920

"Hungry as the man who died on the Ridge; and he was shot."
—Bay Bulls saying

Drawn Etch'd & Pub.d by Dighton. 12. Charing Cross. March

Exploring Bay Bulls

Killing walrus, c. 1605

First recorded in 1592, the name "Bay Bulls" or "Bay of Bulls," likely refers to an animal found in the area, possibly the *bull* walrus, but more likely the *bull-bird* (common dovekie). In those years when icefloes prevented access to St. John's, early-arriving ships would have skirted the floe's edge—prime bull-bird habitat—as they approached Bay Bulls. After a taxing voyage, it is likely that the immense bull-bird flocks wintering in the leads of the icefield did double duty, as a navigational aide, and a source of fresh meat. Some think bull walrus may be the "bull in the bay." Before they were hunted to extinction in the 16th century, walrus may have hauled out onto the Flats, at the entrance of the harbour.

Holy Trinity Cemetery

In the easternmost (and oldest) of two small Anglican cemeteries bordering Gun Ridge Road, it is possible to trace the outline of Holy Trinity Church. The church, dedicated on May 24, 1864 by Bishop Edward Feild (1801-76), was one of two small Anglican chapels constructed on the Southern Shore during a period of missionary fervour. The second, in Aquaforte, still stands. According to the community historian Paul O'Neill, sectarianism prevented the unloading of material at Bay Bulls, so the chapel's lumber was landed at Gun Ridge where, with difficulty, it was hauled up Church Hill. This slander is disputed by other residents, who remember only good relations between the faiths. Sectarian excitement of some sort likely surrounded the chapel's construction for, on his 1864 map, Commander Orlebar places the chapel on "Heretic Hill." In a similar spirit, Gun Ridge was often referred to by Catholics as "Protestant Town."

Many of the first settlers of Freshwater and Gun Ridge are commemorated on the gravestones surrounding the church, including John Hall (1821-1901), Thomas Pack (1810-76), Catherine F. Pack (no dates given) and George Thomas Pack (1836-89), all native to Devon. In the 1930s, a new cemetery was opened a few

Dovekies

Common Dovekie

The common dovekie (*Plautus alle all*), the smallest member of the auk family, is the Arctic's most abundant bird, nesting in the tens of millions on fjord slopes in northwestern Greenland, and to a lesser degree in Iceland and the European north. For the peoples of the high Arctic, this starling-sized bird (19-23 cm) was a major food and clothing resource. Following breeding season, flocks of dovekies scatter to wherever ice and open water mix. From October to May, the tiny birds rest on floes and bob amid the slob ice for plankton, tiny fish and crustaceans. They are a well-known indicator of ice, hence their nickname "icebird." In Newfoundland, dovekies are commonly called bull-birds, possibly because of their thick neck, or small size, or because, with only bull-birds in the game bag, a hunter was certain to return with a "load of bull." Like puffins, bull-birds need a run to take off and are relatively helpless when confined in a small cove, or by ice. In such places they are easily scooped up with a long-handled net, or "conked" by a rock, a favourite hunting technique of young boys. Bull-birds were a welcome sight in the cooking pot whenever storms prevented extended hunting. Many East Coast Trail communities have a "Bull Cove" on their outskirts, likely because such coves were frequented by the young, or could be inspected in poor weather.

"An appetizing odor ca from the oven, where couple of fine fat bull birds, part proceeds o successful day's gunni in punt, a day or two before, were yielding their juices."

—*TELEGRAM CHRISTMAS, 188*

metres to the west. The abandonment of Gun Ridge in the 1950s exposed the church building to vandalism and, in 1969, the church joined the congregation's westward migration to Bread and Cheese. An arched entranceway, panelling from the chancel and several windows were saved and incorporated into the new church.

Before 1926, school was taught in an attic in Gun Ridge. From 1926 to 1949, a one-room Anglican school operated across from the cemetery on a plot of land now used for parking. Students maintained a flower garden in front of the building. The school closed in 1949 and its pupils trekked 6 km to Bay Bulls for eight years, until the old school was dismantled and rebuilt in Bread and Cheese in 1958. From 1966 onwards, the children of Bread and Cheese were bused to the Roman Catholic school in Bay Bulls.

Gun Ridge students, c. 1948

Holy Trinity Church

HOLY TRINITY CHURCH IN 1950

"Crowded, the church would hold about 40 people. Walls, ceiling and benches are of natural pine. Under a three-lance stained glass window and bearing a brass cross, candlesticks and freshly cut flowers, stands the small altar with an evidently home-embroidered frontal drape of simple and effective design, all ready for the parson's occasional visit, and speaking plainly of the important part church plays in the lives of these people."

—J. Harry Smith, *Newfoundland Holiday*, 1952

Holy Trinity Cemetery in 1922

"A lovelier spot is hard to find, and I am sure that those Devonshire men in picking out the place must have remembered the old land. Here the goldenrod is thickly clustered, the wild Convolvulus rears its head in abundance, in the autumn the mountain ash's red berries lend a charm, and in the cooler days, the wild cherries' leaves, growing golden, are like tongues of fire amongst the deep green of the pungent fir and spruce, pointing skyward, natural lights to the Great Creator and Arbiter of Life."

—F. T. Jardine, "The Trail of the First Settlers of Bay Bulls," SHORTIS V, 1922

Holy Trinity Cemetery in 1950

"The air is heavy with incense of roses, great purple-red single blooms on lusty dark-leafed bushes standing four or five feet high. Brought here long ago, perhaps, by some English man or woman with a longing for a flavour of home in a new land, they now impress their grateful presence on the air of this and almost every village we have so far walked through."

—J. Harry Smith, NEWFOUNDLAND HOLIDAY, 1952

Bread and Cheese Point

Bay Bulls Harbour—capacious, close to St. John's and free of ice—was a convenient place to gather vessels into a protective convoy whenever conflict threatened the fishery. Men-of-war returning from patrol, or assigned to convoy duty, anchored in deep water just inside of Bread and Cheese Point, in compliance with the British Admiralty directive that a warship maintained "at the ready" had to drop anchor with "three points of the compass exposed to the wind," i.e., could pick up wind from three out of four directions and quickly tack out of a harbour to respond to attack. The merchant ships awaiting convoy anchored farther up the harbour, near Stanleys River.

The settlement of Bread and Cheese acquired its curious name from nearby Bread and Cheese Point. The Royal Navy issued each able seaman a pound (450 grams) of bread and a gallon (4.5 litres) of beer a day. Three days a week, oatmeal, butter and cheese were issued in lieu of meat. The point was breezy, free of nippers and lay close to where ships anchored, so it was an ideal spot for off-duty seamen to retire on cheese days with their noontime rations and rum. It was out of the purview of officers, a feature important

Chain at Bread and Cheese Point and Twelve O'Clock Hill

ROYAL NAVAL WEEKLY RATIONS AT SEA (1704)

Sunday & Thursday:
Bread, 1 pound
Beer, 1 gallon
Pork, 1 pound
Pease, 1/2 pint

Monday, Wednesday & Friday:
Bread, 1 pound
Beer, 1 gallon
Oatmeal, 1 pint
Butter, 2 ounces
Cheese, 4 ounces

Tuesday & Saturday:
Bread, 1 pound
Beer, 1 gallon
Beef, 2 pounds

Off-duty sailors

Contemplating a sailor's life, 1878

to a sailor in possession of an extra tot of rum, bargained for on the sly, for seamen were lashed if caught drunk.

A ration of bread and cheese to an infantryman signified a regiment on the march. There are "Bread and Cheese" creeks and rivers in Massachusetts, Rhode Island and Maryland, all places where British regiments succumbed to revolutionary onslaught while eating lunch. The "Bread and Cheese" inland from Ferryland was used by hunters as a rest stop.

Bread and Cheese Point extends further into the harbour than other points, and in 1942 an anti-torpedo net was secured to the point to protect ships awaiting overhaul at the repair facility in the harbour. Visiting the point in the late 1940s, J. Harry Smith noted "the remains of the great steel cable booms and buoys that prevented entry of enemy ships and submarines . . . carefully tidied up and protected as though there might be a chance of being used again some day." A remnant of the chain is still in place. U-boats probed the harbour entrance but, thanks to the net, there were no attacks. The Coadys of Cape Broyle, returning from delivering sand to St. John's during the war, hove to at the mouth of the harbour and, looking over the side, saw a German submarine under their boat. Morning came and the U-boat was gone. John Rice, home on leave, remembers watching several destroyers swiftly leave Bay Bulls Harbour on a mission to intercept a U-boat spotted offshore.

Twelve O'Clock Hill

There are two Twelve O'Clock Hills, a Twelve O'Clock Knob and a Twelve O'Clock Nap on the Southern Shore, each located south of a cove frequented by fishing admirals and the Royal Navy.

Sextant

Upper deck of U-190

FORTUNES OF WAR

U-190, launched in Germany on June 3, 1942, was one of 144 type IXC/40 boats sent out to disrupt and destroy allied shipping. The submarine made six forays into the Atlantic but sank only two vessels: the 7,015-ton British merchant ship *Empire Lakeland* on March 8, 1943, and the minesweeper HMCS *Esquimault* on April 16, 1945. The *Esquimault*, on patrol outside Halifax Harbour, was the last Canadian vessel sunk by enemy action during the Second World War. With the war winding to a close, the minesweeper's crew failed to notice that the ship's radar had picked up a U-boat lurking off Sambro Light. Fleeing the minesweeper, *U-190* launched a single T-5 Gnat acoustic torpedo from a stern tube. The *Esquimault* sank so quickly that it failed to send out a distress signal and eight men went down with the ship. Seventy men made it to the lifeboats, but 44 perished from exposure during the eight hours it took for the HMCS *Sarnia* to come to the rescue.

Following this attack, *U-190* Commander Hans-Edwin Reith set a homeward course that was interrupted, on May 8, by an order from the German High Command to dump ammunition and hoist a "black flag of surrender." (Admiral Karl Dönitz refused to

Twelve O'Clock Hill in Bay Bulls is across the harbour from Bread and Cheese Point. A naval ship's day began (and ended) at noon with the striking of "eight bells" and the formal recording of position and date in the ship's log. A glance at the hill was a sailor's way of telling time. With "the sun over the yard-arm" (and the hill), the day's work was over, the main meal was served and each able-bodied seaman was issued a cup of the hard stuff: brandy until 1687; then rum until 1740; then rum mixed with water, i.e., "grog" thereafter.

British Admiralty maps name the Nipple, a hillock slightly southeast of Twelve O'Clock Hill. Naval officers generally retreated below decks for their first tot or "tipple" of the day when the sun was over the *fore*yard-arm, that is to say, at eleven, not twelve. In Bay Bulls, this was when the sun was over the Nipple.

U-190 *moored below Twelve O'Clock Hill and the Nipple*

U-190 in Bay Bulls Harbour

Many Newfoundland workers and fishermen took an "elevener," i.e., a reviving tot of rum, served either straight or mixed with spruce beer. Only able-bodied seamen, it would seem, had to wait until twelve.

Kate Point

The small roadside park at Kate Point, formerly Woody Point, with its welcome bench and dignified memorial, was constructed in 1996 by the wife and children of Patrick T. Coady (1931-94). Captain Coady and his crew of four were lost on October 13, 1994, when the 15-metre-long *Patrick & Elizabeth*, fishing for turbot 70 km east of Bay Bulls, encountered a fierce squall and disappeared in six-metre waves and 107-km/hr winds. Coady was a generous-spirited, widely respected captain who blessed threatening waves and who was "determined about fishing," meaning he was willing to take chances. For the memorial, five granite boulders were transported from the resettled Placentia Bay community of Bar Haven, Coady's birthplace, and set in the shape of a ship's prow. The Newfoundland-Bulgarian sculptor Luben Boykov cast the bronze figure of a gannet emerging from the tallest stone like a ship's figurehead, symbolizing the meeting of the material and spirit realms.

surrender his fleet using the traditional white flag, so a Royal Navy negotiator said, "Fly the black flag, then!" The black flag, favoured by pirates and anarchists, commonly signals, "No quarter!") British warships secured the U-boat and crew on May 11, 850 km off Cape Race. They escorted the submarine into Bay Bulls on May 14, where it was docked for three weeks.

U-190 was ultimately commissioned into the Royal Canadian Navy and served for two years as an anti-submarine training vessel. On October 21, 1947, three naval ships and 20 aircraft celebrated the 150th anniversary of the Battle of Trafalgar by ceremoniously sinking *U-190* over the wreck of its last victim. *U-190* was painted red and white to make it a more photogenic target for the press. The *U-190's* periscope is one of many Second World War treasures displayed at the Crow's Nest Officers Club in St. John's. Club patrons use it to scope out Water Street.

UNWILLING FISHERMEN

The success of the American Revolution in 1782 threw Bermuda into turmoil, for the island lost its economic mainstay, the transport of goods from colonies on the eastern seaboard to Caribbean plantations. In 1787, 300 Bermudian slaves shipped north in sloops to catch and land fish on Newfoundland's east and south coasts. Local fishermen were hired to secure rooms, provide fishing instruction and cure fish. The initiative was widely suspected as a ploy by American merchants to gain access to Newfoundland's fish trade, or to mask smuggling.

The slaves out-rowed and out-fished their Newfoundland counterparts and, unlike the freeborn, could be ordered out in foul weather. The sloops returned the following year, this time with fewer slaves, but were served notice nonetheless by Governor John Elliot (1730?-1808) that they were in violation of *Palliser's Act of 1775*, which barred British colonials living elsewhere in the Americas from landing and curing fish in Newfoundland. The Bermudians attempted to ship Newfoundland fish south **green** (salted, but not dried) in subsequent years, but the uncured fish spoilt.

The park was formerly the site of a four-gun battery, most likely one constructed at Woody Point by public subscription in 1779. When Northside Road was widened through Blacks Hollow, a cannon that had long lain next to the road was winched to the top of the road cut. A faint footpath up the south-facing side of the cut leads to the cannon, which is of the same type as the two large cannon supporting the gates of Saints Peter and Paul Church.

Immediately below Kate Rock, a rock knob on the westernmost edge of Bread and Cheese, a small grotto faces east. Father Francis J. Mullowney (1910-84) served for 44 years as a parish priest in Oderin, Lamaline and Trepassey before retiring to his family home in Bread and Cheese in 1980. The priest spent his retirement years travelling. He returned from one

18th-century Bermudian sloop

trip with the statue of the Blessed Virgin Mary that is now sheltered in the grotto, which was built as a memorial by friends shortly after Father Mullowney's death.

Blacks Hollow

It is well known in Bay Bulls that the road past Kates Rock is haunted by three ghostly black men who stroll Blacks Hollow at night. Some say the men were eaten by starving shipmates when a stranded Spanish ship wintered in the harbour without supplies. Others claim the men died at sea and were buried in the hollow because their religion was unknown. It is not known if the black ghosts generally wander eastwards towards the "black Protestant" settlement of Bread and Cheese, or westwards towards "papist" Stanleys River, home turf of three unshriven Royal Navy deserters, who died in 1793. The deserter ghosts were seen by Queen Maloney as recently as the 1920s, marching in procession from their place of death on Stony Ridge to their burial plot in a small cemetery next to the Alley.

The house in Blacks Hollow is haunted by an old woman, one who feels *such* affection towards young children that her face appears in the window—but only if the *very* young walk by. She, like the black men

Father Mullowney's memorial grotto

"A ghost story what was told to me was about Blacks Hollow, where years ago hundreds of people used to get slaughtered and tortured, like getting fingers chopped off and getting your tongue cut out. And it is believed now when you walk past it, a cold wind will be there."

—L. J. Maloney, *ECTA Community Map Project*, 1998

Blacks Hollow

CHRISTMAS DAY, BAY BULLS, 1753

Around 8:00 p.m. on December 25, 1753, the planter Martin Doyle, much in liquor, was fetched home by his son and an apprentice. The group arrived to find Doyle's house invaded by servants, some dancing about in a wild humour, others sitting on the **settle** (wood couch) in front of the fire, well into their fourth or fifth flip. Doyle's wife retired while the severely inebriated Doyle attempted to evict the Christmas celebrants before some, or all, bedded down for the night.

One of the revellers, Milos Keefe, turned aggressive, threw a flip in the fire and threatened to do the same to Robert Garmer, the man who had planned to drink it. Doyle would later testify that he accidentally stabbed Garmer while attempting to heave Keefe out the door. Another witness claimed Garmer stepped outside to make wind and water and returned to the house bleeding profusely, the offending cutlass being seen in Doyle's hand shortly after. Before, or possibly after Garmer received his fatal wound, Keefe assaulted Doyle and his wife with a fire-tongs, an instrument kept in the fire to warm flip. Justice Brookes charted new legal territory, two months after the affair, by ruling Doyle could not be convicted of murdering Garmer, for though he was seen holding the cutlass, no one had witnessed the blow. Brookes also ruled that, though innocent, Doyle should pay court costs.

and deserters, was a ghost with a job to do, for she discouraged the children of two religions from co-mingling. Once a child had reached adolescence, the ghosts added an appealing horror element to evening promenades and trysts. The tradition continues, for the late Father Mullowney was seen recently by a babysitter, stretched out on a daybed in his Kate Rock residence.

Pepperelli Point

Past Kate Point the coast bends northwest, forming a shore that is protected year round from ocean swells. Here, a low-lying promontory, known as Pepperelli Point, faces the harbour's finest anchorage and was a first-rate spot to establish a *planter's room* (an extensive fishing premises). It is likely that Pepper Alley—these days just called the "Alley"—was named first and the point later.

"Pepperelli" is a corruption of "Pepper Alley," originally a lane in Southwark, London, next to London Bridge, renowned for its pugilistic displays, both organized and spontaneous. The London alley was popular with seafaring folk, for stairs led directly from the Thames to the lane's taverns. In the 1820s, "a trip down Pepper alley" was a slang term for a knock-out, and today's boxers are still "peppered" with blows. Like London's Pepper Alley, Pepper Alley in Bay Bulls led from a district of taverns to a more secluded spot, where disputes could be settled in a manly fashion, without official intervention.

Any place where convoys and naval ships collect is likely to be a party town. The first licensed tavern in Bay Bulls dates to the 1640s; as governor of the Colony of Avalon (1637-54) Sir David Kirke actually obliged planters to open taverns so he could collect licensing fees. In 1670, James Yonge enjoyed such a

Sailors carousing

good time in Bay Bulls, "living a jolly life" with four fellow Plymouth surgeons, that the group's liquor and dainties—meant to last to the fall—were consumed by April 16. The partying doctors ignored the smallpox raging through the community. In 1726, one out of every six Bay Bulls planters kept a tavern.

In 1729, Governor Henry Osborne appointed Nathaniel Brookes, a planter from Topsham, Devon, residing at Pepperelli Point, as the first Justice of the Peace and "winter magistrate" of Bay Bulls. By 1750, Brookes' jurisdiction had expanded to include maritime law and property disputes. Brookes settled altercations in a manner that brought him to the frequent attention of governors. In 1751, for example, Governor Bernard Drake heard complaints that Brookes was claiming other men's property in Witless Bay and on Ship Island (also called Isle Spear), and Madame Brookes appeared before the governor to protest that a sea captain had encroached upon the Brookes plantation. In 1753, Governor Hugh Bonfoy heard a petition against Madame Brookes, who the year before had materialized suddenly with a boat crew, pulled down a neighbour's cattle fence and erected a flake. In 1756, Brookes officiated at the wedding of Nicholas and Elinor Coombs. The following year, Governor Richard Edwards received a petition from Elinor complaining that her husband

18TH-CENTURY LIBATIONS

RIP: Spruce beer with spirit, usually rum; also called callibogus.

FLIP: Rip sweetened with sugar and heated with a red-hot poker or fire-tongs; a drink associated with the seafaring life.

EGG FLIP: Flip with egg added; also called egg calli.

KING CALLI: Spirit added to freshly brewed spruce beer while the beer was still hot.

Royal Navy officers assigned to the Newfoundland Station had a low opinion of resident justices and viewed Newfoundland's planter class in general as an ignorant lot. In 1745, one officer penned the following anonymous accolade to Justice and Madame Nathaniel Brookes. The year before, Justice Brookes had been appointed to a newly created vice-admiralty court, which ruled on matters related to shipping and the sea.

A Seat Imperial

No mortared bricks in smouldering flames prepared;
No Parian marble the proud fabric reared;
No lofty turrets, reaching to the sky,
Reproached the newfound soil with luxury,
But poles, and dirt, boxes of slaughtered cod
The sides composed, the roof was rinds and sod.

At either end (his worship else had choked)
A headless hogshead for a chimney smoked;
While through the front seven shattered windows stared,
With paper some, and some with rags repaired.
Four sturdy poles, overlaid with twigs of birch,
Projecting from the entrance, formed a porch.

Profuse of odours, here the housewife good
Her platter washed, and here the hogs' trough stood;
More odourous still, before the sunny pile,
Livers of fish lay rotting into oil.
Less stank that liver which next Tobit's bed
The angel burned, when the choked devil fled.

Oh Toby, hadst thou, here, first met thy bride
E'en then, perchance, the devil himself had died,
Yet, here, o'er cods and men, Nathaniel rules
The seat Imperial of the Bay of Bulls.

had been "induced" into moving in with Ellen Williams. The governor ordered Brookes to make Nicholas "either live with his wife or give her a maintenance." In 1766, the Justice learned that two of his servants had slept together and deducted the value of the intercourse from the male's wages. Governor Hugh Palliser ruled that Brookes should return the withheld money, and ordered the woman deported.

Nathaniel Brookes presided over the "whole business of the district" for 48 years; his son James held office for a scant two. In 1779, Governor Edwards (back for a second term) queried the new justice's handling of funds and James responded that he would be returning to England shortly. The governor appointed an immediate replacement and suggested James not trouble him with a courtesy visit before his departure.

Briarcliff, the attractive house now on Pepperelli Point, was constructed by George C. Whiteley Jr. (1908-90), a young scientist hired by the Marine Biological Research and Fishing Station at Stanleys River. It is said Whiteley built the house in a Cape Cod style to please his American wife. Whiteley, grandson of William H. Whiteley (1834-1903), the inventor of the cod trap, went on to a distinguished career as a teacher and yachtsman. Other owners have included Oliver Vardy (1906-80), J. R. Smallwood's fugitive deputy minister of economic development, and the historian, actor and CBC radio producer Paul O'Neill (1928-).

Governor Hugh Palliser

Governor Richard Edwards

17th-century jug

Joan Clays Hill and cemetery, c. 1917

Joan Clays Hill

The 249-metre-high hill above Bay Bulls is now called Stony Ridge, or "the Ridge" for short, but appears as "Joan Clays Hill" on an English map of 1689. The ridge's southernmost prominence still goes by this name. The name was extended, inexplicably, to "Joan Clais Hill of Bergen" on a Dutch map of 1693. A planter named Joan Clay resided in Bay Roberts in 1675; she was one of several female planters in Newfoundland at the time. Her association, if any, with Bay Bulls is unknown. Possibly, a tavern led to the naming of the hill, for "joan" is an affectionate term for a woman and to take a drink is to "wet your clay." Sometime before 1864, an American party placed an American man (cairn) and flag on the highest point of Stony Ridge. The height has been called American Man ever since. As previously recounted (at **13.3 km** on Spout Path), Commander Orlebar renamed the cairn after himself.

The old Roman Catholic cemetery at the base of Joan Clays Hill, informally known as the "Alley cemetery," contains large headstones commemorating Jeremiah, 33, and Francis Brien, 28, both killed during the "Great Gale of 1846." The gale destroyed 40 boats in Bay Bulls. The Brien brothers succeeded in rescuing the crew from one ship in peril, only to be crushed to death when the storm blew a stage head roof onto

---

MEDICARE DURING PROHIBITION IN THE 1920S

"If you wanted a bottle of wine or liquor, you had to have what was known as a 'script' from your Doctor. You paid him $1.00 for it. You then had to take the script to a Bond Store in St. John's and pay for your bottle and come home on the train. The doctor was paid $5.00 a year from each household. The script was a little side money for him. He came on a moment's notice and you 'treated' him before he left. There were no MCP cards then.
He drove in his horse and buggy and the horse would always take him safely home with his dog and pipe. Today he's resting with his people on the Hill."

—Queen Maloney, "Memories of the Thirties in Bay Bulls," *The Seniors' News*, August 1990

heir boat. There are headstones for Mary, the mother, who died in 1830, and for brothers Martin, 33, and John, 34. Michael, the father, was severely injured by the falling roof. If a headstone was erected for him, it has not survived.

Also, the long-serving surgeon, magistrate, customs officer and road commissioner Dr. John L. McKie (1784-1869) is commemorated with a stone. Dr. McKie's professional career included treating smallpox victims during "The Winter of the Rals" in 1817. He retired as Justice of the Peace in 1864, after 51 years at the post. In McKie's day, few patients could pay the fees set for treatment. Generally, the government solved this problem by multiplying a doctor's appointments until the stipends added up to a living; hence Dr. McKie's long list of appointments. The first Roman Catholic chapel in Bay Bulls likely stood near the cemetery, possibly within the cemetery's bounds. Roman Catholic institutions were prohibited in Newfoundland until 1784, so the chapel cannot have been built before this date.

Rescued 18th-century crucifix, Saints Peter and Paul Church

Year of the French

On September 2, 1796, a French raiding squadron composed of seven ships of the line and two frigates was sighted off Bay Bulls. Most settlers immediately took to the woods where, it is said, the most cautious spent the winter. Two days later, his direct assault on St. John's having failed, Rear Admiral Joseph de Richery (1757-99) landed a force in Bay Bulls unopposed. The French set fire to most of the community the next day, including the Anglican and Roman Catholic chapels. A zealous parishioner fled into the woods with an Italian-carved, mahogany figure of Christ, saved from the Roman Catholic chapel.

> "It is said, likewise, that Richery has sailed from Cadiz, with his seven sail, and 12 sail of Spanish ships of the line under Solano, but nobody knows where. If they fall in with the British, that will probably bring matters to a crisis; but John Bull will trash them both at sea, to the end of time, if they do not inveigle Pat [Ireland] out of his hands. I wish to God Carnot was as sensible of this as I am. Well, here I am, and here I must remain, and I am as helpless as if I were alone, swimming for my life in the middle of the Atlantic."
>
> —Theobald Wolfe Tone, *Diary*, June 13-14, 1796

Theobald Wolfe Tone

Some claim it was Richery's intention to capture St John's from Bay Bulls, that is, until a quick-thinking prisoner informed him that St. John's was defended by 5,000 well-armed men. A French force reconnoitered as far as Frenchmans Camp, near Bay Bulls Big Pond, erecting cairns at kilometre intervals, but explored no further due to the poor state of the path. Local tradition paints the admiral as a gallant. During his stay, he occupied the dwelling of the Irish planter Nicholas Coady on Pepperelli Point and the house was spared destruction. Richery also spared a *tilt* (hut) near Stanleys River owned by an Irishman named Nolan, whose wife had just given birth to twins. It is said that the French were softened by the sight of Nolan holding a child on each knee. Or, alternatively, moved by the grizzled fisherman's brave attempt to defend his domicile with a sharpened pitchfork. Richery returned a cow to an elderly woman: some say she refused to budge from her chair until it was returned; others claim she rowed out to his ship to demand it back.

Overly embroidered as these stories now seem, they may well be true. Richery had good reason to befriend the Irish of Bay Bulls. On December 11, 1796, three months after leaving Bay Bulls, his squadron joined a 43-ship fleet carrying an invasion force of 14,450 French soldiers to Bantry Bay, Ireland, in aid of Theobald Wolfe Tone (1763-98) and the United Irishmen Rebellion. Understandably, as he was on his way from Cadiz, Spain, to Brest, France, on a mission to liberate Ireland, Richery kept his stop-over in Newfoundland brief. Most likely he crossed the Atlantic to raid the Newfoundland fishery, a mission that had failed the previous year (1795) when his squadron set off for an unknown destination, only to be chased back to Cadiz by the Royal Navy.

18th-century recruits

The Alley

The Alley, or Alley Road, running between Stanleys River and Joan Clays Hill, marks the beginning of the old footpath to St. John's. The path led up the Ridge, then followed high ground for 43 km, through bog and barren. Hard scrabble routes of this type were called "Indian paths." Notoriously steep, narrow and overgrown, the path was walked five times by invading French forces, and was chosen as an avenue of escape by two centuries worth of soldiers, seamen, servants and convicts tired of being ordered around. It remained the only way to St. John's until William Sweetland, in 1835, surveyed a valley route more suited to carts and carriages.

In October of 1793 three seamen from the HMS *Boston* deserted ship in St. John's and set out for Bay Bulls. They came to within 5 km of Bay Bulls before losing the path and perishing in the cold. Their bodies were found on the Ridge the next spring and interred in a small cemetery, between the Alley and Stanleys River. "As tired as the men who died on the ridge," is still a common expression in Bay Bulls. In 1975, three skeletons, most likely those of the soldiers, were unearthed at the site during a road upgrade.

STRATEGIC THINKING, 1796

"The French inquired of him the distance from there to St. John's and how the road was. He informed them that the road was very bad and narrow and that only one man could go on it at once, and that it was impossible to take cannon. On this, the officer said they did not intend to take cannon, but to march as quickly as possible, summon the garrison to surrender, and put to death every one. He was asked what strength was in St. John's. He informed them, 5,000 at least, and that had they attempted the harbour they would not have succeeded as there was a boom and a chain across it. The officer to whom he was speaking went to Admiral Richery and they conversed together and from that time he thinks all thought of attacking St. John's was given up."

–John Morridge, *Declaration*, September 29, 1796

An Indian Path Excursion, 1794

"I shall conclude my account of Indian paths by stating that about 4 years ago the purser of the "Rose" frigate, then on this station, being at Bay of Bulls, a distance of about 20 miles from St. John's, came to the resolution to walk it. He did so, but under circumstances not a little laughable, for he lost his shoes, tore the skirts of his coat off and, what was worse than all, rended his breeches in such a manner as decency forbid him entering St. John's until after night had set in."

—THE NEWFOUNDLAND JOURNAL OF AARON THOMAS

Highway into Bay Bulls, c. 1917

Stanleys River, c. 1917

Stanleys River

The Alley runs up the eastern side of Stanleys River; Marsh Lane runs up the western side. Men from Bread and Cheese used to gather outside Jerry Williams' Goods Store, located between the two roads. Up until the 1940s, Jerry Williams & Co. workers did not receive money for their labour, but were given a slip of paper with a certain amount on it and were sent up to the Goods Store to pick out a matching sum of supplies. Jerry Williams rebuilt after the fire of 1937, but in the late 1940s sold out to East Coast Fisheries. With the switch to frozen product, the property fell into disuse and was pulled down.

Sometime between 1867 and 1872, Job Brothers & Co. constructed a factory that converted fish offal into fertilizer, most likely in the Stanleys River area. In the 1890s, Hamilton Weeks, a Prince Edward Island native, conducted business from a premises and house owned by Job Brothers, on the east bank of the river. In addition to his employment as general merchant and agent for Job Brothers, Weeks was a Justice of the Peace, notary public and vice-consul. In 1895, customs agents raided Weeks, finding 150 kilos of tobacco in his St. John's residence and 37 undeclared pairs of rubber boots in Bay Bulls. Judge Daniel Prowse (1834-1914) presided over the Weeks

The Factory  *Factory ladies packing fish*

hearing. A few days before the trial was scheduled to begin, Prowse was caught smuggling a dozen bottles of claret from a French warship, and fined. Some sources say Prowse sentenced Weeks to six months in jail, others say that Weeks, too, got off with a fine. In either case, he was back working for Job Brothers in Bay Bulls the following year.

Hamilton Weeks' daughter Edith (1882-1964) was the first Newfoundland-born woman to train as a doctor and surgeon, and the first woman to practise medicine in the colony. After training in Toronto, she joined the staff of the General Hospital in St. John's in 1906, spending summer weekends with her parents in Bay Bulls, where she attended to patients from a room in the family home. She ran a second informal clinic in a Witless Bay parlour, which she reached using the family carriage, pulled by a superannuated racehorse named Flying Cloud. In 1910, Hamilton Weeks sold off his interests and moved to British Columbia. Dr. Weeks met her future husband during the move, and spent the rest of her life in his homeland of New South Wales, Australia.

Fish out of Water

In 1916, the Newfoundland American Cold Storage & Manufacturing Co. built a state-of-the-art fish freezing and drying plant—called "the Factory" for short—at the mouth of Stanleys River. A small electrical station and dam on Main River powered the plant's blast freezers and dryers. Codfish landed from schooners or purchased from local fishermen were skinned, salted, washed and dried in electric-powered dryers, then packed into 500-gram tins for shipment to Africa. The plant also packed fish cakes and fish in casks. In 1919, the dam that generated power for the

Factory freezing chamber   *Plant Office No. 5*

Factory broke, and the bankrupt company sold its premises to A. Harvey & Co. It was 1927 before electrification came again to Bay Bulls.

In 1931, Newfoundland, long a laggard in the field of ocean research, opened the Marine Biological Research and Fishing Station in Bay Bulls, the British Empire Marketing Board providing 50 per cent of the funding. Bay Bulls was likely picked because the Factory, empty and available, was equipped with machinery for freezing, smoking, drying, cod liver oil manufacture, canning and fishmeal production. The station's laboratory and living quarters were on the top floor, an experimental cannery was located on the second and the ground floor was used to store nets, pumps, boats and other equipment.

The Scottish biochemist Harold Thompson commanded the station's research staff, composed of senior Scottish scientists Norman L. Macpherson and Sheila T. Lindsay, and four fishery researchers with Newfoundland roots: Nancy Frost, Allen Johnston, George C. Whiteley and Anna M. Wilson. The station hired a half-dozen support staff from Bay Bulls. The station became a hardship post during the winter, for it was isolated from the life of the capital. Some locals believed—and still do—that the station was a secret American research facility "experimenting on mice, rats and chickens"; others valued the new ideas staff brought to the community. A Sea Scout troop, founded in 1932 by the station's Scottish technician, Andrew Proctor, grew to 76 members by 1935. Proctor taught the boys soccer, and the troop staged Christmas concerts to raise funds for Christmas hampers for the poor. Under the supervision of Robert Frampton, the scouts built a 15-metre-long boat in the "School House," a well-equipped carpentry shop next to the station, operated by Frampton and his sons Robert and Louis.

STANLEYS RIVER SHIPWRECKS

In April of 1696, the 346-ton, 32-gun naval frigate HMS *Saphire*, commanded by Thomas Cleasby, shepherded a convoy of fishing ships from Ireland to Newfoundland. On September 9, the *Saphire* was on patrol near Cape Race when it spotted a French fleet headed for St. John's. Cleasby beat a course north to warn the town of attack but, encountering storm winds, sought refuge in Bay Bulls Harbour. The same wind prevented the French fleet from reaching its objective and the fleet commander, Jacques-Francois de Mombeton de Brouillan, governor of Plaisance (Placentia), followed Cleasby into Bay Bulls Harbour on September 11. Cleasby led a spirited English defense from four makeshift forts on the north and south sides of the harbour.

HMS Dartmouth, *a fifth-rate naval frigate, 1690*

Oil factory and J. Williams & Co. premises

Thompson, as director of the station, embarked on a challenging five-year programme of pure science, product research and fisheries education. His scientific staff tested the effectiveness of nets, studied the effects of water temperature and currents on plankton production and fish migration, looked for ways to improve canning, freezing and curing, and studied the manufacture and marketing of fishmeal, cod liver oil and malt extract. Two fisheries officers assigned to the station visited outports to demonstrate improved fish harvesting and processing methods. During the summer, the station offered study scholarships and the staff taught marine biology courses to student teachers.

Newfoundland as a self-governing dominion disappeared in 1934; the station's funding vanished the following year. The Scots departed, Thompson to direct fisheries research in Australia. The Newfoundland-born food chemist William F. Hampton (1908-68) was hired to head a much-diminished institute. To pare down costs, the station remained operational during the summer only and the lease on the *Cape Agulhas*, the station's research vessel, was terminated. On April 19, 1937, a fire started in a cod liver oil refinery operated by Tors Cove Trading near the station. The fire spread, in succession, to the fishing premises of J. Williams & Co., the de-activated station, the "School House"

Cullys Bottom, looking towards Riverhead

where the Sea Scouts had just finished their boat, a pickling plant used to salt beef and, lastly, the Frampton residence. The fire destroyed not just the station's records, library, collections and samples but also most of the natural history collection of the Newfoundland Museum stored in the station's laboratory as a budgetary measure, the Commission of Government having converted the museum into government offices. The Commission of Government built a new station in St. John's in 1940, directed initially by Hampton. In 1944, Hampton moved on to General Seafoods and its Birdseye Fisheries Laboratories in Massachusetts, where he invented the fish stick.

The Cove

On February 3, 1987, wind and ice carried away stages and boats below the high point on Northside Road known as the Cliff. Past the Cliff, the road descends to Cullys Bottom and crosses Cullys Brook. This pint-size waterway stepped into the historical limelight in 1881, when 85 men petitioned the House of Assembly for back wages, claiming they had been engaged to repair Cullys Bottom Bridge. The contractor had absconded with the $450 government allocation. Next to the brook, Con O'Brien built Bay Bulls Sea Products, a fish plant that seasonally

By mounting all his guns seaward, Cleasby turned the *Saphire* into a fifth, floating battery off Stanleys River. De Mombeton de Brouillan landed troops on the harbour's north and south shores and, judging the fight lost, Cleasby scuttled and set fire to the *Saphire*, which exploded and sank in 18 metres of water, 100 metres from shore. Cleasby, with 35 men, retreated down woods paths to Ferryland, where he again fought and was defeated by the French on November 10.

The wreck of the *Saphire* was discovered and pilfered by divers in the 1960s. Following a trial dig in 1974, the wreck was declared a provincial historic site. Parks Canada underwater archaeologists partially excavated the wreck in 1977, recovering over 2,500 artifacts, before covering the *Saphire* with sandbags to discourage further pilfering. The remains of two naval store hulks, the 420-ton HMS *Asia* and the 400-ton HMS *Loyalty* have been tentatively identified to the east of the *Saphire*; both foundered off Stanleys River on April 7, 1701.

Pipe from HMS Saphire

Sea Forest Plantation

Christened "the pig of the sea" by aquaculturalists, a codfish weighing one kilogram, penned in an untroubled environment, and fed a rich diet of male caplin, can double in weight and quadruple in value in 60 to 90 days. The Sea Forest Plantation corral—which has floated in Bay Bulls Harbour since 1985—can produce up to 350 tonnes of premium fresh cod on a year-round basis. Cod caught in the summer, when prices are low, can be sold during the winter when prices and yields have risen.

In theory, cod ranching should thrive. In practice, large scale ranching proved uneconomic between 1986 and 1991, when there was plenty of cheap wild cod for the taking. With the collapse of the fishery in 1992, cod ranching had to cope with the loss of wild stock to corral.

A full scale, commercial cod hatchery has yet to be tested. Undeterred, in 1993, Sea Forest Plantation secured sufficient public sector funding to open a cod hatchery in a leased fish plant in Placentia. There, the company trained 226 displaced fishery workers to become cod ranchers. On May 21, 1997, on the eve of launching 400,000 marketable fish to 300 independent farmers, poised to create a 6,000-tonne industry generating

Ship in haul-out at HMCS Avalon, *Bay Bulls*

employed 450. A football field-sized blaze took out the core of the plant in 1983. O'Brien rebuilt, only to lose his plant to a second fire in 1995.

The shoreline immediately past the brook, facing the church, has gone through numerous transformations. In 1942-43, the Royal Canadian Navy (RCN) acquired the former Williams & O'Driscoll property on the site and constructed a ship repair facility and supply base. The base was administered as part of HMCS *Avalon*, St. John's. (Naval bases are commissioned as ships, and so have ships' names.) At the heart of the facility was a marine railway and dry dock, used to maintain and repair the hundred or so Allied warships deployed to escort convoys and chase U-boats. In addition to its 2,700-tonne capacity *haul-out* (dry dock), the base had a machine shop, barracks, administration building, sick bay and officers quarters. A floating anchorage stretched far out into the harbour.

After the war, the Fogo Island firm of Earle & Sons turned the RCN facility into a saltfish drying and packing operation. In 1978, the property was expropriated so that it could be turned into a marine service centre for research and offshore surveillance vessels. Nothing initially came of this plan. From 1997 to 2001, Pennecon Ltd., a Penney Group subsidiary, filled in 3.6 hectares of the harbour adjacent to Cullys Brook and Riverhead, creating the Bay Bulls Marine Terminal, a $2 million offshore oil service and docking facility designed to service and repair large offshore oil rigs.

Saints Peter and Paul Church

From 1784 to 1811, a Roman Catholic priest visited Bay Bulls twice a year from St. John's to minister to the flock. The French burnt the settlement's first chapel in 1796. A second, described as "respectable" by a visiting governor's attaché in 1831, was likely in place by 1811, the year Father Timothy Browne (1785-1855) took up residence in Bay Bulls until his manse and chapel in Ferryland could be repaired. Father William Whitty (1791?-1823) assisted Father Browne in Bay Bulls between 1817 and 1822.

Bishop Fleming created St. Patrick's Parish, extending from the Goulds to La Manche, in 1833. Some say he did this to humiliate Father Browne, whom he loathed as a reprobate and rival. During the 49-year incumbency (1833-82) of Dean Patrick Cleary (1796-1882) the parish was administered from Witless Bay. It is likely this decision was made on the advice of Bishop Fleming, who feared a repetition of the state of affairs in Ferryland, where Father Browne caused scandal by hobnobbing with the local Protestant gentry. Unlike Bay Bulls, Witless Bay was exclusively Catholic. In his later years, Dean Cleary developed so strong an aversion to Bay Bulls that he officiated there only when circumstance compelled.

The Church of Saints Peter and Paul was the work of Dean Nicholas Roche (1842-1916), Dean Cleary's nephew, who served as the Dean's curate for 10 years (1867-77) before moving into his own residence in

$25 million in sales and employing over 800, the hatchery burned down. The Bay Bulls pen still holds breed stock. Recent hatchery activity has focused on high-end market species such as halibut, yellowtail flounder and witch flounder, and on re-launching the 1993-97 initiative.

Dean Patrick Cleary with his nephew, Rev. Nicholas Roche, c. 1867

Saints Peter and Paul Church and St. Patrick's School

Father Patrick J. O'Brien, c. 1938

Bay Bulls in 1877. Shortly after, in 1882, Dean Roche succeeded Dean Cleary in Witless Bay. Saints Peter and Paul was consecrated by Dean Roche in 1890, but it was not until 1922—32 years later—that a parish was created to go with the church. In 1916, Father Patrick J. O'Brien (1859-1940) was assigned St. Patrick's following the death of Dean Roche. Father O'Brien was born in Bay Bulls and shifted to his home community in 1921, a decision that provoked a storm of protest from the residents of Witless Bay, who "didn't want to be the tail of the Bay Bulls dog." They petitioned for a priest of their own and in 1922 the parishes of Bay Bulls and Witless Bay were formally separated.

Father O'Brien was one of the shore's great eccentrics and is remembered still with many stories. As a young man, he patented a prize-winning torpedo boat design that he lobbied the British Admiralty to adopt during the First World War. Later, as a priest, he built a prototype and offered the design without charge to hard-toiling Newfoundlanders. During the building of St. Patrick's Convent and School House, next to the church, it is said Father O'Brien performed Mass at 5:00 a.m., so he could spend the rest of his day with the carpenters. Father O'Brien's pride in the convent continued after the Sisters of Mercy took up residence in 1921. Any sister who hammered a nail into the wall had to contend with an irate priest. The convent and passageway that connected it to the church were demolished in 2002.

In 1929, two years after electrical power was introduced into the community, Father O'Brien installed keyboard-operated electrical chimes in the west steeple, and reduced the height of the east steeple, it is said, so that his parishioners could fully appreciate the sound. In 1937, he created the community's most remarked-upon attraction, the four "cannonized" saints that support the metal gates before the church. The two larger cannon are British, the two smaller are said to be French. In addition to designing boats and stained glass windows, and painting portraits, Father O'Brien designed and dug his own tomb, which is just inside the cannon gates. A little to the west, in front of the former convent, Father O'Brien erected a statue of the Archangel Michael, in memory of his nephew Michael O'Brien, who was killed during the last days of the First World War. Another great eccentric, Father O'Brien's grandniece Dorothy Fanning, later Dorothy Wyatt, resided in the rectory as a child. From 1973 to 1981, Wyatt served as mayor of St. John's. Her record-setting tenure as a woman councillor (1973-2000) concluded with her extraordinary re-election, posthumously, to St. John's City council in 2000.

Cannon gates, c. 1938

Dorothy Wyatt, 1985

"CANNONIZED" SAINTS

West to East:

☆ Holding a bishop's crosier: St. Patrick

☆ Holding a key: St. Peter

☆ Holding a sword: St. Paul

☆ With roses and crucifix: St. Teresa

Saint Peter and Saint Paul share a feast day, June 29. All fish caught on this day are donated to the church.

THE BEST SHOPLIFTER IN IRELAND

In 1786, a new prison colony was established at Botany Bay, New South Wales, Australia, to deal with the surfeit of convicts in English and Irish prisons sentenced to transport. On June 14, 1789, 114 men, boys and women were brought in carts from Newgate Prison, Dublin, to the waterfront and taken aboard the **Duke of Leinster**, fitted out as a prison ship and captained by Richard Harrison. Two of the convicts were 13-year-old boys, and two were 14-year-olds. Nearly all aboard had been convicted of petty theft. John O Neal, 20, was described as "the best shoplifter in Ireland" on his docket, an attainment he likely granted himself.

The official destination of the ship was, and to this day remains, a mystery. The convicts most likely believed they were bound for Botany Bay. Newfoundland was sighted four weeks after setting sail, by which time typhus had broken out among the convicts and Captain Harrison was eager to rid himself of his cargo. On the night of July 15 he put 97 ashore at Bay Bulls, with few provisions, and dropped the last 17 in Petty Harbour the next morning, with no supplies at all.

During their stay in Bay Bulls, the convicts burned down a storehouse and dwelling owned by Richard Hutchings (1740?-1808), one of the colony's leading dealers in bread and flour. Small groups straggled up the "Indian path" to St. John's, to the alarm of Governor Mark Milbanke (1723-1805) and the town's property owners.

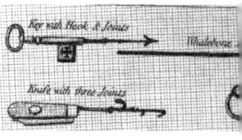

A town-wide conflagration was narrowly averted, but there was a rash of petty theft, and typhus—likely spread by the convicts—killed 200 out of a population of 2,500. The 12 female convicts roamed where they chose, and soon became a scandal. Sixty-three of the males were rounded up and confined—in theory—to a plantation on the barrens north of St. John's; in practice, the drink and food used to mollify the prisoners did not prevent extended leave-taking. One of the boys, John Farrell, disappeared from the official tally in August, as did, eventually, 33 other prisoners, generally those with surnames, such as Lee, Lawler, Pendergast, O'Brien and Keough, pointing to kinship with the local Irish population.

Governor Milbanke eventually commissioned Captain Robert Coysh to return the convicts to Ireland. On October 24, 1789, 74 manacled men and boys, and 6 women, set sail in the brigantine *Elizabeth & Clare*. Governor Milbanke spent £775 on the trip, paying for the passage, manacles and clothing, this last item traded by the exasperated convicts for rum. Milbanke recouped £184 from the merchants of Newfoundland. Back in Newgate, Dublin, the convicts discovered their aborted trip did not count against their sentence, and a prison riot ensued. A small number were eventually transported to Botany Bay.

Riverhead

Men used to gather at the bridge next to Mike Ryan's general store at Riverhead to discuss the day's activities. The war memorial, across from the shop, was originally erected for Jack Frampton, who died during the July Drive of 1916, the first Bay Bulls man to be killed during the First World War. Following the Second World War, other names were added. Across the road, the Parish Hall was considered "large and up to date" in 1955, when it was used regularly for movies and concerts. It now serves as the community museum.

Carpenters Cove

Sir David Kirke is said to have constructed a fort in Bay Bulls in 1638. It is likely he needed one, if his aim was to collect the five per cent tax from foreign vessels specified by his charter. It is not known if this fort still existed, in 1665, when Admiral Michiel Adrianzoon de Ruyter (1607-76) sacked Bay Bulls on behalf of the Dutch Republic. A 1693 map shows fanciful forts on North and South Head, but ground evidence for these structures is lacking. In 1696, four forts were hastily constructed in response to the approach of Mombeton de Brouillan's fleet.

In addition to the French sack of 1696, Bay Bulls was burned by the French in 1705, 1708 and 1796, leading some to pronounce Bay Bulls the most torched town in the British Empire. The French raid of 1762 is often included in the tally; however, on this occasion the French, under Chevalier d'Arsac de Ternay, confined their depredations to storehouses and other waterside structures, slaughtering livestock and seizing boats, but leaving the main settlement

CHRISTMAS CONCERTS IN THE THIRTIES

"Bay Bulls was then in three sections: the Northside, Centre Section and the Southside. The ladies held the dances in their turn and parents and children went to the one dance in the Parish Hall. Aldon Williams and Bert Pack were the fiddlers and Joe Williams was the accordion player. They played square dances, lancers and step dances while someone sang a few old songs. They then passed the hat around while Arthur Hearn raffled a few cakes to pay the fiddler. No band or taped music, then. We were a happy crowd, the days that used to be."

—Queen Maloney, "Auld Lang Syne," *The Seniors' News*, December 1987

Admiral Michiel de Ruyter

18th-century gunner

intact, possibly because 24 Irish servants joined in the cattle killing and looting.

Bay Bulls escaped destruction, too, during the American War of Independence (1775-83). Before the Revolution, Newfoundland was provisioned for the most part by Yankee ships; during the Revolution, the same ships returned as Yankee privateers. American raiding was particularly fierce in 1778-79. In October of 1778 Captain Robert Pringle, the colony's resident naval engineer, showed a committee of 60 anxious Bay Bulls' planters and by-boat keepers the best spots to build defensive batteries. Pringle drew up plans for a six-gun battery at the head of the harbour, just north of Carpenters Cove, and the battery was constructed promptly by public subscription. The following year the committee requested additional cannon, probably for a second Pringle-designed battery at Kate Point. Both batteries were destroyed by the French in 1796. The battery rebuilt at Carpenters Cove following the attack had only three guns.

In 1780, the French assembled a fleet, again under Chevalier d'Arsac de Ternay. Captured papers pointed to Newfoundland as the fleet's target. During the height of this invasion scare, a ship was moored at Riverhead, Bay Bulls, to guard the "Indian path" supplementing the Royal Artillery detachment already stationed in the community, consisting of a corporal, two gunners and six soldiers. The detachment was

Stages, Carpenters Cove

supplied by boat, and relieved every two weeks. The two Bay Bulls batteries were garrisoned in addition by local volunteers, who received naval pay, rations and grog.

The Bay Bulls detachment was expected to apprehend deserters as well as resist Yankee revolutionaries. The men saw action only once. On October 24, 1779, Michael Darrigan and four drinking companions, with shovels and a cutlass, murderously assaulted Cornelius Gallery in St. John's. Darrigan was immediately arrested and imprisoned in chains in a Royal Navy sloop in St. John's harbour. A few days before Christmas, three friends helped Darrigan escape. The fugitives stole a skiff, rowed to Bay Bulls and were spotted attempting to seize a brig. The Royal Artillery detachment pursued the gang into the woods, where they were caught, huddled around a fire in a thicket. Darrigan bolted but was captured, and was tried and hung the following September; his accomplices were deported to Ireland.

The Trepassey Line

The steep slope above Carpenters Cove has been called variously Williams Hill, Partridgeberry Hill and Scotts Hill. The Trepassey Line, a branch rail line operated by the Reid Newfoundland Co., did not descend into Bay Bulls, but followed the contour of the hill to a station immediately south of Quays Road.

Sir Michael Cashin opens the Trepassey Line, 1914

Bay Bulls by Train, 1915

"Of course it was a grand rush to catch the 5:30 [p.m.] train and of course the Reid Nfld. Co., as usual, tried to pack 100 persons in a car designed for 50. Thanks to R.J.K. we got another car locked on and were, consequently, a quarter of an hour late in leaving. Stopping at Waterford Bridge and Brennock's, the run to Bay Bulls was made in an hour and a half. At the station the acquaintance of J.G.H. was made, who immediately turned himself into a lady's maid and general protector. Our load from the station was lightened by his kindness and the muscles of our arms relieved of a great strain. 8:30 brought supper for which we were not only hungry, but ravenous—good bread and butter, ham, raspberry jam and cream. Mrs. Williams escorted us to Mrs. Delaney's where we roomed. J.G. was on the watch and, failing to secure a motor boat, took us for a walk as far as Bread and Cheese—everybody knew Jack, consequently his friends were made welcome."

—Diary of the late Miss Ada Horwood of St. John's, August 21, 1915

Trepassey Line under construction, September 14, 1911

A short section of this route (near the tennis court) has become Southside Road. The line to Trepassey, at 110 km, was the longest of several branch lines promised by People's Party leader E. P. Morris during his successful election bid of 1909. The lines created jobs, but were an economic folly. Between 350 and 1,000 men worked on the Trepassey Line from 1911 to 1914, generally starting once the fishery slackened, and continuing until first snowfall. The line opened to great fanfare in September of 1914. A return ticket to Trepassey cost three dollars, a sum kept low so the line could compete with the coastal boat service. In spite of this incentive, passenger and freight traffic was slight, and the poorly maintained line had deteriorated substantially by the end of the First World War. Regular service ceased in 1920. In 1923, the Newfoundland Government assumed the line's yearly operating loss, replaced the train with a trolley-like day coach and, in 1924, cut winter service. The line closed for good in August of 1931, and the rails were pulled up and sold for scrap the following year. According to local tradition, the steel was sold to Germany, where it was used to make shells and torpedoes, some of which were fired back at Newfoundland. The landmark tank that supplied water to the engine is long gone, but the station's concrete platform is still visible; Dick Power used the station as a blacksmith's forge until the 1950s. Past the station, the old rail route becomes Track Extension Road, then a well-worn woods track that arcs around Twelve O'Clock Hill to Witless Bay.

Maggoty Cove

In an era when fish dried on flakes, all Newfoundland settlements were malodorous and fly-plagued. Evidently, to the nose of the uninitiated, some coves were truly appalling: both Bay Bulls and St. John's have a Maggoty Cove. In Bay Bulls, the name dates to at least 1773. Maggoty Cove was too unsheltered to support a fishing establishment of any size, though in the early 1800s the firm of Moore & Shapley conducted business in Shapleys Cove, possibly Maggoty Cove under a more respectable name.

The Keys

Since the 18th century, *key* (a reef) and *quay* (a constructed barrier), though they are pronounced the same, have been spelt differently. The Keys, Bay Bulls, illustrates how a well-intended reform can magnify, rather than reduce, confusion. Hikers turn onto Quay Road, to go to the Keys, a settlement west of Quay Point; mistakenly called "Quail Point" on 19th-century charts. A half-dozen families once lived at the Keys. The location of the homesteads can be surmised from the terraced house foundations, fieldstone walls and hollows left by root cellars. Over the years, the abandoned buildings were burned or salvaged for wood. The fields served as a landmark for fishermen; the easternmost meadow was used to locate Green Meadows, one of the more oddly named fishing berths along the shore. The lightkeeper Harold Stone was one of the Keys' last residents, and is said to have ploughed up cannon balls in his field while setting potatoes.

Keys Meadow, Joan Clays Hill in the background

ACKNOWLEDGEMENTS

The author would like to thank Petty Harbour-Maddox Cove residents Reg Best, Luke Bidgood, Reg Carter, Mildred Carter, Donny Chafe, Harry Chafe, Richard Clements, Gordon Clements, Clar Hamilton, the late Laurence Kieley, Vince Lee, Sarah (Chafe) Pack, Cyril Whitten, Derm Whitten, Fred Whitten and Kevin Whitten, and Bay Bulls residents Henry Frampton, Eugene Maloney, the late Queen Maloney, Harold Mullowney, Gerry O'Brien, Neil O'Brien, John Rice and Herb Stone for their detailed recollections. The author would also like to thank Grade Six students Kristen Barter, Chris Doyle, Nick Gallant, L.J.Maloney, Dennis O'Dea, Colin Rice, Mike Ryan and Stephanie Williams for their maps and reports on Bay Bulls.

Fellow writers and researchers Libby Creelman, Nathalie Djan-Chékar, Laura Karr and Patrick Ryan contributed substantially to the manuscript in its early stages. The author is also indebted to Norm Catto, Nathalie Djan-Chékar, Mark Graesser, Roberta Hicks, Art King, William Kirwin, John Maunder, Bert Riggs, Julia Schwarz, Darlene Scott, Peter Scott and Alan Stein for their searching questions and painstaking review of the text. Randy Batten, Elliott Burden, Jim Candow, Larry Dohey, Neil Ellis, James Hiller, Phil Hiscock, John Ketchum, Pat O'Brien, Elizabeth Ohle, Maggy Piranian, Marilyn Porter, Pat Rivers and Roger White offered timely facts, advice and imagery. East Coast Trail Association executive members Tim Crosbie, Susan Gardiner, Neil Hardy, Randy Murphy, Wayne Spracklin, Doug Youden and Wanda Cuff Young spent innumerable evening hours battling for the project and its funding. Ed Hayden and Darlene Scott represented the association through the writing and editing process, ably shepherding the project through administrative hurdles. This book owes a great debt to my wife, Julia Schwarz, whose patience, care and knowledge sustained both the author and manuscript through numerous metamorphoses.

Like the trail, this guide is a work in progress. If this book lures its readers into fresh acts of remembering and research, then it has succeeded. Please write or e-mail the East Coast Trail Association with your corrections, suggestions, observations and thoughts.

ILLUSTRATION CREDITS

Drawings by Agnes Marion Ayre are reproduced courtesy of the Agnes Marion Ayre Herbarium, Memorial University of Newfoundland. Etchings by Philip Henry Gosse and his grandson Philip Gosse are reproduced courtesy of the Centre for Newfoundland Studies, Memorial University of Newfoundland. Fern illustrations by Susan J. Meades are reproduced courtesy of the Canadian Forest Service and Department of Forest Resources & Agrifoods, Government of Newfoundland & Labrador. Drawings by Dawn Laurel Nelson and Samantha Smith originally appeared in *Handy Guide to the Mammals of Newfoundland*, *Handy Guide to the Seabirds of Newfoundland* and *Handy Guide to the Whales, Dolphins and Seals of Newfoundland*. Illustrations by Roger Tory Peterson originally appeared in *The Birds of Newfoundland* by Harold S. Peters & Thomas D. Burleigh, co-published by the Department of Natural Resources, Province of Newfoundland, and Houghton Mifflin, Boston, 1951, and are reproduced courtesy of the Newfoundland Museum. Photographs by Gerald Pocius originally appeared in *Heritage '74 Festival of Youth Project: Petty Harbour-Maddox Cove*, and are reproduced courtesy of Gerald Barnable, Bonnell Public Relations, the Department of Tourism and the Memorial University of Newfoundland Folklore and Language Archive. Photographs by Ned Pratt originally appeared in Don Beaubier and Cle Newhook, *Precious Metals: Historic Silver from Newfoundland Churches*, Art Gallery of Newfoundland and Labrador, 1997. Bird and plant illustrations by A. Glen Ryan are reproduced courtesy of the Parks & Natural Areas Division, Government of Newfoundland & Labrador. Illustrations on pages 23, 38, 39, 81, 90, 135, 136, 171, 175, 182, 187, 203 and 204 are reproduced in full in D. W. Prowse, *A History of Newfoundland*, MacMillan & Co., 1895 (Mika Studio Facimile Edition 1972). Etchings on pages 2-3, 65, 74-75, 83, 115, 155, 182 and 186-7 are reproduced in full in Charles P. de Volpi, *Newfoundland, a Pictorial Record*, Longman Canada Ltd., 1972.

Exploring Petty Harbour

2-3 Rev. William Grey, detail from "Petty Harbour," *Sketches of Newfoundland and Labrador*, 1857.
4-5 Petty Harbour, National Library of Canada (#C019955).
6 Detail from "The Stage and Fishermen's Dwellings," *The Graphic* (Museum Catalogue #983.127.5).
6 Maddox Cove, Provincial Archives of Newfoundland and Labrador (#B2-197).
6 Gerald Pocius, Maddox Cove pier (MUNFLA 97-844-24).
7 Two girls in pinafores rounding the Point, 1886, National Archives of Canada (#PA210051).
8 Darlene Scott, the Point.
9 Introducing customers to live lobster, courtesy of the Bidgood family.
10 Fishing boats, National Library of Canada, 1909 (#C65043).
12 Storm damage, 1966, courtesy of Harry Chafe.
13 Storm damage, 1966, courtesy of Harry Chafe.
13 Gerald Pocius, breakwater, 1974 (MUNFLA 97-844-12).
14 Gerald Pocius, under a flake, 1974 (MUNFLA 97-844-14).
15 Gerald Pocius, landing at a stagehead, 1974 (MUNFLA 97-844-17).
15 Gerald Pocius, mending nets, 1974 (MUNFLA 97-844-18).
16 Beaches stagehead, c. 1909, National Archives of Canada (#PA210059).
17 Gerald Pocius, the Beaches, 1974 (MUNFLA 97-844-2).
18 Gerald Pocius, Petty Harbour barrels, 1974 (MUNFLA 97-844-12).
18 Todd Chafe, rind stripper, ECTA collection, artifact courtesy of Petty Harbour Museum.
18 Todd Chafe, carpenter's plane, ECTA collection, artifact courtesy of Petty Harbour Museum.
19 Dog delivering cookies, courtesy of the Bidgood family.
20 Fish sign, courtesy of the Bidgood family.
20 Roger Bidgood with fish, courtesy of the Bidgood family.
20 Bidgood's plant, courtesy of the Bidgood family.
21 Dog delivering bread, courtesy of the Bidgood family.
21 Rider Del & F. Kearny Sr., detail from "Two Dogs" (Museum Catalogue #R984.32.6).
22 Eric Chafe on his "truckley," c. 1941, courtesy of Sarah Pack.
22 Maggie Bidgood and customer, scene from *John and the Missus*, courtesy of the Bidgood family.
23 Bishop Michael Anthony Fleming, courtesy of the Archives of the Roman Catholic Archdiocese.
23 Laurence Kiley Jr., courtesy of Michael Kieley, *Kieley Family History*, c. 1990.
23 Governor Henry Prescott, Prowse, p. 448.
23 Dr. Edward Kielly, Prowse, p. 446.

24 The Mass House, c. 1900, courtesy of Harold Chafe.
25 Peter Gard, Mass House, 2004.
25 Mass House altar, courtesy of Centre for Newfoundland Studies Archives (Collection 137, #7.04.002).
26 Old St. Joseph's, 1955, courtesy of the Archives of the Roman Catholic Archdiocese.
26 Ned Pratt, 1845 chalice from Petty Harbour.
27 St. Joseph's altar, 1955, courtesy of the Archives of the Roman Catholic Archdiocese.
28 Peter Gard, the Pancake and the Cribbies, viewed from Gull Hill, c. 1986.
29 Dean Roger Tierney, courtesy of the Archives of the Roman Catholic Archdiocese.
30 "An Unconscious Victim of the Camera," Petty Harbour, 1886, William and Lois Pinkey Collection, National Archives of Canada (#PA139028).
31 Simeon H. Parsons, "Indian Rock, Petty Harbour," courtesy of Centre for Newfoundland Studies Archives (Collection 137, #7.04.003).
32 T. Crompton Bury, "Fisherman's Cabin, French Shore," *Harper's Weekly*, 1890 (Museum Catalogue #R984.32.16).
32 Samuel Collings & J. Barlow, detail from "Attic Miscellany: Manning the Navy," 1780.
33 "Street in Petty Harbour," 1886, National Archives of Canada (#PA139021).
34 R. H. Holloway, "View of Houses, gardens, Petty Harbour," c. 1890, courtesy of Centre for Newfoundland Studies Archives (Collection 137, #7.04.004).
35 Seal skinner, courtesy of Centre for Newfoundland Studies Archives.
35 Picnicking on Mount Pleasure, courtesy of Sarah Pack.
37 "Boys from Petty Harbour," courtesy of Jim Kennedy. From left to right: Tommy Doyle, Michael Kiley, Ron Doyle, John White, Jim Kennedy, Jimmy Kiley, John Doyle and Ray Walsh.
37 Parsons Studio, "Ellen Doyle Howlett (1827-1916)," 1898, courtesy of Jim Kennedy.
38 Quebec soldier, Prowse, p. 245.
39 Simeon H. Parsons, detail from "Petty Harbour," courtesy of Centre for Newfoundland Studies Archives (Collection 199, #1.008).
39 Pierre Le Moyne d'Iberville, Prowse, p. 215.
40 Power house site, c. 1886, National Archives of Canada (#PA210050).
40 Recently completed power house, c. 1900, courtesy of Donny Chafe.
41 Reid Newfoundland Co. ad, M. Baker, J. Miller Pitt and R. D. W. Pitt, *The Illustrated History of Newfoundland Light & Power*, St. John's, 1990.
42-43 "Pipeline Petty Harbour," 1926-27, Provincial Archives of Newfoundland and Labrador (#A17-130).
42 Gerald Pocius, power house, 1974 (MUNFLA 97-844-23).
44-45 "View of North Side from Bridge," Provincial Archives of Newfoundland and Labrador (#A9-172) joined with "View of South Side from Bridge," Provincial Archives of Newfoundland and Labrador (#A9-175).
44 Peter Gard, Chafe House, 1978.
45 "Babe" Chafe carrying tea in her buggy, courtesy of Robert Chafe.
46 Joe Carter, detail from "Weir's Store," 1979, collection of Peter Gard & Julia Schwarz.
47 Family of Augustus Chafe, 1910, courtesy of Robert Chafe. From left to right: Gus Chafe; children Gilbert, Gus Jr., Ed, Mike, Laura and Tom; Mary ("Babe") Chafe.
47 Todd Chafe, Jacob Chafe's commemorative watch, ECTA collection, artifact courtesy of Newfoundland Museum.
48 Todd Chafe, "Late Night Landing," ECTA collection, 2001.
49 Peter Gard, "The Stand," 1996.
49 Ned Pratt, Williams communion cup.
50 St. Andrew's with Island Rooms, Provincial Archives of Newfoundland and Labrador (#A9-177).
50 Rev. Thomas Martin Wood, courtesy of Centre for Newfoundland Studies Archives (MF-331).
51 School theatrical, courtesy of Jim Kennedy.
52 Peter Gard, Ruby Church, 2004.
52 Two girls in pinafores seated beside the Long Run, National Archives of Canada (#PA178502). They likely accompanied the photographer, for they can be seen rounding the Point on p. 7, and mixing with local children on p. 58.
53 Petty Harbour hearse, courtesy of Jim Kennedy.
53 Detail from "Little Daisy," H. Hallet & Co., Portland, Maine, 1880 (Museum Catalogue #978.68.8).
54 Solomon Chafe's cottage with Mrs. Chafe, 1886, National Archives of Canada (#PA139020).
55 Piling faggots on a flake, c. 1955, courtesy of Sarah Pack. From left to right: Mary Weir, Jean Chafe and Bernice Chafe.
56 "Looking down the Harbour, Petty Harbour, 13 September, 1886," National Archives of Canada (#PA139024).
56 Peter Gard, Tom Best in front of Fisherman's Co-op, 1986.

57 Cod on stage head, courtesy of Provincial Archives (VA6-69).
58 Todd Chafe, fishing shed, ECTA collection, 2001.
58 "On the Street of Petty Harbour," 1886, National Archives of Canada (#PA139018).

Motion Path

59 Philip Gosse, detail from "Explosion on Board a Buccaneer Ship," *The History of Piracy*, 1932.
61 J. W. Hayward, detail from "Interviewing Newfoundland Fishermen as to the Presence of Cruisers Inshore," *Harper's Weekly*, 1887 (Museum Catalogue #R984.32.10).
62 Philip Henry Gosse, pitcher plant, p. 301, *The Canadian Naturalist*, 1840.
63 Peter Gard, above Council Cove, 1988.
63 Agnes Marion Ayre, Virginia rose.
64 Motion Bay excursion, courtesy of Sarah Pack.
64 A. Glen Ryan, dwarf huckleberry, adapted from *Native Trees and Shrubs of Newfoundland and Labrador*, 1995.
65 Robert Dudley, detail from "Interior of Mess Room, 1858," Day & Son Ltd., London, 1866.
65 A. Glen Ryan, leatherleaf, adapted from *Native Trees and Shrubs of Newfoundland and Labrador*, 1995.
68 Peter Gard, tracks in a flashet.
69 Peter Gard, Siles Cove starrigans.
70 Siles Cove shoreline, ECTA collection.
70 Samantha Smith, harp seal.
71 Darlene Scott, Paddy Root.
71 Peter Gard, dragon's mouth orchid.
72 A. Glen Ryan, spotted sandpiper, adapted from *Some Newfoundland Birds*, 1997.
73 Peter Gard, Big Rocks erratics.
74-5 J. W. Hayward, detail from "Breaking Out through the Ice," *Harper's Weekly*, 1884.
75 "Fishermen Recovering Bodies in the Gulch, January 23rd and 24th," *Frank Leslie's Illustrated News*, 1877 (Museum Catalogue #R984.32.15).
76 Peter Gard, niche habitat, pond near Long Point.
76 Scott Chafe, yellow pond lily.
78-9 Peter Gard, Motion Head erratics.
78 English pikeman, 1660 (Museum Catalogue #975.33.1).
78 "Cod Fishing on Shoal Ground," *Ballou's Pictoral Drawing-Room Companion*, c. 1860 (Museum Catalogue #R983.127.4).
80 Samantha Smith, polar bear.
81 Slaying a white bear, Prowse, p. 59.
82 Todd Chafe, flat ass kettle, ECTA collection, artifact courtesy of Petty Harbour Museum.
83 N. Tetu, detail from "Shooting Ruyder Ducks," *Canadian Illustrated News*, 1871.
83 Peter Gard, fly-way, Lower Cove Head.
84 Darlene Scott, Kettles Cove.
84 Peter Gard, Lower Cove cliffs.
84 Peter Gard, niche habitat, Piccos Gulch.
85 Peter Gard, Piccos Gulch shoreline.
86-87 Peter Gard, overgrown otter rub, Piccos Gulch.
86 Samantha Smith, river otter.
88-89 J. W. Hayward, detail from "In the Highway of Commerce," *Harper's Weekly*, 1882 (Museum Catalogue #R984.32.5).
89 Detail from "Recovering the Bodies from the Gulch," *Frank Leslie's Illustrated News*, 1877 (Museum Catalogue #R984.32.15).
90 French soldier, c. 1705, Prowse, p. 219.
90 Canadian soldier on raquets, Prowse, p. 243.
91 Todd Chafe, jigger mould, ECTA collection, artifact courtesy of Petty Harbour Museum.
91 Detail from "Cod Caught by a Jigger," *The Graphic*, 1874 (Museum Catalogue #983.127.5).
92 Roger Tory Peterson, northern harrier, detail from Plate 7 (Museum Catalogue #984.13.7).
93 Neil Hardy, Hearts Cove Ridge from the air.
93 Darlene Scott, Lower Cove from Burkes Head.
94 SS *Regulus*, courtesy of Centre for Newfoundland Studies Archives (Collection 137, #24.02.001).
96 Darlene Scott, Hearts Point Cove Ridge.
96 Darlene Scott, view of crevasse.
97 Darlene Scott, Hearts Point.
98 Susan J. Meades, spinulose wood fern.

99 Susan J. Meades, cinnamon fern.
99 Susan J. Meades, bracken fern.
100 Susan J. Meades, sensitive fern.
101 Susan J. Meades, New York fern.
102 Joseph Beete Jukes, courtesy of Centre for Newfoundland Studies Archives (MF-032).
102 Peter Gard, Shoal Bay copper mine.
102 Agnes Marion Ayre, plumboy.
104 Peter Gard, quartz breccia, Salmon Head.
105 Peter Gard, felsenmeer, Miner Point.
105 Peter Gard, quartz veins, Salmon Head.
106 Barbara Gard, Newfoundland red fox.
107 Philip Gosse, detail from "Captain Bartolemew Roberts and His Two Ships off Guinea," *The History of Piracy*, 1932.
108 Peter Gard, Shoal Bay Road, approaching Nippers Harbour.
109 Philip Gosse, detail from "Captain Bartolemew Roberts and His Two Ships off Guinea," *The History of Piracy*, 1932.
110 Royal Navy sloop of war, courtesy of Centre for Newfoundland Studies Archives (MF-213.2.13).
111 Peter Gard, gulch near Doubloon Pool.
111 Patrick Ryan, rip-up clasts.
112 Charlotte E. Holmes, adapted from "mosquitoes," *Common Insects of Oxen Pond Botanical Park*, 1975.
112 Peter Gard, Raymonds Gulch.
114 Philip Henry Gosse, "Swell among Ice," *The Ocean*, 1860.
115 C. Parsons, "Fishing Adventures - The Spout off Cape Broyle [sic]," *Harper's New Monthly Magazine*, March, 1861.
116 Peter Gard, the Spout in winter, 1996.
117 Agnes Marion Ayre, haircap moss.
118 Peter Gard, drook near Raymond Head.
118 Peter Gard, sandstone ledges near Raymond Head.
119 Peter Gard, Queens River bridge.
120-21 Peter Gard, New York aster.
120 Agnes Marion Ayre, rough-stemmed goldenrod.
121 Agnes Marion Ayre, bog aster.
122 Wayne Andrews, Queens River discontinuity.
123 Peter Gard, coastal heath near Red Rocks.
123 Peter Gard, Red Rocks.
124 Peter Gard, Island of Long Point.
124 Detail from "Lowering the Sailor Patrick Coombs over the Cliff," *Frank Leslie's Illustrated News*, 1877 (Museum Catalogue #R984.32.15).
125 Peter Gard, heath at Long Point.
126 Peter Gard, hanging rock.
127 Ed Delaney, alignment of the Thoroughfare with the Spout.
127 Peter Gard, blow-back stream.
128 A. Glen Ryan, black spruce, adapted from *Native Trees and Shrubs of Newfoundland and Labrador*, 1995.
129 Neil Hardy, aerial view of two gulches.
129 Peter Gard, cavern entrance.
130 Peter Gard, landing rock removal gear, 1995.
130 Peter Gard, rock blocking the Spout, 1995.
130 Peter Gard, rock removal, 1995.
131 Alan Kenworthy, the Spout blowing.
135 Alan Kenworthy, the Spout blowing, from above.
135 Bishop John Inglis, Prowse, Supplement, p. 6.
136 Cyrus W. Field, Prowse, p. 637.
137 D. C. Hitchcock, "The Spout," John Mulally, *The Laying of the Cable or Ocean Telegraph*, 1858.
139 Wayne Andrews, hikers admiring a blow.
139 Darlene Scott, Spout rainbow.
140 Wayne Andrews, Top of the Spout.
141 Peter Gard, eagle on sea stack.
142 Peter Gard, sea stack camouflage.

142 Peter Gard, jump at Landing Place.
142 Peter Gard, ledges at Landing Place.
144 Wayne Andrews, Drop Cove Rock.
144 A. Glen Ryan, sheep laurel, adapted from *Native Trees and Shrubs of Newfoundland and Labrador*, 1995.
145 Peter Gard, Iron Doors.
146 Peter Gard, the Chaver.
146-7 Agnes Marion Ayre, detail of white birch.
147 Alan Kenworthy, sea arch.
148 Peter Gard, Shag Rocks and cliffs at dusk.
149 Peter Gard, the Oven.
150 Peter Gard, Sculpin Island.
150 Peter Gard, *roche moutonnée*.
151 Peter Gard, Freshwater falls and cove.
152 Peter Gard, North Head sunset.
153 Frampton house, Freshwater, courtesy of Bay Bulls Historical Foundation.
153 Wayne Andrews, musk mallow in bloom, Freshwater.
154 Peter Gard, Freshwater cart track.
154 Peter Gard, Freshwater bridge.
155 C. Parsons, detail from "Fishing Adventures - Riding out a Northeaster," *Harper's New Monthly Magazine*, March, 1861.
156 Ocean sunfish, courtesy of John Maunder.
156 Dawn Nelson, basking shark.
157 "550 pound Tuna," courtesy of Centre for Newfoundland Studies Archives.
157 Philip Henry Gosse, "Sea Serpent, or the Enalicsaurias Hypothesis," *The Romance of Natural History*, 1862.
158 Patrick Ryan, Dungeon Cove.
158 Todd Chafe, fisherman's lunch box, ECTA collection, artifact courtesy of Petty Harbour Museum.
158 Peter Gard, North Head light.
158 Patrick Ryan, lighthouse door.
159 Peter Gard, North Head transition.
161 Pat Rivers, fossil Aspidella.
161 Patrick Ryan, the Beamer.
162 "Rosa Praed," Rosa Campbell Praed, *My Australian Girlhood: Sketches and Impressions of Bush Life*, London, T. Fisher Unwin, 1902.
162 HMS *Cordelia*, 1898, courtesy of Centre of Newfoundland Studies (Collection 177, #3.05.040).
163 Peter Gard, Bull Cove.
163 James Gillray, detail from"The Nancy Packet," published by Robert Wilkinson, 1784.
164 Dawn Nelson, greater black-backed gull.
164 Useless Bay, from the Flats, ECTA collection.
165 Peter Gard, Seven Island Cove.
165 Peter Gard, Pulpit Rock with nesting gull.
165 Raspberry Bottom, ECTA collection.
166 Darlene Scott, witches' broom.
167 Ed Delaney, Punter, Ed's Newfoundland dog, on the Cape Boone steps.
167 John Maunder, eastern dwarf mistletoe.
168 Bert Pack, courtesy of Gladys Benson.
169 Gun Ridge before resettlement, courtesy of Gladys Benson.
169 Peter Gard, Gun Ridge, 1998.

Exploring Bay Bulls

171 Dighton, detail from "Descriptions of Battles by Sea and Land," March 1801 (Museum Catalogue #980 970).
172-3 Bay Bulls, courtesy of Bay Bulls Historical Foundation.
172 Killing walrus, Prowse, p. 60.
174 Dawn Nelson, common dovekie.
175 Gun Ridge students, courtesy of Sarah Pack.
175 Holy Trinity Church, courtesy of Bay Bulls Historical Foundation.

176 Wayne Andrews, roses in bloom, Holy Trinity Cemetery.
177 Peter Gard, chain at Bread and Cheese Point, with the Nipple and Twelve O'Clock Hill.
178 Detail from George Cruickshank, "Saturday Night at Sea."
178 Adapted from *Nova Scotia United States Lights & Tides Tables*, 1878 (Museum Catalogue #989.35.75).
179 Todd Chafe, sextant, ECTA collection, artifact courtesy of Newfoundland Museum.
180 Upper deck of *U-190*, National Archives of Canada (#PA134169).
180 *U-190* moored below Twelve O'Clock Hill, courtesy of Sarah Pack.
181 *U-190* in Bay Bulls Harbour, National Archives of Canada (#PA178935).
182 C. Parsons, "Fishing Adventures - Tall Fishing," *Harper's New Monthly Magazine*, March, 1861.
182 18th-century Bermudian sloop, Prowse, p. 345.
183 Peter Gard, Father Mullowney's grotto.
183 Peter Gard, Blacks Hollow.
185 George Cruikshank, detail from "Sailors Carousing," Greenwich Hospital, 1825.
185 Man with tankard, detail from George Cruickshank, "Six Pence a Day."
187 Hugh Palliser, courtesy of Centre for Newfoundland Studies Archives (MF-231.4.05).
187 Governor Richard Edwards, Prowse, p. 349.
187 Todd Chafe, jug from HMS *Saphire*, ECTA collection, artifact courtesy of Newfoundland Museum.
187 J. Becker, detail from "Trinity Bay and Hearts Content," *Frank Leslie's Illustrated Newspaper*, September 9, 1865.
188 House and flake next to old cemetery, courtesy of Harold Mullowney.
189 Peter Gard, rescued crucifix, Saints Peter and Paul Church.
190 Theobald Wolfe Tone, *Wikipedia* (en.wikipedia.org).
191 18th-century recruits (Museum Catalogue #975.325).
192 Highway into Bay Bulls, *c.* 1917, courtesy of Harold Mullowney.
193 Stanleys River, *c.* 1917, courtesy of Harold Mullowney.
194 The Factory, courtesy of Harold Mullowney.
194 Factory ladies packing fish, courtesy of Harold Mullowney.
195 Factory freezing chamber, courtesy of Harold Mullowney.
195 Plant Office No. 5, courtesy of Harold Mullowney.
196 J. Williams & Co., with cod liver oil factory in background, courtesy of Harold Mullowney.
196 HMS *Dartmouth*, a fifth-rate naval frigate, 1690, courtesy of the Sisters of Mercy, Bay Bulls Convent.
197 Cullys Bottom, looking towards Riverhead, Provincial Archives of Newfoundland and Labrador (#A17-44).
197 Todd Chafe, pipe from HMS *Saphire*, ECTA collection, artifact courtesy of Newfoundland Museum.
198 Ship in haul-out at HMCS *Avalon*, Bay Bulls, courtesy of Bay Bulls Historical Foundation.
199 C. D. Chisolm, Dean Patrick Cleary with his nephew, Rev. Nicholas Roche, *c.* 1867, courtesy of the Archives of the Roman Catholic Archdiocese.
200 Saints Peter and Paul Church, and St. Patrick's School, courtesy of Bay Bulls Historical Foundation.
200 Father Patrick O'Brien, *c.* 1938, courtesy of the Archives of the Roman Catholic Archdiocese.
201 Cannon gates, *c.* 1938, Provincial Archives of Newfoundland and Labrador (# VA7-23).
201 Peter Gard, Dorothy Wyatt, 1985.
202 "Barrington Picking the Pocket of J. Brown, Esq., of Brandford," *Memoirs of George Barrington, containing every Remarkable Circumstance, etc.*, London, 1790.
202 Robert Pool and John Cash, "The New Prison (Newgate)," *Views of the Remarkable Public Buildings, Monuments, and other Edifices in the city of Dublin*, Dublin, Dublin Society, 1780.
203 Admiral Michiel de Ruyter, Prowse, p. 197.
204 18th-century gunner, Prowse, p. 371.
204 Stages, Carpenters Cove, courtesy of Bay Bulls Historical Foundation.
205 Sir Michael Cashin opens the Trepassey Line, 1914, Provincial Archives of Newfoundland and Labrador (#B1-99).
206 Trepassey Line under construction, September 14, 1911, Provincial Archives of Newfoundland and Labrador (#A22-158).
208 Wayne Andrews, Keys meadows, Joan Clays Hill in background.

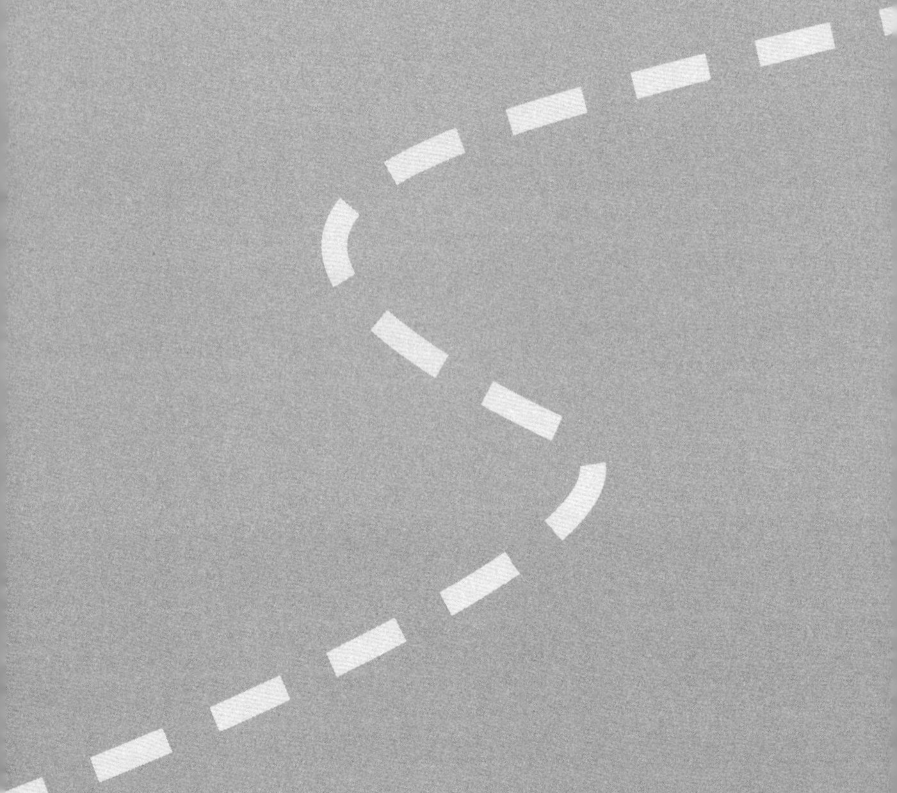

EAST COAST TRAIL USERS CODE

Do not use mountain bikes, horses or motorized vehicles on the trail, except on sections that are roads or established paths.

Respect the peace and quiet, privacy and property of people living along the trail.

Respect wildlife. Observe animals from a distance. Do not feed wild animals. Take special care that neither you nor your dogs disturb nesting birds.

Keep dogs under vocal or physical control at all times. Leash dogs when approaching communities and when approaching or passing other hikers.

Leave the trail cleaner than you found it. Carry out all litter.

Use designated campsites where available. A **NO OPEN FIRE** policy applies to campsites.

Carry a backpacking stove for your cooking needs. Do not light fires on or near the trail.

Woodcutting is forbidden within 50 m of the trail. Report violations to the appropriate authority.

Do not damage live trees by blazing, breaking branches or stripping bark.

Respect delicate ecosystems. Keep to the marked route.

Switchbacks protect fragile slopes. Stay off shortcuts and other "volunteer" paths.

DO NOT RISK HIKING CLIFFSIDE PATHS WHEN CONDITIONS ARE ICY OR SLIPPERY.

Enjoy your visit, tread lightly on the land and leave no trace.

Trip Tips

TRIP PLANNING

Check that you have the following:
- trail map
- adequate food & water
- head covering
- clothing to protect against wind, cold & rain
- extra socks
- sunscreen with a high SPF
- insect repellent
- pocketknife
- emergency kit
- first aid kit

FIRST AID KIT
- moleskin
- tensor bandage
- tweezers
- scissors
- needle
- oval eye pad
- bandaids
- topical antiseptic
- pain medication

EMERGENCY KIT
- matches
- candle / fire-starter
- rescue poncho / blanket
- high energy food
- flashlight
- extra batteries
- compass
- whistle

Make sure someone at home knows your plan & intended time of return. Let them know you're back. Most walkers cover 2 to 3 km per hour. Time your start to get out well before dark. Pre-plan & repackage meals to reduce litter. Blisters & strained muscles ruin many hikes. Begin at a warm-up pace, gradually increasing speed. A walking stick provides good balance & reduces knee & ankle fatigue. Wear comfortable, broken-in footwear with good ankle support & tread. High coliform counts are common in Newfoundland streams. As a precaution, bring water to a rolling boil, and/or carry purification tablets or a filter. If camping in the rough, choose an off-trail site that won't be damaged by your stay. Minimize alterations. Before leaving, erase all evidence of your visit. Open fires degrade & threaten the environment. If you encounter a fire site, scatter the evidence to discourage other fires. Pack salt or baking soda for cleaning needs, or use biodegradable brands of toothpaste & soap. Use designated latrines. Otherwise, dig a 15-cm deep "cat hole" at least 50 paces away from the trail & at least 100 paces away from a campsite or water body. After use, refill & replace original sod on top. Scatter pet waste off the trail. Paths will be wet & streams swollen early & late in the season. Avoid spring & fall hiking if conditions are not to your taste. Walk through wet areas rather than widening them by creating bypasses. Respect cliffs, ice, waves & cold weather. Know your limits & the limits of your gear. When in doubt, turn back. Keep a change of clothes & shoes in your car.

Yes, I want to help build and maintain the East Coast Trail!

- [ ] by becoming a member

    — individual / family ($25)
    — business ($100)

- [ ] by making a donation
    — $35
    — $50
    — $100
    — other $

- [ ] by becoming a patron and adopting one km of trail
    — $1,000

- [ ] by volunteering for

    — fundraising
    — special events
    — trail maintenance
    — the newsletter
    — the executive
    — leading hikes
    — office support

Name _____

Address _____

_____

Province / State _____

Country _____

Postal Code _____

E-mail _____

Telephone _____

- [ ] Visa - [ ] Cheque

Visa # _____

Expiry date _____

Signature _____

Become a part of the East Coast Trail Association

Please send your payment with completed form to the ECTA at:

The East Coast Trail Association
P.O. Box 8034
50 Pippy Place
2nd Floor
St. John's NL
Canada
A1B 3M7

For more information visit our website at:

www.eastcoasttrail.com

BECOME A PART OF SOMETHING SPECIAL...

How do you create a 420-km long hiking trail? One step at a time

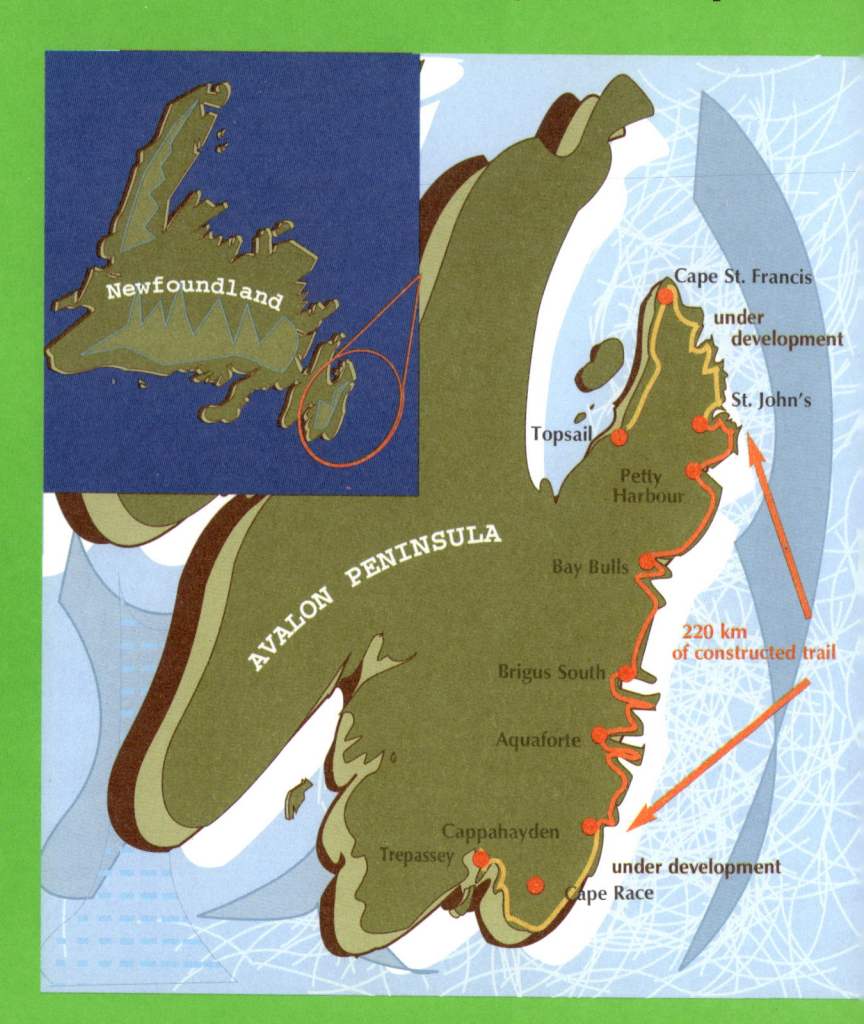

Newfoundland

AVALON PENINSULA

Cape St. Francis
under development
St. John's
Topsail
Petty Harbour
Bay Bulls
220 km of constructed trail
Brigus South
Aquaforte
Cappahayden
Trepassey
Cape Race
under development

Over the past decade, more than 1,200 hikers worldwide have shown their support for the East Coast Trail by joining the East Coast Trail Association (ECTA). The East Coast Trail is 100 per cent volunteer-driven and volunteer-maintained. An average of 200 hikers work on improving and maintaining the trail each year; another 500 hikers participate in recreational and fundraising events. If you love the trail as much as we do, please add your name to the growing ECTA membership list, help out at an event, purchase an ECTA product and / or make a donation (the ECTA is a registered charity).